D1624028

The Politics of the Pantomime

Regional identity in the theatre, 1860–1900

The Society for Theatre Research

The Society for Theatre Research, founded in 1948, brings together those interested in the history and technique of the British theatre, and it encourages research into these subjects. Lectures are held in London and members receive the Society's illustrated journal, *Theatre Notebook*, as well as (at least) one book annually. The Society makes substantial Research Awards and in 1998 instituted the Theatre Book Prize. New members are welcome. Details of subscription rates and a list of past publications appear on the Society's website – www.str.org.uk – or may be obtained by writing to: The Society for Theatre Research, PO Box 53971, London SW15 6UL.

The Politics of the Pantomime

Regional identity in the theatre, 1860–1900

Jill A. Sullivan

University of Hertfordshire Press

The Society for Theatre Research

First published in Great Britain in 2011 by
University of Hertfordshire Press
College Lane
Hatfield
Hertfordshire
AL10 9AB
UK

© Jill A. Sullivan 2011

The right of Jill A. Sullivan to be identified as the author of this work has been asserted by her in accordance with the Copyright, Designs and Patents Act 1988.

All rights reserved. No part of this book may be reproduced or utilised in any form or by any means, electronic or mechanical, including photocopying, recording or by any information storage and retrieval system, without permission in writing from the publisher.

British Library Cataloguing in Publication Data
A catalogue record for this book is available from the British Library

ISBN 978-1-902806-88-4 hardback
ISBN 978-1-902806-89-1 paperback

Design by Alma Books Ltd
Printed in Great Britain by Henry Ling Ltd

Contents

Illustrations

Abbreviations

BCL	Birmingham Central Library (Local Studies Library)
BL	London: British Library: Lord Chamberlain's Plays
MA	Manchester Archives: Theatre Collection
NA	Nottinghamshire Archives
NLSL	Nottingham Local Studies Library

Acknowledgements

A large number of people have enabled me to explore the world of Victorian provincial pantomime and I am delighted to be able to formally thank them all. This book began life as a PhD thesis and I am profoundly grateful for the support and guidance that I received from my primary supervisor Josephine Guy and also Joanna Robinson, both at the University of Nottingham; my examiners Helen Freshwater and, particularly, Jim Davis for their encouragement and continued interest in my work; the Society for Theatre Research and Jeffrey Richards for his interest and enthusiasm in the initial ideas for the book; Jane Housham, Sarah Elvins and readers at the University of Hertfordshire Press; staff at the British Library, St Pancras, especially Kathryn Johnson and her colleagues in the Manuscript Department; the British Library at Colindale; the John Johnson Collection, Bodleian Library, Oxford; Birmingham Central Library, Local Studies Library and the Birmingham City Archives; Nottingham Central Library, Local Studies Library; Nottinghamshire Archives; Manchester City Library, Manchester Archives Theatre Collection staff, particularly Annie Morland, and staff in the Local Studies Library; the Public Records Office; Bromley House Subscription Library, Nottingham; and the Devon and Exeter Institution which became my writing space in the last months of completing this book. For advice, help and information, I would like to thank colleagues in the Department of English Studies at the University of Nottingham, and the Department of English and Film at the University of Exeter; David Mayer for sharing his ideas on Victorian pantomime and for the loan of selected books of words; Shaf Towheed, Rosy Aindow, John Plunkett, Ann Featherstone, plus fellow delegates at conferences in England and America for the many helpful recommendations and comments that I have received from them. Thanks are also due to all my friends and converts to the joys of pantomime, especially Ursula, Linda and Taro, for their generous hospitality during the many research trips to

London and Manchester; and finally but most importantly to my parents: my mother who shared my love of theatre but who never saw the outcome of my studies and my father for his support, humour and understanding.

An earlier version of the section in Chapter 3 on the financial records of the Theatre Royal, Nottingham was previously published as 'Managing the Pantomime: Productions at the Theatre Royal Nottingham in the 1860s', *Theatre Notebook*, 60/2 (2006), pp. 98–116. Similarly, an earlier version of the case study in Chapter 4 on Chamberlain and politics at the Theatre Royal, Birmingham has been published as 'Local and Political Hits: Allusion and Collusion in the Victorian Pantomime', in J. Davis (ed.), *Victorian Pantomime: A Collection of Critical Essays* (Basingstoke, 2010).

Introduction

At the beginning of February 1886, the *Birmingham Daily Post* carried an advertisement for the Theatre Royal pantomime, the central feature of which was an extended quote from *Theatre*:

'Robinson Crusoe' at the Birmingham Theatre Royal is, in my estimation, far and away the best of the provincial pantomimes in general excellence of scenery, costumes, and acting, to say nothing of its music, which surpasses that in all other productions in point of melody and liveliness. Let me advise such of my readers as care to see a brisk, well-constructed, amusing, and thoroughly enjoyable pantomime, to lose no time in finding their way to Euston, and travelling thence by the well-ordered, fast, and punctual trains of the London and North-Western Railway to Birmingham, there to see 'Robinson Crusoe' at the Theatre Royal. I will answer for it that the pantomime at the Birmingham Theatre Royal is the best to be seen in the country this year.[1]

The *Theatre* reviewer engaged a metropolitan audience in his promotion of a regional pantomime. His 'estimation' of the quality of the pantomime prepared the visitor for certain standards of production, and his list of requisite elements, of 'melody and liveliness' in a 'brisk, well-constructed, amusing, and thoroughly enjoyable pantomime', neatly summarised aspects of the performance for potential audiences. The trains out of London are as brisk as the pantomime and those of the metropolis who venture beyond Euston are guaranteed an efficient journey and gratifying theatrical experience. The potential local and regional audiences of Birmingham and the Midlands may have espied other promotional aspects in their regional newspaper previews: the status of the theatre locally (not the 'Theatre Royal' of a London paper, but the familiar 'Royal'); the reputation of the manager and his author; and a range of references that

1

could be appreciated by a local audience. The Theatre Royal manager chose to include this review in the context of local theatrical competition and the history and identity that he had established for his theatre. For the London critic and reader this review would not have carried those inferences. The foregrounding of scenery, costumes, acting and music in the quotation does not give a true sense of the nature and variety of provincial pantomimes; there is an implicit assumption that, essentially, all pantomimes are the same, albeit produced to different standards. For many years, theatre historiographers regarded Victorian provincial pantomime in a similar light: they focused on London, in particular giving preference to the histories of the patent theatres and, to an extent, assuming homogeneity of those productions that occurred beyond Euston station. In this book I intend to redress this imbalance and to examine pantomime productions in the three urban centres of Birmingham, Nottingham and Manchester in order to establish the variety and traditions that characterised provincial pantomime. In particular, I will illustrate how the managers of each theatre appealed to their audiences by reflecting specific aspects of regional and local identity in the annual production.

The prevalent assumption regarding provincial homogeneity arguably has its foundations in the relatively small quantity of material that has been published on the Victorian pantomime. Whilst, until now, it has not been the sole subject of an academic work, our understanding of the developments and structure of the pantomime after the 1830s owes much to Michael R. Booth's *English Plays of the Nineteenth Century*, vol. v: *Pantomimes, Extravaganzas and Burlesques* which, together with *Victorian Spectacular Theatre 1850–1910* and *Theatre in the Victorian Age*, dominates studies of the genre.[2] Victorian pantomime has tended to attract greater attention in relation to ideological concerns with, for example, empire in the late nineteenth century, gender roles, and sexuality,[3] but Thomas Postlewait's recent reminder of the value of empirical work, in *An Introduction to Theatre Historiography* (2009), foregrounds the fact that although the cross-dressed, music-hall influenced Victorian pantomime has attracted ideological debate, little new empirical evidence has emerged on which to found new discussions. It is instead the pantomime of the eighteenth and early nineteenth centuries that has tended to attract greater comment, dominated by David Mayer's 1969 work, *Harlequin in His Element: English*

Pantomime 1806–1836, together with John O'Brien's *Harlequin Britain: Pantomime and Entertainment 1690–1760* and Jane Moody's *Illegitimate Theatre in London 1770–1840*, which have provided a broader contextual base for the pantomimes of Georgian London.[4] There has been a fascination with the silent harlequinade: in 'The State of the Abyss: Nineteenth Century Performance and Theatre Historiography in 1999', Jane Moody made a crucial point when she stated that, 'It is disconcerting to realize that many of the authoritative surveys of theatrical forms, published over three decades ago, have never been succeeded, let alone challenged.'[5] Foremost amongst those surveys, she argued, was Mayer's *Harlequin in His Element* and yet her proposed extension to the range of genres studied did not promote the exploration of pantomime beyond the time range established by Mayer.[6]

Whilst the early history of pantomime is fascinating and the work by Mayer and O'Brien in particular has established and developed valuable evidence for our understanding of the genre, the absence of an extensive body of work on the Victorian pantomime has been perturbing. I would suggest that much of the critical reluctance to address the range of later pantomimes stems from an uncritical acceptance of nineteenth-century judgements about the genre. Clement Scott, for example, in 'The Lost Art of Pantomime' mourned the harlequinade that he thought 'lost for ever'. He remembered the Georgian pantomimes of his youth and, in particular, he recalled the acting of Grimaldi, who had revitalised the role of Clown in the early part of the century.[7] Scott was not alone in recalling Grimaldi's acting talents. In 1872, J.R. Planché had also recalled the early pantomimes: 'there was some congruity, some dramatic construction … and then the acting! For it was acting, and first-rate acting.'[8] Planché was quoted by Leopold Wagner in *The Pantomimes and All About Them* in 1881, the latter additionally perceiving the acting of the harlequinade as good training for the 'legitimate drama'.[9] Finally, J. Wiston, who had been a manager of Drury Lane Theatre in the early nineteenth century, commented that 'Grimaldi was a better clown. He made it a more intellectual performance.'[10] National and local newspaper articles of the nineteenth century reiterated the concept of the 'lost pantomime', recalling Grimaldi and finding his performance superior to those in the later harlequinades.

The focus on Grimaldi's performance can be linked to contemporaneous debates regarding the status of drama. In *New Readings in Theatre History*,

Jacky Bratton succinctly outlined the nineteenth-century concept of the 'decline of the drama' and the critical separation of popular theatre and dramatic literature in the early nineteenth century. Bratton acknowledged that such divisions can still influence theatre history, identifying melodrama as having been particularly susceptible to dismissal by exponents of the dramatic integrity of theatre.[11] Further, Simon Shepherd and Peter Womack in *English Drama: A Cultural History* referred to the redefinition of pantomime in the eighteenth century as an art form.[12] They argued that the specifics of mime and its inheritance from the Italian *commedia dell'arte* lent pantomime an historical and cultural authenticity, and it is, I argue, this perception of authenticity which underlies the reminiscences by Scott, Wagner, Planché and the innumerable nineteenth-century essayists, about Grimaldi's acting abilities. The incorporation of spectacle and song after the 1840s epitomised for many critics not only the perceived degradation of theatre but also, and crucially, the degradation of the genre, an attitude which seems to have influenced modern studies of the genre.[13] In particular, J.R. Planché's despair at the increasing emphasis on spectacle inaugurated by the transformation scene, and E.L. Blanchard's condemnation of the perceived abuse of his scripts by theatre managements, plus the critic William Davenport-Adams's disgust at the importation of music-hall stars, instilled a sense that Victorian pantomimes offered little beyond glitter and morally dubious music-hall songs.[14] By contrast, pantomime producers have always accepted the intrinsic variations of the genre. Indeed its survival throughout three hundred years has hinged on its adaptability and on theatre managers' awareness of changing tastes and expectations. O'Brien has highlighted the fact that such manoeuvrings had been at the root of pantomime's success a hundred years earlier, and Gerald Frow, writing in 1985, observed that 'pantomime has *never* been what it was'.[15]

In addition to the influence of nineteenth-century judgements about artistic worth, I would also suggest that Victorian pantomime has been regarded in much the same critical light that for many years fell on melodrama and the music hall. In the light of judgements based on the literary worth of drama, those genres were disregarded for many years, to be rediscovered and re-valued as a result of the post-1960s developments in cultural studies; they have since claimed what David Mayer in 1977 perceived as 'academic respectability'.[16]

However, Victorian pantomime – and more especially the provincial productions – has been largely excluded from that momentum. There is a sense perhaps that productions at established cultural centres, such as the Theatres Royal, have a more limited research value when set alongside the dynamic politics of the working-class music hall. In 1997, Peter Holland referred briefly to a possible and influential 'cultural contempt for the [pantomime] form in contemporary society'.[17] There exists therefore a curious tension: of pantomime being interpreted in the nineteenth century as commercial, popular (vulgar) and inartistic, and a later twentieth and twenty-first century interpretation of it as popular (mainstream) and therefore politically uninteresting. It has effectively been caught in a cultural and critical pincer movement.

Although the provincial pantomime has languished in critical commentaries, there was always an awareness of the range and quality of productions. In *English Plays*, Booth cited Leopold Wagner's 1881 comment on the importance of regional pantomime and the latter's brief listing of the main centres such as Birmingham, but there has remained until very recently a critical reliance on London performance and production. Shepherd and Womack succinctly address this issue of 'metropolitan domination' in their introduction to *English Drama*. They argue that 'Since the late sixteenth century, theatrical production in Britain has been organized in an increasingly unitary system whose centre, socially, economically and politically, is London.' The authors appreciate that while 'this hierarchy has been continually deplored and resisted' and 'there are times … when theatre is more inventive, popular and energetic at the edges than it is at the centre, that fact doesn't shift the structural relation in itself'.[18] This 'hierarchy' in relation to pantomime has been evident in works throughout the twentieth century. More especially, it is a hierarchy that invariably defers to a single theatre – the Theatre Royal, Drury Lane – and which depends on inherited assumptions. In 'Imperial Transgressions', Jim Davis cited a nineteenth-century review in the *Star* newspaper, in which the Drury Lane pantomime was described as a 'national institution'.[19] Similarly, Booth, in his 'Introduction' to volume five of *English Plays*, stated that 'Drury Lane … dominated English pantomime in the last twenty years of the nineteenth century' and cited *Theatre* of 1882, which claimed that 'Drury Lane pantomime is an English

Institution'.[20] However, the most interesting comments on this topic were made by A.E. Wilson back in 1934:

> The history of pantomime must inevitably resolve itself into a history of Drury Lane. It was on the boards of the 'national theatre' that some of the first pantomimes appeared and earned the support of the public, and it was there that pantomime assumed the character of a fixed institution. Pantomime was looked for there as a matter of course … and it was from there that it drew its peculiar character. The principal changes effected in its form nearly all emanated directly or indirectly from it, and consequently the feeling that this historic theatre is the national home of pantomime has descended from one generation to another … I make no apology, therefore, in dealing with the subject of pantomime generally for dwelling so much upon the history of Drury Lane.[21]

Wilson also cites a contemporaneous report, this time from the manager of the Britannia Theatre in Hoxton, who claimed that 'The other theatres of London and the provinces were influenced by Drury Lane.'[22] Wilson's work, alongside that of David Mayer, was cited by Michael Booth in 1991 as one of the two principal works on nineteenth-century pantomime to date, and Peter Holland referred to Wilson as 'the most important critic of panto in the middle of [the twentieth] century'.[23] Wilson's work is certainly valuable and contains extremely useful information about the structure of pantomime, certain performers and performance traditions. However, his promotion of Drury Lane has placed an unnecessarily large foundation stone for later approaches to the pantomime. Further, works such as Wilson's *Christmas Pantomime* have a direct lineage from nineteenth-century publications on theatre history, in particular R.J. Broadbent's *A History of Pantomime* and Leopold Wagner's *The Pantomimes and All About Them*.[24] The breadth of coverage suggested by Wagner's title belies the fact that the book was in fact dedicated to Augustus Harris, then manager and pantomime producer of Drury Lane, thus indicating the trajectory of Wagner's argument. The Drury Lane theatre was of course important and its pantomimes influential, but that fact should not be permitted to overshadow pantomimes produced at

6

other theatres, especially those in the provinces. Although Drury Lane set a benchmark for production trends, those trends were not slavishly followed, and provincial theatres such as the Theatre Royal at Birmingham actively strove to establish their own unique identity. In *Theatre in the Victorian Age* Booth highlighted the fact that improved transport in the nineteenth century meant that audience members could and often did visit the theatre in more than one town.[25] Certainly evidence from provincial newspapers demonstrates that Christmas and pantomime excursion rail trips were advertised in Manchester, Birmingham and Nottingham, enlarging the potential topography of audiences to all the outlying areas, towns and cities. Nottingham advertised trips to the pantomime from Sheffield, Leicester and Derby, as well as routes from Lincolnshire; the Birmingham theatres advertised rail trips across the Black Country and Derbyshire, to Malvern and Worcester; and Christmas trips to Manchester were advertised from Sheffield and Liverpool, the manager of the Theatre Royal in the 1890s boasting audiences 'from as far south as Swansea … Carlisle in the north, and Hull in the east'.[26] If economic conditions were favourable to audiences visiting more than one theatre, managements would have endeavoured to offer different elements in their pantomimes. It is far more useful therefore to regard Drury Lane as the setter of national trends that were subject to regional differences and influences and which were tailored to the tastes of local audiences.

I mentioned above the altered critical perspective on the music hall and melodrama in the 1960s and 1970s, which focused on the political implications of those genres. At the time, much of the work on regional, mainstream theatres was arguably still influenced by the more traditional historical approach of surveying repertoire and casts. Anxious to establish regional theatres in terms of their relative status (the performance of Shakespeare, or the visits of notable London actors for example), those former overviews provided little engagement with the concept of theatre as commercial enterprise, or regional audiences. Since the 1980s, such methods have begun to be revised, led by Kathleen Barker's 1982 thesis 'The Performing Arts in Five Provincial Towns 1840–1870', which remains a leading example of research into provincial theatres, including the Theatre Royal at Nottingham. Other work on nineteenth-century provincial theatre has focused on Leicester, York, Manchester and Macclesfield, offering new and valuable insights into repertoire, audience and theatre management.[27] And work on music hall in the provinces has also provided new contextual evidence and methodological approaches to the study of audience, notably Dagmar Kift's *The Victorian Music Hall*.[28] Amongst recent trends to address global theatre, the relevance of the provincial theatre has been further raised by Jo Robinson, who argues against the temptation to 'abandon or denigrate the local ... which can offer us access to a variety of cultures' and provide complementary yet unique studies.[29]

Much work remains to be done, however, and in this current project I intend to draw critical attention back to the provinces in an examination of pantomime productions at a selection of theatres in Nottingham, Birmingham and Manchester between 1860 and 1900: the Theatres Royal of Manchester, Nottingham and Birmingham, the Prince of Wales Theatre in Birmingham, and the Queen's Theatre, the Prince's Theatre and aspects of the Comedy Theatre in Manchester. This selection is not comprehensive in terms of the legitimate theatres in each city, but it focuses on the principal theatres that were functioning throughout the second half of the century.

During this period, provincial theatre managements gradually ceased to engage regular stock companies and, increasingly, hosted touring versions of London productions. This changing pattern of production (which occurred during the late 1870s at the Nottingham and Manchester theatres and 1880 at the Theatre Royal, Birmingham), has perhaps led to a perceived uniformity of provincial touring houses, but such a viewpoint belies subtle differences that were manifested in the production of the annual pantomime. The content and promotion of those pantomimes drew on notions of regional identity and status that were unique to each house. Examination of the productions at Nottingham, and the nature of the competition between theatre managements within Manchester and Birmingham and the subsequent differences in production styles, reveals that the strategies of pantomime production across the towns drew on specific features and preferences that were influenced by the local socio-economic and political clime, far more so than in the main season of programming.

Both Nottingham and Birmingham are situated in the English Midlands, which was a region of established agriculture and developing industry in the nineteenth century. By 1861, Nottingham, in the east of the region, was a small town surrounded by villages and hamlets, with a population of 75,000.[30] To the south were the agricultural districts of the Dukeries, and to the north and west the mining communities of Mansfield and district and the Erewash Valley, which stretched into Derbyshire. The physical expansion of Nottingham had been impeded until the mid-1840s by the desire of the town fathers to protect their meadow land beyond the ancient town boundary. Despite the growth in population, residential and factory building had been forced to remain within the boundary, leading to the creation of some of the worst slums and tenemented areas in England.[31] Local industry was therefore spread between the town and nearby villages, which expanded as workers moved out of the overcrowded town. The Nottingham Enclosure Act of 1845 finally paved the way for town development and in 1877 the local Borough Extension Act created the 'consolidation of the industrial parishes for administrative purposes',[32] making the later growth of Nottingham the result of incorporation rather than the development of suburbs witnessed in other towns and cities of this period. This growth can be seen in the population figures recorded in the censuses of 1871 (87,000 for the town plus 52,000 for the environs) and 1881, at which point the census recorded an inclusive figure of 187,000.[33] Industry in Nottingham centred on the production of hosiery and lace, but both products were particularly susceptible to the vagaries of fashion and foreign competition, and it was not until the 1880s that the range of local production started to expand, noticeably into the alternative industries offered principally by the Raleigh bicycle factory, John Player tobacco products and Jesse Boot's pharmaceutical supplies and shops, all of which ensured a wider and more varied economic base for the town.[34]

The growth of Birmingham and its neighbourhood parishes had not suffered from such land constrictions and by 1861 the town parish of Birmingham was almost four times the size of Nottingham, with a town population of 296,000 plus 55,000 in the 'environs' of 'Aston, Handsworth, King's Norton, Northfield and Yardley'.[35] The growth of Birmingham and its nearby parishes made it one of the largest urban centres in the country, what the historian Simon Gunn has referred to as one of the 'provincial metropolises', alongside Manchester, Liverpool and Leeds.[36] To the west of the town were the mining and iron-producing districts of the Black Country, consisting of parts of South Staffordshire and North Worcestershire and stretching from Wolverhampton in the west up to Walsall in the north and south to Stourbridge.[37] The mines of the Black Country provided the basic materials for the manufacture of finished metalware products in many small towns in the West Midlands. However, those towns tended to concentrate on a specific product, becoming, over time, particularly vulnerable to trade fluctuations. By contrast, Birmingham had established an extremely varied trade base and although local production was dominated by the four main manufactures of guns, brassware, jewellery and buttons for much of this period, the variety of individual products within those classifications, and a propensity for innovation and adaptability, ensured that there was always some successful branch of trade even in periods of national depression.[38]

Manchester, in Lancashire, north-west England, had been a centre for cloth production and trade long before the impact of mechanised cotton production processes that were first introduced in the Industrial Revolution of the late eighteenth century. Those developments and the subsequent influx of workers led to a rapid expansion of the city in the first half of the nineteenth century. Manchester's economic growth was linked to its geographical situation: the revolutionary steam-powered mills drew on the waters of the Pennine rivers, and comprehensive canal and rail links – not to mention the Ship Canal completed in 1894, which displaced Liverpool's role as the primary port for the city – enabled a flourishing trade based as much on commercial distribution as production. Whilst cotton (and silk) production formed the core industry of the town, the commercial success of Manchester also enabled a local growth in banking as well as chemical and machine-making industries linked to the cotton factories. Similarly, trade imports and distribution included industrial materials and food. By the late nineteenth century, the city centre had become a hub of retail businesses and commanding warehouses, whilst the middle classes moved further afield to more salubrious suburban addresses in Cheshire and Lancashire. In the early nineteenth century the town grew rapidly, the population quadrupling between 1801 and 1851, at which point the census figure was 316,213, and whilst it lacked the official boundary restrictions experienced in Nottingham, the escalating population meant that living conditions for many were squalid, restricted to the worst parts of town near the polluted rivers Irwell and Medlock.[39]

Each of the three towns (each town achieved city status at a different time during the second half of the century: Manchester in 1853, Birmingham in 1889 and Nottingham in 1897) therefore had a distinct identity and my examination of regional pantomime necessarily employs a micro-historical methodology in the study of the range of theatres in each city.[40] For theatre historians writing in the twenty-first century it has become standard practice to engage with the environment in which performances were produced. Further, and thanks notably to Tracy C. Davis's seminal work *The Economics of the British Stage 1800–1914*, which not only addressed theatre business practices but also sought to engage with regional archive materials, the historiography of Victorian theatre has been reinvigorated in the last ten years by consideration of what in 1989 Michael Booth called 'the *business of theatre*'.[41] My research therefore engages with the socio-economic and political contexts, available financial evidence, promotional materials, scripts (published and manuscript) and newspaper reports for the range of theatres. It is this business aspect of regional pantomime production that forms the focus of my study: how theatre managers produced and promoted pantomimes for their local and regional audiences. However, although the expectations of audiences and – in terms of topical referencing – their experiences framed the writing and presentation of each pantomime, I have not sought to empirically establish those audiences. Rather, I have used the textual evidence of reviews, promotional materials and the scripts to source a notion of audience, a notion that defined the managerial policies at each theatre. Jim Davis and Victor Emeljanow briefly address this concept in *Reflecting the Audience: London Theatregoing 1840–1880*. In noting the local places referred to in the Pavilion Theatre pantomimes in 1844 and 1859, they suggest that 'None of this proves conclusively that the theatre was attracting a primarily local audience, but it does suggest that managements were aware of the drawing power of depicting local settings on stage.'[42] The audience-drawing power of pantomimes at regional theatres depended on more than scene settings: references to local issues, traditions and the promoted status of theatres, managers, authors and location all formed a part of the theatre-going experience.

It is not my intention to attempt a recreation of nineteenth-century pantomime productions, nor is my argument overly concerned with the performance of pantomime. Indeed such an attempt would be fraught with difficulty as the genre was (and is) by its nature mutable: surviving scripts are only indicative of what happened on stage as, in performance, lines would be cut or changed, topical references were updated, and there was a vast amount of ad-libbing and unrecorded stage and comic 'business'. This central problem, which threatens to undermine any reading of the pantomime script, was highlighted by Michael Booth in his 1981 work *Victorian Spectacular Theatre*. Booth stressed that in order to understand Victorian pantomime more fully it is necessary to draw on additional evidence from the contemporaneous newspaper reviews, whose descriptive passages of the first-night performance frequently give a clearer indication of elements such as the *mise-en-scène* than is apparent from the scripts.[43] His recommendation is invaluable, but an engagement with the nineteenth-century newspaper reviewer also offers alternative ways of studying the Victorian pantomime than simply establishing the visuals of performance. Central to my argument in this book is the use of promotional materials in the nineteenth century and the evidence they contain of regional business practices. Therefore, throughout I have addressed the review as integral to the promotional strategies employed by the theatre management. In his 1987 book *The Rhetorics of Popular Culture: Advertising, Advocacy and Entertainment*, Robert L. Root stated that 'Reviewing is a rhetorical act'; whatever the subject matter, 'the critical review always involves a recommendation, whether implicit or explicit, and an attempt to convince readers of the reliability of that recommendation'.[44] According to Root's definition, there is a subtle difference between reviewing and criticism. The former contains description, evaluation, substantiation and recommendation, whereas the latter allows for a more personalised 'analysis and interpretation'.[45] Root establishes the rhetoric of the reviewer as one of advocacy, which seeks to provide reassurance for the reader in his expression of artistic knowledge. Certainly the pantomime reviewers often incorporated a brief history of the genre, or specific terminology as regards the ballet, but I am less concerned with this aspect of the reviewer's writing than with the relationship between his role as advocate and the promotional materials organised by the theatre management. Root separates the advocacy of the critical review from advertising, but during the run of a nineteenth-century pantomime, the distinction could become much less specific. Most of the newspapers cited in this book continued to review the pantomime after the first-night performance. In this matter, the role of the reviewer could become almost as mutable as the production itself; the emphasis of the reviews could change to promote particular aspects of the production or to realign public perception and expectation.[46] Often a second review would be printed after two or three days to assess changes in performance and, even if the initial review had been disapproving, this later review would invariably be much more positive. Indeed, negative reviews were not sustained throughout a run. In turn, further reviews printed during the pantomime season could become little more than extended advertisements, containing anticipatory comments regarding the length of the run, additions to the cast or new costumes for the ballet. These promotional reviews ran in tandem with the advertisements, both featuring the predominant elements of the production. Indeed, the reviewer could pre-empt the advertisements, suggesting that such and such a change might be forthcoming, to be followed a few days later by a front-page advertisement promoting that very change. Helen Freshwater has acknowledged that for theatre historians the review is often the sole means of accessing a past production but questions both the assumed objectivity of the newspaper reviewer when he writes of 'our' reaction and the 'we' of the audience, and a tendency for audiences to 'imagine that reviewers' long experience of theatre going lends their judgements a special cultural authority'.[47] I do agree that sweeping inclusions can be misleading, and the reviewers' eager adoption of that 'special cultural authority' can be particularly off-putting in reviews of pantomime, for example in the repetitive histories given each year in many of the previews. However, the use of 'our' and 'we' can often be integral to the intentional promotion of the theatre in terms of claiming status in the town ('our theatre') and it can also (as I discuss in Chapter 4) infer a political collusion in the referencing in certain pantomimes. Such readings are also possible, as Jacky Bratton has established, for other promotional materials such as the playbill, and the issue of how audiences 'read' such matter is crucial to an understanding of how theatres and particularly authors were promoted in relation to the pantomime.[48] Further, the press previews and reviews of the pantomimes frequently printed excerpts from the scripts to highlight particular references; they could also comment on the effectiveness of delivery and the responses by the audience (of value in terms of partisan political comments) and, sometimes, they recorded the impromptu 'gag' of comedians or snatches of topical songs. The combination of such materials, especially in the last instance (and even allowing for the subjective perspective of the reviewer), does offer an occasional bridge between the static text and evidence of performance.

This book therefore draws heavily on textual evidence, not as a substitute for lost performances, but more as a means to re-evaluate the importance of pantomime for local theatres. A central element of this reassessment is the pantomime scripts that have survived in the form of the 'book of words'. These books contained a version of the script that was on sale to the audience in the theatre. (It has also emerged from letters of complaint in the local press that books of the songs were sold in the streets, the street sellers shouting their wares noisily to the annoyance of passers-by.) The majority of the books of words remain in local library collections and, where none are known to have survived, the Lord Chamberlain's Plays collection at the British Library contains a selection of manuscript versions in addition to some extant copies of those printed books of words that were submitted for licensing. The fact that both the book of words and the manuscript copies were not entirely representative of the production during the run does present a methodological problem, as Michael Booth has established. However, whilst the extant versions of the scripts may not constitute an accurate definition of the production in performance, they do provide extremely important evidence as to the potential audience at which the production was being targeted by theatre managers. More specifically, the topical referencing (in terms of both style and subject matter), even allowing for cuts and changes, represented a specific range of interests and affiliations, particular to the city and each theatre, and a reading of available scripts across the period has enabled patterns and trends of referencing to emerge. Those issues and trends, whether related to civic affairs, trade, party political debates, the use of dialect or entrance prices to the local art gallery, all combined to present a sense of regional and local identity, and to reflect the relevant reference points for the range of potential audiences. Regional identity emerges from the individual and communal lived experiences of those within a particular region[49] and, similarly, the theatres in this study did not present homogeneous off-shoots of London productions but vibrant and individual performances.

This book is organised into two overarching sections, the first dealing with spectacle and the second with referencing. Within the first part, Chapter 1 provides an overview of the format of pantomime production in the period, with a particular focus on the transformation scene and the harlequinade. These two components were inherited from the Georgian and early-nineteenth-century pantomime, and their sustained incorporation was a vital element in terms of audience expectations and the subtle differences of local and individual productions. The argument then turns in Chapter 2 to the individual theatres in each town, examining the nature of pantomime production at theatres with differing financial and logistical capabilities, and how some of the more established and financially confident theatres could incorporate success, creative ability and the ensuing status into the promoted local identity of the theatre. In seeking a different kind of status, financially less able theatres adapted elements of spectacle to create their own identity in the face of competition. These features were supported by the local press and over time the promotional materials effectively introduced new ideas of tradition, relating them very specifically to the identity of individual theatres.

The second section of the book focuses on the variety of references in local pantomimes and the way in which a local identity could be projected through the use, not just of spoken references, but of visual representations, themed scenes, tableaux, dance and dialect. In order to clarify my aims in this section I have avoided using the word 'topical' although it is regularly applied to pantomime references. According to the *Oxford English Dictionary* definition, 'topical' can mean 'Of or pertaining to a place or locality; local', as well as 'Of or pertaining to the topics of the day; containing local or temporary allusions'. Topicality therefore engages with the 'topics of the day', 'temporary allusions' and a 'place or locality'. The extant manuscripts and books of words contain a wide variety of references that indicate different interest groups, knowledge and perspectives, including local, national and international references as well as various cultural, slang and everyday references that would have meant different things to different people in the audience. Subjects ranged for example from acts of Parliament, civic buildings, health and living conditions, trade disputes and recession to Rowland's hair oil, the sensation novel in the 1860s, the catchphrase 'Not for Joe', the literary character Mrs Grundy, the resort of Baden-Baden, railway accidents, Madame Tussauds, Cook's Excursions, Tennyson's poetry, Aestheticism, and Crosse and Blackwell pickles and hair dyes, as well as parodies of drama and opera. I am aware that there are references that, at this distance and without the necessary supporting evidence, cannot be identified. Similarly, there is always the danger of misinterpretation, as Clifford Geertz has established in his succinct definition of constructed data.[50] However, even with this caveat in place, a survey of the range of references emphasises that the terms 'local' and 'topical' are far more complex: what exactly constituted 'local' or 'topical' for people living in the three towns in this period, not necessarily in terms of the literal and geographic but in terms of knowledge? Was there an apparent demarcation of knowledge in the Nottingham, Birmingham and Manchester references that defined the appeal to each audience? More specifically still, for whom exactly, amongst the potential audience members, might a subject have been topical? These are important questions in terms of the relationship between the pantomime author/theatre managers and their audiences. With these additional considerations in mind, I have opted to use another, more general concept, that of *social referencing*. This term allows for greater flexibility in the interpretation of what was relevant to whom, and encompasses references to aspects of mid- to late-Victorian culture that, whilst they may not have been topical in the immediate temporal or spatial sense, still act as indicators of potential audiences and their various experiences and understandings. Regarding the issue of audience perspectives, the book draws throughout principally on the work of Susan Bennett, in particular her re-evaluation of Susan Suleimann's theory of the audience's horizons of expectation.[51]

In producing the range of references, provincial managers often opted to engage local authors, and in Chapter 3 I re-evaluate the role of what was often considered the 'hack' writer. The examples of writers such as F.R. Goodyer, John Anderton and George Dance, each engaged for a significant number of years by specific theatre managers, demonstrate that these authors were in reality considered and promoted precisely because of their localness and local knowledge, and became a vital tool in the success of pantomimes at those theatres. This chapter concludes with a selection of what were called 'topical songs'. These were not usually printed, and indeed due to their nature may not have been performed or at least would have been changed to incorporate updated material. Nevertheless, they do provide an additional and interesting insight into managerial consideration of what might be relevant for local audiences, particularly in the case of the Edwin Waugh song, which was never performed as it dealt with unemployment and starvation and was – perhaps naturally – considered too depressing for a pantomime.

Chapter 4 addresses the 'Politics of the pantomime' and the variable nature of party political referencing that took place across the theatres. Often theatres adopted a somewhat neutral pose and avoided such subjects or at least opted to attack all politicians of whatever colour. The main theatres at Birmingham, however, reflected the vibrant and important part that the city politicians – particularly Joseph Chamberlain – played in national politics. Two central case studies in this chapter, of the Theatre Royal and the Prince of Wales Theatre, illustrate once again the importance of authorship for a regional theatre and the extent to which a theatre manager could, over time, establish a particular political allegiance in the visual and verbal referencing of his pantomimes. The chapter addresses the role played by the Lord Chamberlain and Examiner of Plays as well as the nature of the unofficial censorship by the press and audiences. In the Birmingham cases, audience reaction and the lack of official complaint lead me to suggest a level of complicity between managers and their audiences, offering another dimension to the Victorian provincial pantomime.

Notes

1. *Birmingham Daily Post*, 1 February 1886, p. 1. Part of this quotation is cited by Gerald Frow in *'Oh Yes, It Is!': A History of Pantomime* (London, 1985), p. 163.
2. M.R. Booth (ed.), *English Plays of the Nineteenth Century*, vol. v: *Pantomimes, Extravaganzas and Burlesques* (Oxford, 1976); Booth, *Victorian Spectacular Theatre 1850–1910* (London, 1981), and *Theatre in the Victorian Age* (Cambridge, 1991). See also J.C. Morrow, 'The Staging of Pantomime at Sadler's Wells 1828–1860', unpublished PhD thesis (Ohio State University, 1963), which offers a detailed discussion of tricks and transformations; and R. Mander and J. Mitchenson, *Pantomime: A Story in Pictures* (London, 1973), which provides a pictorial overview of pantomime, although their discussion has been superseded by Booth's work.
3. For ideological concerns with Empire, see J. Davis, 'Imperial Transgressions: The Ideology of Drury Lane Pantomime in the Late Nineteenth Century', *New Theatre Quarterly*, 12 (1996). For discussions of sexuality, cross-dressing and gender, see P. Holland, 'The Play of Eros: Paradoxes of Gender in English Pantomime', *New Theatre Quarterly*, 13 (1997); D. Mayer, 'The Sexuality of English Pantomime', *Theatre Quarterly*, 4 (1974); E.M. Eigner, 'Imps, Dames and Principal Boys: Gender Confusion in the Nineteenth-Century Pantomime', *Browning Institute Studies*, 17 (1989); and S.A. Weltman, 'Pantomime Truth and Gender Performance: John Ruskin on Theatre', in D. Birch and F. O'Gorman (eds), *Ruskin and Gender* (Basingstoke, 2002). In addition, the economic and social role of women and children employed in pantomime has been addressed by T.C. Davis, 'The Theatrical Employees of Victorian Britain: Demography of an Industry', *Nineteenth Century Theatre*, 18/1 and 2 (1990); and D. Purkiss, *Troublesome Things: A History of Fairies and Fairy Stories* (London, 2000).
4. D. Mayer, *Harlequin in His Element: The English Pantomime 1806–1836* (Cambridge, 1969); J. Moody, *Illegitimate Theatre in London 1770–1840* (Cambridge, 2000); and J. O'Brien, *Harlequin Britain: Pantomime and Entertainment, 1690–1760* (Baltimore, 2004). See also George Speaight, 'New Light on "Mother Goose"', *Theatre Notebook*, 52 (1998), and 'Harlequinade Turn-Ups', *Theatre Notebook*, 45 (1991). The dominance of the Georgian pantomime has also influenced works aimed at the general reader: N. Robbins's *Slapstick and Sausages: The Evolution of the British Pantomime* (Tiverton, 2002) expended five chapters on the origins and early history of the pantomime to the 1800s.
5. J. Moody, 'The State of the Abyss: Nineteenth Century Performance and Theatre Historiography in 1999', *Journal of Victorian Culture*, 5 (2000), p. 124.
6. *Ibid.*, p. 125. The study of Victorian pantomime has recently been reinvigorated: Jim Davis's conference on Victorian pantomime at Warwick University in 2007 paved the way for a compilation of essays, *Victorian Pantomime: A Collection of Critical Essays* (Basingstoke, 2010). Katherine Newey (Birmingham) and Jeffrey Richards (Lancaster) embarked on a three-year AHRC-funded project on Victorian provincial pantomime in 2009, and a further AHRC-funded project on Scottish pantomime, 'Pantomime in Scotland: Your Other National Theatre' is currently being undertaken at Glasgow University, led by Professor Adrienne Scullion.
7. C. Scott, *The Drama of Yesterday and Today*, 2 vols (London, 1899), vol. ii, pp. 164–87 (quotation p. 164).
8. J.R. Planché, *The Recollections and Reflections of J.R. Planché: A Professional Autobiography*, 2 vols (London, 1872) vol. ii, p. 139.
9. L. Wagner, *The Pantomimes and All About Them: Their Origin, History, Preparation and Exponents* (London, 1881), p. 51.
10. Cited in E.M. Eigner, *The Dickens Pantomime* (Berkeley, CA, 1989), p. 143.

11. J. Bratton, *New Readings in Theatre History* (Cambridge, 2003), pp. 12–13. Similar concerns have also been raised by R. Jackson in *Victorian Theatre* (London, 1989), pp. 2–3, 5–6.

12. S. Shepherd and P. Womack, *English Drama: A Cultural History* (Oxford, 1996), pp. 192–3.

13. A brief but succinct outline of those nineteenth-century expressions of regret regarding the perceived decline of the pantomime are given in Cheesmond, 'Oh No It Isn't: A Functionalistic Re-definition of Pantomime', in R. Merkin (ed.), *Popular Theatres? Papers from the Popular Theatre Conference* (Liverpool, 1996), pp. 220–2. See also a reference to nineteenth-century critical attitudes in Booth, 'Introduction' to vol. v of *English Plays*, p. 2.

14. C. Scott and C. Howard, *The Life and Reminiscences of E.L. Blanchard, with Notes from the Diary of Wm. Blanchard*, 2 vols (London, 1891); Davenport-Adams cited in J. Davis, 'Imperial Transgressions', pp. 147–8, and Mander and Mitchenson, *Pantomime*, pp. 35–6.

15. J. O'Brien, 'Harlequin Britain: Eighteenth-Century Pantomime and the Cultural Location of Entertainment(s)', *Theatre Journal*, 50 (1998), p. 399; Frow, '*Oh Yes, It Is!*', p. 10.

16. D. Mayer, 'Some Recent Writings on Victorian Theatre', *Victorian Studies*, 20 (1977), p. 314.

17. Holland, 'The Play of Eros', p. 196.

18. Shepherd and Womack, *English Drama*, p. x.

19. J. Davis, 'Imperial Transgressions', p. 148.

20. Booth, *English Plays*, p. 54.

21. A.E. Wilson, *Christmas Pantomime* (London, 1934), p. 174.

22. *Ibid.*, p. 202.

23. Booth, *Theatre in the Victorian Age*, p. 209; Holland, 'The Play of Eros', p. 197. See also A. Ruston, 'Richard Nelson Lee and the Victorian Pantomime in Great Britain', *Nineteenth Century Theatre Research*, 11/2 (1983), p. 105.

24. R.J. Broadbent, *A History of Pantomime* (London, 1901). See also A.E. Wilson, *Pantomime Pageant: A Procession of Harlequins, Comedians, Principal Boys, Pantomime-writers, Producers and Playgoers* (London, 1946). Broadbent's book has recently been republished, further extending the dominance of the nineteenth-century histories.

25. Booth, *Theatre in the Victorian Age*, pp. 14–16.

26. 'The Secrets of Pantomime Production. By Our Special Commissioner', *Manchester Weekly Times*, 22 December 1893, p. 8.

27. K. Barker, 'The Performing Arts in Five Provincial Towns 1840–1870', unpublished PhD thesis (University of Leicester, 1982); also 'Bristol at Play 1801–1853: A Typical Picture of the English Provinces?', in D. Mayer and K. Richards (eds), *Western Popular Theatre: The Proceedings of a Symposium Sponsored by the Manchester University Department of Drama* (London, 1977), and *The Theatre Royal, Bristol, 1766–1966: Two Centuries of Stage History* (London, 1974). The earlier work by J.E. Cunningham (*Theatre Royal: A History of the Theatre Royal, Birmingham* (Oxford, 1950)), is somewhat traditional in its approach and is dismissive of pantomime, but he raised awareness of archive records in Birmingham. More interesting is D.A. Reid's study of audience in, 'Popular Theatre in Victorian Birmingham', in D. Bradby, L. James and B. Sharratt (eds), *Performance and Politics in Popular Drama: Aspects of Popular Entertainment in Theatre, Film and Television 1800–1976: Papers Given at a Conference at the University of Kent at Canterbury, September 1977* (Cambridge, 1980). See also: J. Crump, 'Patronage, Pleasure and Profit: A Study of the Theatre

Royal, Leicester 1847–1900', *Theatre Notebook*, 38 (1984); L. Fitzsimmons, 'The Theatre Royal, York in the 1840s', *Nineteenth Century Theatre and Film*, 31/1 (2004); A. Heinrich, *Entertainment, Propaganda, Education: Regional Theatre in Germany and Britain between 1918 and 1945* (London, 2007); K. Newey, 'Early Nineteenth-Century Theatre in Manchester', *Manchester Regional History Review*, 17/2 (2006); and P.A. Talbot, 'The Macclesfield Theatre Company and Nineteenth Century Silk Manufacturers', *Theatre Notebook*, 54 (2000).

28. D. Kift, *The Victorian Music Hall: Culture, Class and Conflict*, trans. R. Kift (Cambridge, 1996); and A. Featherstone, '"Crowded Nightly": Popular Entertainment Outside London during the Nineteenth and Early Twentieth Centuries', unpublished PhD thesis (Royal Holloway, University of London, 2000). Plus: J. Crump, 'Provincial Music Hall: Promoters and Public in Leicester, 1863–1929', in P. Bailey (ed.), *Music Hall: The Business of Pleasure* (Milton Keynes, 1986); and P. Joyce, *Visions of the People: Industrial England and the Question of Class 1848–1914* (Cambridge, 1991), in particular Chapter 13, 'Stages of Class: Popular Theatre and the Geography of Belonging'.

29. J. Robinson, 'Becoming More Provincial? The Global and the Local in Theatre History', *New Theatre Quarterly*, 23/3 (2007), p. 239.

30. 1861 census figure taken from B.R. Mitchell with the collaboration of P. Deane, *Abstract of British Historical Statistics* (Cambridge, 1962), p. 26.

31. J. Beckett, *The Book of Nottingham* (Buckingham, 1990), p. 11.

32. R.A. Church, *Economic and Social Change in a Midland Town: Victorian Nottingham 1815–1900* (London, 1966), p. 236.

33. *Ibid*, plus Beckett, *Book of Nottingham*, p. 11; D. Gray, *Nottingham, Settlement to City*, 2nd edn (East Ardsley, 1969), pp. 66–71; and J. Beckett, *The East Midlands from A.D. 1000* (London, 1988), pp. 225–7. Census figures from Mitchell and Deane, *British Historical Statistics*, pp. 26–7.

34. Church, *Economic and Social Change*, p. 195; and H.E. Meller (ed.), *Nottingham in the Eighteen Eighties* (Nottingham, 1971) p. 11.

35. Mitchell and Deane, *British Historical Statistics*, pp. 24, 27. The census figures were inclusive from 1911.

36. S. Gunn, *The Public Culture of the Victorian Middle Class: Ritual and Authority and the English Industrial City* (Manchester, 2000), p. 12. The *Birmingham Daily Post* referred to 'visitors to the Midland Metropolis' in its pantomime review 'Christmas Entertainments: Theatre Royal' on 26 December 1872, p. 8.

37. G.C. Allen, *The Industrial Development of Birmingham and the Black Country 1860–1927* (London, 1929), p. 3.

38. *Ibid*., pp. 33–4, 43.

39. A. Kidd, *Manchester* (Keele, 1993), pp. 15, 21, 22, 27, 30–2, 105, 144, 145–50.

40. In their introduction to *The Performing Century: Nineteenth Century Theatre's History* (Basingstoke and New York, 2007), the editors T.C. Davis and P. Holland refer to micro-historical processes as 'Marxist-inflected'. This is not, I believe, a universal application, and I use the term in relation to New Historicist rather than Marxist methodologies.

41. T.C. Davis, *The Economics of the British Stage 1800–1914* (Cambridge, 2000). Booth used the phrase 'the *business* of theatre' in his review of John Pick's *The West End* in the article 'Studies in Nineteenth Century British Theatre 1980–1989', *Nineteenth Century Theatre*, 20/1 (1992), p. 53.

42. J. Davis and V. Emeljanow, *Reflecting the Audience: London Theatregoing 1840–1880* (Hatfield, 2001), p. 68. Booth earlier suggested that the East End pantomimes were produced for 'neighbourhood audiences' and had 'their own pantomime traditions' (*English Plays*, p. 54).

43. Booth, *Victorian Spectacular Theatre*, p. 86.
44. R.L. Root, Jr, *The Rhetorics of Popular Culture: Advertising, Advocacy, and Entertainment* (New York, 1987), p. 63.
45. *Ibid.*, p. 64.
46. For a discussion of the combined influence of the theatre manager and the reviewer in altering aspects of a production, see J. Kaplan, 'A Puppet's Power: George Alexander, Clement Scott, and the Replotting of *Lady Windermere's Fan*', *Theatre Notebook*, 46 (1992).
47. H. Freshwater, *Theatre & Audiences* (Basingstoke, 2009), pp. 36, 35.
48. Bratton, *New Readings in Theatre History*, pp. 38–66.
49. See, for example, A.R. Townsend and C.C. Taylor, 'Regional Culture and Identity in Industrialised Societies: the Case of North-East England', *Regional Studies*, 9/4 (1975), and J. Nadal-Klein, 'Reweaving the Fringe: Localism, Tradition, and Representation in British Ethnography', *American Ethnologist*, 18/3 (1991), 'Representations of Europe: Transforming State, Society and Identity', who argue for the relationship between local and regional identity and individual experience. See also the introduction to R. Cowgill and P. Holman, *Music in the British Provinces 1690–1914* (Aldershot and Burlington, VT, 2007), which addresses the notion of the 'provincial'.
50. C. Geertz, *The Interpretation of Cultures: Selected Essays* (London, 1993), p. 9. Although not related to pantomime, the distinction between general and specific knowledge is also usefully addressed in R.D. Altick's essay 'Past and Present: Topicality and Technique', in J. Clubbe (ed.), *Carlyle and His Contemporaries: Essays in Honour of Charles Richard Sanders* (Durham, 1976). In this Altick presents an interesting discussion of the range of references – from the national and well-known to more personal references known only to a few – in the work of Thomas Carlyle. He addresses the problem of assessing the impact of the historical use of topicality at pp. 112–13.
51. S. Bennett, *Theatre Audiences: A Theory of Production and Reception*, 2nd edn (London, 1994), pp. 125–65.

Part One

The Spectacle of Pantomime

1

The gorgeous Christmas pantomime

In late November 1860, theatre managements around the country began their preparations for the Christmas pantomime. Depending on the resources of the individual theatre, the pantomime might be a bought-in production from one of the London or other provincial theatres, a production wholly created in the local theatre, or one that drew on both locally produced and bought-in elements of scenery and script. The decision rested on the financial capabilities of the theatre, the pecuniary skills of the management and the success or failure of the preceding autumn drama season. An astute investment of time and money was crucial as the profit from the pantomime would contribute significantly to the realisation of a successful theatre season for the remainder of the year (as well as potentially providing funds for necessary alterations or repairs to the building). The *Manchester Weekly Times* in its preview of the forthcoming production in 1860 proclaimed that:

> What would become of us if it were not for our pantomimes? so say all of us, managers the most earnestly, for pantomime has become – 'O tempora, O mores' – the sheet anchor of the drama. If it were not for that raddled face and those spangled pantaloons, what would become of Shakespeare and Sheridan. The former bring grist to the mill, the great immortals gobble it up.[1]

John Knowles, the proprietor of the Theatre Royal, Manchester echoed these sentiments at the 1866 Select Committee on Theatrical Licenses and Regulations, stating that 'in most country towns, pantomime is … the sheet anchor of the drama at the present moment'.[2] It was crucial, then, that theatre managers provided not simply an annual pantomime, but one that both corresponded to specific expectations regarding the format and reflected national and local innovations. Traditions and variation, national patterns and local identity all shaped productions at the theatres in Manchester, Birmingham and Nottingham.

By the 1860s, the audiences of the Midlands and North West who visited their local theatres at Christmas were partaking in particular theatrical traditions and developments that epitomised pantomime productions by mid-century.[3] Throughout the period the theatre managements in all three centres adhered to the basic format of pantomime, which comprised the 'opening', culminating in a transformation scene, followed by a short harlequinade, and concluding with an optional finale, sometimes a ballet or tableau such as 'Shadow and Sunshine' at the end of *Harlequin Sinbad the Sailor; Or, the Red Dwarfs, The Terrible Ogre, and The Old Man of the Sea* (Theatre Royal, Birmingham, 1865) or 'Flora's Home Amid the Honey Bouquets in the Garden of the Fairy Queen', which concluded *Robinson Crusoe* at the same theatre two years later, in 1867.

During the 1860s and 1870s, the pantomime would often be preceded by a short opening play, usually a comedy or farce, a practice which lasted until the discontinuation of the stock company at the local theatres. At Manchester and Nottingham this change occurred in the late 1870s, but the Theatre Royal, Birmingham was – according to its manager Mercer Simpson – the last provincial theatre to engage a stock company: not until the 1880–1 theatre season did he have an entire season that comprised touring theatre companies.[4] By 1880 the pantomime at all theatres took up the entire bill and three to three and a half hours appears to have been the accepted length of a performance. In 1890, the *Birmingham Daily Gazette* commented that a rehearsal of *The Forty Thieves* had been 'compressed into a little over four hours'. The reviewer suggested that 'with a judicious cut here and there, we fully expect to see it squeezed into the usual three and a half hours'.[5] However, there were exceptions: the 1862 production of *The House That Jack Built* at the Manchester Theatre Royal lasted an exceptionally short two hours, whereas *The Queen of Hearts* at that theatre in 1884 exhausted its first-night audience with a five hour performance. Such excesses were not unknown at Drury Lane, but at the provincial theatres pantomimes of this length would have been edited after the first night.

Traditionally, the pantomimes opened on Boxing Day and, as Jim Davis has recently highlighted, this night combined the fashionable and the popular, with theatres up and down the country packed with expectant audiences.[6] This particular tradition was not comprehensively adhered to: the multiple and highly competitive theatre managements in Manchester regularly opened their pantomimes prior to Boxing Day, sometimes by as much as a week or ten days. Most theatres shut for a rehearsal week prior to the first night, but such measures rarely guaranteed a flawless performance. Scenery would stick, the dancers were not necessarily performing in unison and lines were forgotten. Both press and audiences alike were sympathetic; the difficulties of the first night – often compounded by the piece overrunning until past midnight – were also regarded as yet another tradition. What would have been unforgivable in opera or drama was permitted at the pantomime. Very occasionally a public dress rehearsal would be held, such as that at the Theatre Royal, Nottingham in 1866, but all theatres would have staged a formal rehearsal for the press and invited guests a few days prior to the opening night. Subsequent previews, prompted by the theatre management, emphasised features that were also central to the initial newspaper advertisements. The promoted features highlighted the often extravagant expenditure on productions: between 1860 and 1900 this emphasis slowly shifted from scenic spectacle to the names of the specially engaged company, including stars of the burlesque and music-hall stage, variety acts and, by 1900, the biograph.

As the following chapters will illustrate, theatre managements all faced the annual dilemma of providing their audiences with particular elements of nationally recognised traditions, such as the transformation scene and the harlequinade, as well as responding to the latest innovations in spectacle and effects, whilst aiming to sustain audience figures for the two- or three-month run and conclude the Christmas season with a profit. In order to maintain audiences and income, many theatres resorted to what was termed the 'Second Edition' and, very occasionally, a 'Third Edition' in late January or early February. This later edition of the pantomime could include new songs, comic 'business' and new costumes; sometimes one or two new sets would be provided, or some of the pantomime roles recast. On rare occasions, if both the press and public had remained unforgiving after the first night, the pantomime might be completely rewritten. At some theatres, for example the Prince's Theatre in Manchester, the Second Edition itself became a tradition. The revised version was reviewed in the local press as another stage in the organic development of a good pantomime, one that was to be expected of that theatre. In marked contrast, the management at the Theatre Royal in Birmingham refused to openly acknowledge that the pantomime needed revising, and although new features may have been added after Christmas, it was never advertised as a Second Edition. The local press again supported this decision; when in February 1894 the pantomime was revised to include new songs and jokes, the *Birmingham Daily Post* merely commented that such small changes were always necessary in a pantomime.[7]

By mid-century the productions were dominated by the opening, which consisted of between ten and twelve scenes. It was invariably based on a well-known story or fairy tale and recurring popular titles in this period included *Dick Whittington*, *Robinson Crusoe*, *Aladdin*, *Blue Beard*, *Babes in the Wood* and *The Forty Thieves*. By the 1860s, the first two scenes of the pantomime often followed a specific pattern: Scene 1 would be a 'dark' scene featuring nefarious magicians, evil spirits and ogres plotting to thwart the hero within settings such as 'The Magician's Study in the Temple of the Thundering Winds', which opened the Nottingham pantomime of *Aladdin* in 1866, or 'The Storm King's Lair under the Deep Blue Sea', which began *Robinson Crusoe* at the Theatre Royal, Birmingham in 1878. The dark scene would be followed by a second, contrasting scene wherein the Fairy Queen counterplotted to aid the hero. Such oppositions established the moral outcome of the story, with the attributes of the demons and fairies being sustained by the characters in the main plot: the hard-working and virtuous hero and heroine, and the profligate baron or wicked uncle.[8] This scene order had been established in the pantomimes of the late eighteenth and early nineteenth centuries and was regarded by the newspaper reviewers as traditional, but, as Michael Booth has noted, the sequence could be reversed in pantomimes produced after the mid-nineteenth century.[9] Certainly, evidence from the provincial theatres illustrates variations in the scene ordering of pantomimes of the 1860s and 1870s. For example, in 1867 at the Theatre Royal, Birmingham, the opening scene to establish the pantomime story of *Robinson Crusoe* was interrupted by 'Mischief'; the first, celebratory scene in *The Fairy Fawn* (1872) was similarly interrupted by the uninvited bad fairy 'Argentina', and the opening scene of the Comedy Theatre production of *Dick Whittington* in Manchester in 1887 included both the good and wicked fairies debating the future of the hero. Equally, the ill-will of demons could be enacted by mortal villains in the opening scene, such as Idle Jack in *Dick Whittington* of 1870, or the family solicitor in *Puss in Boots* of 1875, both staged at the Theatre Royal, Birmingham. The 1869 and 1876 productions at Nottingham opened with the fairy scene, and in *Blue Beard* (1877) the 'Abode of the Goblin King' was moved to Scene 2 whilst the pantomime opened in Toyland, populated by a selection of topically well-informed and disgruntled dolls. In *The Pantomimes and All About Them* (1881), Leopold Wagner stated that many librettists had stopped including an opening demon scene, but evidence from Manchester and Birmingham shows that the traditional opening dark scene, whether solely the domain of demons or interrupted by good fairies, was in fact sustained into the 1890s.[10]

The remaining eight or ten scenes of the pantomime opening pursued the story of the title, the pantomimes of the mid-century culminating in another 'dark' scene where the hero and heroine were trapped (recalling the Georgian and early Victorian harlequinades in which Harlequin customarily lost his magic bat and had to be rescued).[11] Once again the fairy appeared, to release the heroes and punish the wrongdoers, and the transformation scene followed marking the end of the opening. Whereas in pantomimes at the beginning of the century the short, spoken opening was a prelude to the longer, mimed activity of the harlequinade, by the 1860s the opening contained full, scripted dialogue. Portions of the libretto were printed and available to the audience as a 'book of words', which were on sale in the theatre for 1d at Nottingham and 2d at the Birmingham and Manchester theatres.[12]

The opening did not simply tell the tale; it was an opportunity for scenic display, grand ballets, music and comedy. Much of the last involved burlesque, so much so that the opening was often referred to as the 'burlesque opening'.[13] A popular genre that had emerged in the 1850s and 1860s, burlesque 'was a compound of music hall, minstrel

Cover of the 1883 book of words from the Theatre Royal, Nottingham, *Little Bo Peep*.

show, extravaganza, legs and limelight, puns, topical songs, and gaudy irreverence'.[14] In particular, burlesque was predicated on parody and satire, and pantomime plots increasingly included liberal imitations of well-known plays and operas. The pantomimes at Nottingham, for example, could include parodies of Shakespearean drama, such as that of *Macbeth* in 1876 ('Is this a corkscrew I see before me') or of *Othello* in *Little Red Riding Hood* (1873):

> BARON. 'One more, one more – when I have plucked thy rose'
> GRANNY. Oh! Where's my handkercher? let's blow my nose.[15]

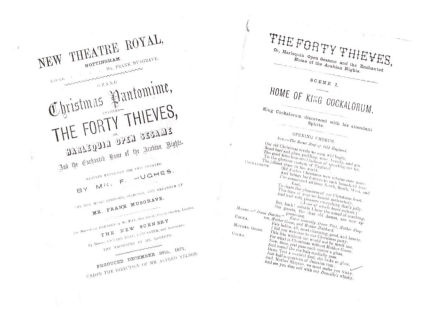

Book of words from the Theatre Royal, Nottingham, *The Forty Thieves or, Harlequin Open Sesame and the Enchanted Home of the Arabian Nights* (1871).

The Nottingham pantomimes also included burlesques of Gilbert and Sullivan's *Trial by Jury* (in *Babes in the Wood* of 1878) and *Ruddigore* (in the 1887 version of *Babes in the Wood*).[16] The script of the 1887 production of *Beauty and the Beast* at the Prince's Theatre, Manchester was littered with character references to *Hamlet*, as well as to nautical melodramas and Gilbert and Sullivan operettas. *Harlequin Graceful; or, the Fair One with the Golden Locks* at the Theatre Royal, Nottingham in 1876 featured the Dame busy with her laundry tub: 'Tubby or not tubby is not the question / ... Scouring o' dirty linen, there's the rub.'[17] By 1891, a version of *Robinson Crusoe* at the Nottingham Theatre Royal mercilessly parodied the conventions of melodrama and pantomime throughout:

Atkins. I am the villain, but of course you know so.
They shot a blaze of lime-light on to Crusoe.
Lights up for heroes – that's the only way;
Red fire and discord for the villain of the play.[18]

Increasingly in the second half of the nineteenth century the opening became the site for spectacular effects, initially epitomised in the transformation scene. Whilst in pantomimes of the early nineteenth century this scene indicated the crucial transformation of figures in the opening into the harlequinade characters (achieved by the removal of outsized masks and costumes), by the 1860s this aspect of the scene had become a token gesture, with the emphasis instead falling on the transformation of the scenery.[19] The reinvention of the transformation scene had been primarily influenced by William Beverley, resident scenic artist at the Lyceum Theatre in London. In 1849 Beverley had designed a concluding scene for J.R. Planché's fairy extravaganza *The Island of Jewels*. This scene had featured 'the novel and yet exceedingly simple falling of the leaves of a palm tree which discovered six fairies supporting a coronet of jewels'.[20] Planché described in his autobiography how Beverley was subsequently required to produce ever more spectacular scenery: 'Year after year Mr. Beverley's powers were tasked to outdo his former out-doings. The *last* scene became the first in the estimation of the management.'[21] Planché noted how this aspect of the extravaganza was quickly incorporated into the transformation scene of the pantomimes, thereby turning the formerly simple transition into 'the great feature of the evening'.[22] Each year witnessed another variation on Beverley's original concept and by the mid-1850s pantomimes around the country featured transformation scenes, incorporating adult and juvenile dancers placed in and around glittering variations on crystal hives, outsized gilded and decorated banana or palm leaves, and a variety of flowers, shells and bulrushes. The standards set by the London theatres meant that local theatre productions were, to a certain degree, in thrall to consumer anticipation regarding the quantity of tinsel and gorgeous fabrics in their pantomimes, and the consequent expense of this scene for theatre managements was reflected in the prominence of the transformation scene in advertisements and – certainly into the early 1870s – the press reviews of the opening night. Lengthy descriptions extolled the extravagance of scenes such as 'Halls of Shadows and Sunshine', the title of the transformation scene in the 1867 pantomime *Robinson Crusoe* at the Birmingham Theatre Royal:

This latter scene is, of course, a marvel of splendour. Its chief component elements are golden bulrushes of every hue and size, arranged in a series of receding quatrefoil frames.… The central group consists of a silver clad fairy, in mid-air, supported cariatyd [sic] fashion by a number of inferior spirits who gradually float downwards in an expanding circle. Behind the central figure is a huge sun, consisting of a silver globe emitting substantial golden rays but its glories are presently eclipsed by the intervention of a huge golden trellis work, rising nearly to the flies, and decorated with living fruit, in the shape of lightly clad fairies. In the wings and foreground other fairies are attitudinising, some in stationary and others in revolving clusters of bulrushes, upon which the many coloured electric light plays with dazzling and ever changing effect. The production of this spectacular triumph, yesterday, was hailed by the large audience present with immense enthusiasm, and the manager and Mr. Roberts, the artist, were summoned forward to receive the public felicitations.[23]

In 1868, the transformation scene 'Queen of the Night and Her Maids of Light' was reported by the critic of the *Birmingham Daily Post* to be a scene of 'dazzling splendour'. Despite doubting his own abilities to describe the scene, the critic continued:

the general form of the tableau is a series of Persian arches fringed with large bell-shaped flowers, and flanked by cabriole-shaped wings. In the distance is a rustic arcade through the arches of which naiads appear against a glittering green background. The extreme distance is occupied by a huge revolving sun in fret work, and the wings are encircled with metallic revolving stars whose radii reflect the hues of the electric light. The centre space is occupied partly by a descending group of fairies supporting a huge golden crescent, which remains poised in mid air, and from beneath by the leading fairy figure richly clad, ascending out of an open trellis work bower. The foreground is occupied by banks of flowers, and all the vacant parts of the design are filled up with richly attired fays in sculpturesque attitudes and draperies. The effect of the whole under the glow of the coloured fires and electric light is resplendent beyond conception.[24]

The 1861 transformation scene at the Manchester Theatre Royal had been similarly impressive. 'The Cascade of Liquid Diamonds in the Valley of Sparkling Gems' used the entirety of the stage:

> The stage of the theatre is opened to its utmost extent of, we believe, some eighty feet from the footlights. In the extreme distance are high rocks of gold, over which falls a sheet of real water, that, rolling down, spreads itself over a broad and inclining surface, upon which are liberally strewed golden nuggets, precious stones, so rich and rare that the eye is dazzled with their brilliance as they flash and sparkle under a blaze of light. Anon the silver flood takes all the hues of the rainbow, as though the surface over which it rushes was illuminated from beneath; again its silvery face looks deeply transparent, and again and again it is clothed in rainbow beauty. At the same time, the golden banks of the stream are lighted up, and upon golden pedestals (one of which is worth a journey to California in shoes filled with dried peas) there are floated into this gorgeous arena groups of the loveliest of lovely maidens, all decked out in costume of richest material and colour.[25]

During the 1860s new, rival theatres opened – the Prince of Wales Theatre in Birmingham and the Prince's Theatre in Manchester – and each of these theatres also strove to provide the necessary glittering conclusions to the opening of their pantomimes. Indeed, under the management of Charles Calvert, the Prince's Theatre, Manchester displaced the more established house. Once the Prince's had opened in 1864, the Theatre Royal transformation scenes ceased to inspire extensive press notices and the Prince's Theatre provided the Royal with a formidable rival for the remainder of the period. For the 1866 pantomime of *Robin Hood*, a team of artists led by Thomas Grieve, one of the principal London scenic artists, created a transformation scene of which

> The first view represents an enchanted lake, the moonlight playing upon its transparent waters, bedecked with silver lilies. This occupied the foreground. In the extreme distance the figure of the angel 'Bon Accord' is seen. It would be almost impossible to describe all the numerous and complicated changes that take place, and we can do

no more than briefly allude to the magnificent effect of the shower of jewels, the brilliancy of the shifting lights, the splendour of the fairies who fill the scene at the end, the angel with her outstretched wings, and, chief of all, the centre group, representing a colossal épergne of silver, with the three horses life-size, and on which are seated 'Robin,' the 'King,' and 'Maid Marian.' There is a novelty and a grandeur about this scene that cannot fail to make the pantomime memorable.[26]

Lovely maidens at the Theatre Royal had been transposed into 'splendour' at the Prince's Theatre; the central effect there was colossal grandeur. In 1873, the transformation scene at the Prince's was a grand representation 'of the daring attempt of Endymion to scale the heights of Mount Latimus, the descent of Diana, and Endymion's dream'.[27] Spectacular transformation scenes that created new and exciting variations on the traditional format continued at the Prince's Theatre. The 1874 version featured a 'River of Glass' with 'Cupid's State Barge' and in 1876 the 'imposing' transformation scene 'The Dream of the Sphynx' comprised three tableaux, concluding with the 'triumphal entrance of Sinbad's fairy barge'.[28]

SCENE FROM THE PANTOMIME AT THE PRINCE'S THEATRE, MANCHESTER—("SINBAD").

Prince's Theatre Manchester pantomime of *Sinbad* (1876), in the *Illustrated Sporting and Dramatic News*.

The picture in the *Illustrated Sporting and Dramatic News* highlights the shift of emphasis in transformation scenes at the Prince's. The trio of fairies, which here provides a background picture, would have traditionally been centre stage, at the conclusion of a series of unfolding and highly decorated mechanisms, but here the front of the stage is dominated by the life-sized barge. Whilst this last feature repeated the successful motif of the 1874 production, the illustration suggests that Sinbad's boat sailed on water not glass; droplets fall from the suspended oars manned by children in remarkably English sailor suits. The use of water for spectacular stage effect had been established in 1860 by Dion Boucicault's incorporation of a water tank for the dramatic conclusion of *The Colleen Bawn*. The eclectic nature of pantomime quickly adopted this stylistic feature, and a succession of streams, waterfalls and ponds recurred in the more expensive productions of the second half of the nineteenth century. Indeed, the fact that the Prince's Theatre management continued to include a range of novel elements in their transformation scenes as well as a plethora of additional features in the opening marked out the financial capabilities of the establishment. The Prince's Theatre was not simply concerned to rival local productions; its management boasted a national status. Press advertisements promoted the 'METROPOLITAN REPUTATION' of the theatre, exhibiting quotes from the principal local as well as London press. The claim that 'The expense of the Manchester pantomime has probably cost more than all the London Christmas pieces combined' was undoubtedly exaggerated puff, but the theatre, under Calvert's immediate management and later legacy, certainly reigned amongst the leading provincial houses.[29]

As mentioned at the start of this chapter, in achieving a spectacular pantomime, managers could draw on local as well as London talents. Sometimes the full range of sources for scenery and mechanical effects was played down, to prioritise the promotion of local resources, but provincial theatres did not always attempt to conceal the metropolitan sources of their spectacle. Such inclusions did not usurp local creative talents, but their promotion could instead be used to underscore the status and particular identity of the individual theatres. For example, the Grieve family designed and executed scenery for the Theatre Royal, Covent Garden and other major theatres, and Thomas Grieve regularly painted and supervised scenes for Calvert's Shakespearean revivals and pantomimes in Manchester.[30]

Importantly, those original scenes were created specifically for the Prince's Theatre rather than being bought in from an older production, and the provenance of scenery and artist formed a central part of the advertising strategy for the theatre. Similarly, the 1867 transformation scene at the Theatre Royal, Birmingham cited above had been painted by David Roberts, the Grieves's main rival, who created scenery for the Theatre Royal, Drury Lane.[31] At the Prince of Wales Theatre in Birmingham in 1864, the management actively promoted the fact that the transformation scene had been painted by James Gates of the theatres Royal Lyceum, St James's and Adelphi, and John Johnson of the Surrey Theatre. The latter's 'REGISTERED SCENIC EFFECTS' were central to advertisements. Johnson again provided the transformation scene for the 1865 production and it was promoted as 'JOHNSON'S MAGNIFICENT TRANSFORMATION AND BALLET SCENES'.[32] A reviewer in the *Birmingham Daily Post* called the scene 'another bit of London on provincial boards', but the phrasing of the review suggested not simply that the management had bought in the scene, but that its contribution to the pantomime conferred a certain status on the theatre, implying that its management had the financial ability to create a production equal to anything in the capital.[33] The source of pantomime scenery and its promotion could prove effective not simply in terms of press and playbill advertisements. Both Grieve and Roberts appeared at the first nights of the pantomimes at the Manchester and Birmingham theatres and took a bow at the end of the respective performances. To be able to produce the artists, the embodiment of creative skill, physically alongside the manager, with both men acknowledging an enthusiastic audience, was a symbolic moment. In that bow, manager, artist, pantomime and theatre were as one in their achievement and the audience who were witness to the event partook in that celebration. The presence of the creative team on stage at the end of the opening-night performance enabled what Philip Auslander has phrased as the 'socio-cultural value attached to live presence', the éclat of being present at a particular and defining event.[34] For first-night audiences, the combined visual effect of expensive scenery and a London artist at their local theatre confirmed the status and particular identity of that theatre.

The Manchester Theatre Royal management also actively promoted the scenic effects of their pantomimes but, lacking the financial liberality of the Prince's Theatre management, the Royal transformation scenes sometimes reflected the effect of competition. In 1872, the final scene was simply a transparency – albeit 'magnificent' – of St George and the Dragon 'as represented on our gold coinage and surrounded by an illuminated gas device' with 'the other six champions ... ranged along the wings'. The *Manchester Guardian* reviewer thought the effect 'very pretty' and 'a pleasing variety on the ordinary style of things'. Indeed, he argued, the more typical transformation scene was 'very apt to be monotonous and tiresome'.[35] This statement reveals the reviewer as an advocate of the theatre, and supportive of change at a time when financial restrictions may not have allowed for greater display, but the audiences were not happy with the alternative style of scene. Whilst theatre managements aimed to influence their audiences with novelties, the pressure of competition and audience expectations could sometimes dictate the presentation of more traditional aspects. Following the experiment of 1872, the Manchester Theatre Royal pantomime of 1873 evinced far greater spectacular resources and returned to the more traditional format of the transformation scene. The reviewer in the *Manchester Guardian* effortlessly reverted to praise for the revised style, and upbraided the theatre the following year for not maintaining such a high standard. The sentiments of advocacy prevailed in 1875, however, when the Royal transformation scene, once again a more muted production, was described as 'highly artistic without being too lavish'.[36]

By the late 1870s, reviewers drew on generalities in their descriptions, or omitted the transformation altogether in their comments. This decline reflected the general trend of reviews in the provinces, as attention was drawn away to other features in the annual productions. Theatre managements all experienced conflicting pressures: to balance the desire for tradition with that for novelty, retaining the conventional spectacular final scene whilst incorporating new effects, scenes and, increasingly after the 1880s, expensive stars from the burlesque stage and music hall elsewhere in the opening. Even the detailed reviews of the transformation scenes at the Manchester Prince's Theatre were less frequent after 1880. The seduction of novelties, together with a perception that the transformation scene format had passed from tradition to monotony, interspersed the reviews of other theatres, but even in the 1860s there had been occasional comments that the scene had become somewhat conventional. In 1867, the transformation scene at the Prince of Wales Theatre in Birmingham was recommended to 'the lovers of spectacle' but also described as 'conventional … with its gauze and glitter, its gold and colour, its waving palms and flying fairies'.[37]

For smaller houses, or those with fewer financial resources, for which a range of spectacular features could be neither logistically nor financially viable, even an emphasis on the transformation scene could sometimes be difficult to sustain. For example, the overarching promotion of the transformation scene at the Theatre Royal, Nottingham followed a similar pattern to that at Birmingham and Manchester, with the scene remaining as a central focus of advertisements into the 1870s, but lengthy detailed descriptions tended to be the exception rather than the rule. The theatre had no legitimate rival, apart from the ballet spectaculars at the Alhambra Music Hall in the town, but the financial resources of the theatre management were such that even in the 1860s and early 1870s the transformation scene lacked the lavishness and novelty that attracted reviewers in the larger towns and cities.

After the 1870s, the transformation scene was not discarded by pantomime producers at any of the provincial theatres under discussion. Although reviewers and audiences were diverted by other elements, managements continued to invest in the scene, as evinced by its continued presence in advertisements. In 1892, for example, the *Birmingham Daily Gazette* stated that 'The transformation scene … worthily upholds the reputation of the Royal Theatre for brilliant spectacle.'[38] A factor here may well have been the influence of the Theatre Royal, Drury Lane. The management at that house continued to produce a transformation scene into the 1890s, so other theatres – particularly the major provincial houses – were unlikely to completely discontinue the tradition. The same cannot be said of the harlequinade, however, which experienced different fortunes in the second half of the nineteenth century.

Despite the emphasis by theatre historians on the decline of the harlequinade after Grimaldi's death in the late 1830s, this feature of the pantomime was still important nearly thirty years later. Therefore, as would be expected of a pantomime of the late 1850s, the harlequinade at the Manchester Theatre Royal in the 1859–60 season still commanded attention from the critics, who focused on the tricks and settings, most

AMUSEMENTS.

NEW THEATRE ROYAL, NOTTINGHAM.
Lessee :—Mr. FRANK MUSGRAVE.

MORNING PERFORMANCES.

NOTICE.—To accommodate Families residing in the Counties of Leicester, Derby, and Lincoln, Chesterfield, &c., there will be Two Morning Performances of the Pantomime on the following dates :—
First Morning Performance ....Saturday, Jan. 6th, 1872.
Second Morning Performance, Saturday, Jan. 13th, 1872.

On and after Wednesday, Jan. 10th, 1872,
JUVENILE NIGHT EVERY WEDNESDAY,
When the Pantomime will be played first. Children Half-price to Dress Circle, Upper Circle, and pit. No Half-price to Dress Circle Stalls or Gallery.

This (Monday) evening, Jan. 1, 1872, and every evening till further notice, the curtain will rise at Seven o'clock on the Charming Comedietta, entitled—

A DAY AFTER THE WEDDING,

Supported by Mr. Walter H. Fisher, G. A. Foote, C. F. Marshall, Miss Ada Coates, and Mrs. Bennett.

After which will be produced a Grand New and Original Pantomime, entitled—The

PORTY THIEVES.

Or, Harlequin Open Sesame, and the Enchanted Home of the Arabian Nights.

Written expressly for this Theatre by Mr. FRED HUGHES. The New and Original Music composed, selected, and arranged by Mr. FRANK MUSGRAVE. The New and Elaborate Scenery by Mr. EDWARD RYAN, Mr. LANCASTER, and Assistants. The Gorgeous Dresses designed and made by Mr. SAMUEL MAY, Bow Street, Covent Garden, London. The whole produced under the Direction of Mr. FRANK MUSGRAVE and Mr. ALFRED NELSON. Principal characters by Messrs. F. Marshall, G. K. Maskell, Martinetti, G. A. Foote; Mesdames Lotte Venne, Lee, Martinetti, Patty Kosa, Lennox, Sandretta, Annie Morton, and Hilda Vaughan.

Harlequin	M. Francoal
Columbine	Mdlle. Cerito
Clowns	Messrs. Harry Wright and Martinetti
Pantaloon	Mr. J. Halford
Sprites	The Martinetti Troupe, from the Cirque Imperial, Paris.
Premiere Danseuses	Mdlle. Cerito and Patty Kosa

Box Plan open at Mr. R. B. Earp's, 3, Market Street, Long Row.
Acting Manager and Treasurer......... Mr. J. C. MUSGRAVE.

Newspaper advertisement in the *Nottingham Journal* for January 1872, showing the harlequinade cast.

of which were routines dating back to the harlequinades of the early nineteenth century: 'Many are the tricks upon travellers – many the hair-breadth escapes – frequent the street rows, with the tangled confusion and battle storm of carrots, turnips, cabbages, red-herrings, sucking pigs...' The harlequinade performers on this occasion were engaged in addition to the 'regular stock company' performers, plus Mr J.P. Weston's performing dogs.[39] The following year the harlequinade took up an hour of the performance, once again featuring Mr Weston as Clown ('the favourite of last year'). In 1863 at a third theatre in Birmingham, the short-lived New Adelphi Theatre in Moor Street, the pantomime of *Blue Beard; or, the Genius of Fiction* included 'quite an army of supers to represent the mob' in the harlequinade; indeed this particular army mobilised in late January when their wages failed to materialise.[40]

However, and as indicated in these examples, in engaging separate performers the relationship that had existed in early-nineteenth-century pantomimes between the characters of the opening and those of the harlequinade had disappeared. The hero of the opening no longer became Harlequin, or the heroine Columbine; her father or guardian did not become the tottering Pantaloon and his servant no longer emerged as the anarchic Clown. Michael Booth in *English Plays* dates this change from the mid-1850s and emphasises the gradual division that had occurred in the London pantomimes by the 1860s, between the company who performed in the opening and the separate group of pantomimists who played in the harlequinade.[41] To a large extent, this was also true of the provincial theatres. At the Theatre Royal, Nottingham a team of pantomimists was engaged for the 1866–7 Christmas season and paid as a separate group at £14 per week, with £7 for the rehearsal week.[42] By the 1880s troupes such as the Lupino family were becoming favourites in the provincial theatres: the *Manchester Weekly Times* critic noted in 1879 that the harlequinade performed by the Lupino troupe 'was very lively and amusing' and paid them the dubious honour of stating that their act 'was quite worth staying for'.[43] The Clown in particular (played by established performers such as Little Levite, Little Laffar and Wattie Hildyard) was always highly promoted, earning a benefit performance throughout the period. However, although the correlation of characters no longer existed, the separation of the different groups of performers could be less comprehensive even after the 1860s. A.E. Wilson in *Pantomime Pageant* states that during the stock company years, Clown and sometimes Harlequin were special engagements, but both during and after the cessation of the stock companies at Nottingham, Manchester and Birmingham, the performers who played Clown and Harlequin often took on other roles in the opening.[44] For example, in Manchester Little Levite, the Clown in the Queen's Theatre harlequinade in 1874, also took on the role of the Wicked Fairy's son 'Cockatrice' in the opening. Mr Jean Stanley, who played Harlequin at the Theatre Royal, Nottingham in the 1880s, also played 'King Octopus' in *Little Bo Peep* of 1883, and 'Wehr Wolf' in *Little Red Riding Hood* of 1885.[45] Very occasionally the traditional links between the opening and harlequinade characters were recalled. In the Nottingham version of *Aladdin* in 1886, echoes of the traditional link between the Clown and the disreputable servant of the opening were revived when the Clown, Harry Collier, also played the Emperor's Vizier 'Jin Sling' in the opening.[46]

In addition to the separation of characters, the harlequinade, formerly the principal part of the pantomime, had by mid-century been reduced to just three or four scenes, although the urban settings of these scenes drew on much older traditions. Jane Moody has detailed how the early-nineteenth-century harlequinade featured urban street scenes with easily identifiable shops and businesses. The businesses illustrated provided an opportunity for advertising, the feature embracing the theatre in the commercial world of the urban environment.[47] Until the late 1860s, this element was central to harlequinades, whether performed at the West End, transpontine or provincial theatres. Productions at the Manchester theatres in particular maintained the use of urban and local settings and commercial references into the 1870s. The 1874 harlequinade at the Prince's Theatre, for example, featured a scene combining a reference to local commerce – 'the Depôt in China from which are shipped the MONING AND PAKLIN TEAS, to Black and Green, Piccadilly, Manchester' – with a novel yet entirely unrelated feature, 'THE FUNNY DOGS, IN NEW AND CORRECT COSTUMES'.[48] More usually on playbills and in the books of words, the scene descriptions are generic, such as the 'post office' or the 'butcher's shop', but whether the option for local advertising remained within those generalised settings, or whether advertising within the shortened harlequinade was no longer a viable commercial option, is unclear. Certainly in a review of the Drury Lane pantomime in 1870, the *Era* had commented that 'Thanks to the abolition of the advertising scenes, the harlequinade is better this year.'[49]

Harlequinade settings in the provincial pantomimes also promoted new civic and public buildings and achievements in the town. The 1868 pantomime at the Theatre Royal, Birmingham included a scene with the Town Hall in its harlequinade; in the 1860 pantomime of *Cinderella* at the Manchester Theatre Royal, the penultimate scene of the harlequinade depicted the new Assize Courts; and the Prince's Theatre in 1872 had 'a view of the New Town Hall completed' as the opening scene of its harlequinade, 'an extremely effective one' according to the *Manchester Weekly Times*.[50] The image occurred again in the opening of the 1876 pantomime at that theatre. In a scene supposedly representing the 'Gardens of the Seraglio', 'the painter, in defiance we fear of all laws of Oriental architecture, has constructed his towers *à la* Waterhouse. One portion of the picture has a decided resemblance to the New Town Hall.'[51] The 1872 Queen's Theatre harlequinade included a view of the Manchester aquarium, and the 1877 harlequinade at the Theatre Royal, Manchester included a view of Southport 'with the bathing machines' and one of the Manchester School of Art. Even though the harlequinade as a whole had become compressed and was sometimes omitted from reviews altogether by the late 1870s, there were still occasions on which it had a role to play in constructing local identity in the pantomime; this version for example included other local scenes and 'some capital local hits' in its harlequinade.[52]

After mid-century, there was a perception amongst critics and newspaper reviewers, in both London and the provinces, that the format had somehow stagnated, relying on routines and jokes 'as old as the hills'.[53] Along with the transformation scene, by the early 1870s the harlequinade had ceased to be described. in quite such detail as it had a few years earlier in reviews of any of the theatres, although it continued to be produced and advertised into the 1880s. Indeed, it did not simply wither and die during the later decades of the century. Janice Norwood has recently commented on the harlequinade at the Britannia Theatre in Hoxton, whose management:

bucked the prevalent trend to omit, or at least to reduce substantially, the harlequinade (essentially visual entertainment) in favour of a much longer and more verbal opening. By 1881 Leopold Wagner could write 'we have still in existence a people's theatre, in the East End of London, whose patrons are annually treated to a pantomime of the old sort, quite different from anything to be witnessed at the other houses.'[54]

The harlequinade did survive much longer in both the transpontine and provincial theatres in the nineteenth century than in the West End Theatres Royal of Drury Lane and Covent Garden.[55] It is evident that in the provinces this survival was linked to a combination of the traditions of the harlequinade (the comic policeman, the stolen baby, sausages and butter slides), together with fresh and innovative features, and the individual abilities of particular Clowns who, by their re-engagement at the provincial theatres, could be promoted as local favourites.[56] In 1876, front-page advertisements for the Theatre Royal, Nottingham unusually promoted a 'costly' 'BUDGET OF FUN' in that year's harlequinade and the expenditure was complemented by an extended review in the *Nottingham Journal*. The Clown, Mr J.M. Jones, displayed 'a fertility of invention, which while preserving the time honoured but mischievous proclivities of clown and pantaloon, imparts to the fooleries enough of novelty to keep them abundantly alive'.[57] In 1871 the *Birmingham Daily Mail* remarked of the Theatre Royal harlequinade, that 'Mr. Bibb makes a capital clown, introducing several clever new tricks' and in 1873 the same paper applauded the fact that 'The harlequinade introduces lots of new tricks – regular side-splitters.'[58] Alternative innovations had been reported earlier, in the 1860s. In 1867 the harlequinade at the Prince's Theatre, Manchester featured pantomimists from Drury Lane and the Crystal Palace, plus a local scene of 'Ardwick Green, with the pond frozen over, and troops of sliders and skaters upon it'.[59] The 1874 pantomime at the same theatre was concluded by a harlequinade that was 'long and full of business', including the by now almost obligatory performing dogs.[60] For the Prince's Theatre pantomime of 1877, *Babes in the Wood; or, the Demon Colorado, the Blighted Tuber, & the Harlequin Baron of the Whoa Emma Mine*, the harlequinade was 'diversified' by 'The Bale and Otto Combination' of bicyclists.[61] A Second Edition was promoted in mid-February, with a revised harlequinade, and the addition of new performers, including Russian skaters, was recommended by the reviewer of the *Manchester Weekly Times*. It was, he thought, 'a great deal more interesting, and is much more appreciated, than the buffoonery usually following a pantomime'.[62] Evidently, novelty could be introduced into the harlequinade as long as some of the traditional elements remained, but the shift in emphasis from the harlequinade to the opening had caused this reviewer to make a notable remark. Whereas in earlier decades the word 'pantomime' had usually denoted the harlequinade, in other words the formerly prominent scenes, by the 1870s most people accepted the term as inclusively referring to the entire production. This reviewer in his use of the word effectively reversed a century of tradition by excluding the harlequinade from his definition of a pantomime. Indeed, although the harlequinade remained in the programme until around 1900, the links between the comic scenes and characters and the opening had disappeared long before. If the pantomime as a whole was overrunning, which it frequently did at the first performance, the harlequinade would be omitted and sometimes in the late 1890s it would be entirely replaced by disassociated items such as that selected for the 1898 production of *Cinderella* at the Theatre Royal, Nottingham: a selection of 'Tableaux de Marbre', comprising numbers of stationary figures depicting classical images on a revolving platform.[63]

In the late nineteenth century, critical retrospection regarding the perceived decline of the harlequinade sometimes argued not for a revival that would recall the achievements of Grimaldi, but for a revival of a simpler form of pantomime. The elaborate tricks that had been devised for harlequinades at the turn of the nineteenth century were temporarily forgotten and instead the 'old-fashioned' pantomime was remembered as simpler, somehow more genuine than the lavish excesses of spectacle witnessed each year. In January 1880, an editorial in the *Manchester Weekly Times* noted the range of pantomimes available in London, and the pressure to provide spectacle, often at the cost of the 'old-fashioned form of pantomime, which depended upon legitimate fun and drollery'. If, the piece continued, 'the small theatres would give good old-fashioned laughter provoking pantomimes … they would not so often have to deplore a serious deficit in their treasuries'.[64] Although managers were unlikely to revert to the harlequinade-dominated pantomime of earlier generations, there were some attempts to revive the fortunes of Clown and Pantaloon in the last decades of the century. In 1887, a review in the *Birmingham*

Daily Mail commented that 'Mr. Simpson [at the Theatre Royal] has gone in for a revival in the shape of a merry harlequinade of more than average length', and the book of words for *Dick Whittington* at the Prince of Wales Theatre in 1891 promised 'Ten Minutes of Genuine Old-fashioned Fun' for that year's harlequinade.[65] Nottingham resident Sidney Race, a regular pantomime-goer in the 1890s, noted the quality of productions in his diaries. Race admired the innovation introduced at the end of the Theatre Royal pantomime in 1894, but preferred a 'rollicking, old-fashioned harlequinade', a few years later applauding 'a good one' at the Grand Theatre, with 'capital' work by the Pantaloon and Harlequin, and a Columbine who 'looked a really charming creature and certainly danced well'.[66] There was evidently a fondness amongst provincial audiences for the traditional harlequinade, which theatre managements acknowledged. Their focus, however, remained on the opening and the competitive demands of scenery, costumed processions and star performers, the provision of which created new traditions linked to the resources of each theatre.

Notes

1. 'Theatre Royal – The Pantomime', *Manchester Weekly Times*, 22 December 1860, p. 5.

2. *Report from the Select Committee on Theatrical Licenses and Regulations; Together with the Proceedings of the Committee, Minutes of Evidence, and Appendix* (Shannon, 1970; 1st edn 1866), pp. 246–7. The claim – of pantomime being the 'sheet anchor of the drama' – is well known; Booth, for example, cites it in *Theatre in the Victorian Age*, p. 18.

3. The following discussion of the structure of pantomime in the second half of the nineteenth century, its traditions and developments, draws on Booth's *English Plays*, although his work is largely informed by patterns established at the London theatres.

4. Mercer Simpson made this claim at the 1892 Select Committee hearing: *Report from the Select Committee* (Shannon, 1970; 1st edn 1892), p. 185, in answer to question 2623.

5. 'Christmas Amusements: *The Forty Thieves* Rehearsed', *Birmingham Daily Gazette*, 25 December 1890, p. 8. See also Booth, *English Plays*, p. 43, in which he states that a pantomime production of this period could last from three to five hours.

6. J. Davis, 'Boxing Day', in T.C. Davis and P. Holland (eds), *The Performing Century*.

7. 'Theatre Royal Pantomime', *Birmingham Daily Post*, 6 February 1894, p. 5.

8. The inferred morality of the Victorian pantomime is discussed in Booth, *English Plays*, pp. 20, 45–8, and in *Theatre in the Victorian Age*, p. 200.

9. Booth, *English Plays*, p. 46.

10. Wagner, *The Pantomimes and All About Them*, p. 28. See also Booth, *English Plays*, pp. 55–7.

11. Mayer, *Harlequin in His Element*, p. 30.

12. For an extended discussion of the book of words and its use at a performance event, see J.A. Sullivan, 'Pantomime Libretti and the Victorian Reading Audience', in G. Allen *et al.* (eds), *Making an Audience: Reading Textual Materiality* (forthcoming, 2011).

13. See, for example, 'Christmas Amusements: The Pantomime at the Royal', *Birmingham Daily Mail*, 24 December 1870, p. 8, and, in the same newspaper title, 'Christmas Amusements: The Pantomime at the Royal', 28 December 1874, p. 2.

14. Booth, *English Plays*, p. 38.

15. *Macbeth* parody in BL: Brit. Mus. Add. Ms 53180B: Alfred Davis, *Harlequin Graceful and the Fair One with the Golden Locks, or, the Dame who Lived in a Shoe, and the Little Old Man in the Moon* (1876), Scene 10, p. 37; and *Othello* parody in NLSL: L79.8: F.R. Goodyer, *Little Red Riding Hood* (1873), book of words, Scene 9, p. 24.

16. Burlesque and its absorption into pantomime are discussed by Booth in *Theatre in the Victorian Age*, p. 196. See also *English Plays*, Appendix B, 'Criticism of Burlesque', pp. 470–84; and for a further discussion of the parody of Shakespearean plays in burlesque, see J. Davis (ed.), *Plays by H.J. Byron* (Cambridge, 1984), p. 3.

17. BL: Brit. Mus. Add. Ms 53180B: Alfred Davis, *Harlequin Graceful and the The Fair One with the Golden Locks* (1876), Scene 3, p. 8.

18. NLSL: L79.8: Arthur L. Maddock, *Robinson Crusoe; Or, the Good Friday Who Came on Thursday Half-Holiday* (1891), book of words, Scene 1, p. 8. This feature was not unique to Nottingham, however. In *English Plays*, Booth notes that pantomime could be burlesqued and cites early-nineteenth-century productions (p. 30, n. 2). See also his discussion of the burlesquing of melodrama villains (p. 32).

19. In *Theatre in the Victorian Age*, Booth states that this structure – of the dominant opening and 'vestigial' harlequinade – had become established by the 1840s and 1850s (p. 199).

20. Planché, *Recollections and Reflections*, p. 135.
21. *Ibid.*, pp. 135–6. His comments are cited in Booth, *English Plays*, p. 48. Booth has stated that Planché's comments are 'well-known' and very frequently quoted. See also *Victorian Spectacular Theatre*, p. 80; Mander and Mitchenson, *Pantomime*, p. 29, citing Planché from P. Fitzgerald, *World Behind the Scenes* (London, 1881); Wagner, *Pantomimes and All About Them*, p. 11; and Broadbent, *A History of Pantomime*, p. 184, citing Wagner's quotation of Planché. Fitzgerald also details the machinery of the transformation scene (pp. 90–1) and is cited by Russell Jackson, *Victorian Theatre*, pp. 193–4, and by Booth, *Victorian Spectacular Theatre*, pp. 80–1.
22. Planché, *Recollections and Reflections*, vol. ii, p. 135.
23. 'Christmas Holiday Amusements: Theatre Royal', *Birmingham Daily Post*, 27 December 1867, p. 3.
24. 'Christmas Holiday Amusements: Theatre Royal: *Ali Baba and the Forty Thieves*', *Birmingham Daily Post*, 28 December 1868, p. 5.
25. 'The Christmas Pantomimes. The Royal: *Beauty and the Beast*', *Manchester Weekly Times*, 28 December 1861, p. 3.
26. 'Prince's Theatre', *Manchester Weekly Times*, 22 December 1866, p. 5.
27. 'Prince's Theatre', *Manchester Weekly Times*, 3 January 1874, p. 4.
28. 'Prince's Theatre', *Manchester Times*, 30 December 1876, p. 5.
29. Advertisement, *Manchester Times*, 3 February 1877, p. 1.
30. Mrs Charles Calvert, *Sixty-Eight Years on the Stage* (London, 1911), p. 73. Richard Foulkes also discusses the association with Grieves and his superintendence of work at the Prince's Theatre, in *The Calverts: Actors of Some Importance* (London, 1992), p. 55.
31. Additional information on Grieves and Roberts from *Oxford Dictionary of National Biography*, ed. H.C.G. Matthew and B. Harrison, 60 vols (Oxford, 2004), vol. xxiii, pp. 917–20.
32. Advertisement, *Birmingham Daily Post*, 26 December 1865, p. 1.
33. *Birmingham Daily Post*, 23 January 1865, p. 6, citing 'The British Drama in the Provinces' from the *London Standard*.
34. P. Auslander, *Liveness: Performance in a Mediatized Culture* (Oxford and New York, 2008), p. 66.
35. 'The Christmas Pantomimes: Theatre Royal', *Manchester Guardian*, 23 December 1872, p. 3.
36. 'Theatre Royal', *Manchester Guardian*, 27 December 1875, p. 7.
37. 'Public Amusements: the Theatres', *Birmingham Daily Post*, 2 January 1868, p. 8.
38. '*Cinderella* at the Theatre Royal', *Birmingham Daily Gazette*, 27 December 1892, p. 5.
39. 'Theatre Royal – The Pantomime', *Manchester Weekly Times*, 24 December 1859, pp. 4–5.
40. 'The New Adelphi Theatre', *Birmingham Daily Post*, 26 January 1864, p. 4.
41. Booth notes that in the shift to separate companies there were examples of part exchanges (for example just one or two characters). However, he states that, insofar as the London pantomimes were concerned, the clear division between the two companies was evident by the mid-1860s (*English Plays*, p. 43).
42. The pantomimists' wages are listed in NA: M8814: 'Salary Book No. 2', pp. 30–44; and the rehearsal week payment in M8809: 'Day Book of Accounts for the Administration of Nottingham Theatre Royal 1866–7' (22 December).
43. 'The Pantomimes: *Dick Whittington* at the Theatre Royal', *Manchester Weekly Times*, 27 December 1879, p. 7.
44. Wilson, *Pantomime Pageant*, p. 54.

45. NLSL: RL79.8: Loose collection of playbills (Theatre Royal, Nottingham) 1860–1900: playbills for *Little Bo Peep*, dated 26 December 1883, and *Little Red Riding Hood*, dated 26 December 1885.

46. NLSL: RL79.8: Loose collection of playbills (Theatre Royal, Nottingham): playbill for *Aladdin*, 27 December 1886. See also the 1876 version of *Sinbad the Sailor* at Birmingham, in which Mr F. Newham played 'Stevedore' in the opening and Clown in the harlequinade ('Theatre Royal Pantomime', *Birmingham Daily Post*, 27 December 1876, p. 5).

47. Moody, *Illegitimate Theatre*, pp. 218–19.

48. Advertisement, *Manchester Weekly Times*, 26 December 1874, p. 1.

49. 'Christmas Amusements: "Old" Drury Lane', *Era*, 1 January 1871, p. 14.

50. 'The Christmas Pantomimes. Prince's Theatre – "Forty Thieves"', *Manchester Weekly Times*, 28 December 1872, p. 5.

51. 'Christmas Festivities. Prince's Theatre – "Sinbad"', *Manchester Weekly Times*, 23 December 1876, p. 5.

52. 'The Pantomime at the Theatre Royal', *Manchester Weekly Times*, 5 January 1878, p. 5.

53. 'The Pantomime', *Nottingham Daily Guardian*, 30 December 1884, p. 8. Expressions of boredom occur in Planché, *Recollections and Reflections*, pp. 136–7, and are reiterated by Wagner, *Pantomimes and All About Them*, p. 52. Writing in 1881, Wagner pointed to the lack of originality in harlequinades as the reason audiences were tiring of them. The *Illustrated London News* of 1877 had also commented on the lack of 'originality' in the harlequinade. The latter is cited in Wilson, *Pantomime Pageant*, p. 59. See also Frow, '*Oh Yes, It is!*', pp. 87, 103.

54. J. Norwood, 'The Britannia Theatre: Visual Culture and the Repertoire of a Popular Theatre', in A. Heinrich, K. Newey and J. Richards (eds), *Ruskin, the Theatre and Victorian Visual Culture* (Basingstoke, 2009), p. 150.

55. Wilson, *Pantomime Pageant*, p. 45.

56. The traditional elements of the harlequinade are discussed in *ibid.*, pp. 38–9.

57. 'Theatre Royal', *Nottingham Journal*, 3 January 1877, p. 4.

58. 'Christmas Amusements: The Pantomime at the Theatre Royal', *Birmingham Daily Mail*, 27 December 1871, p. 4, and 'Christmas Amusements: The Pantomime at the Royal', 27 December 1873, p. 2.

59. 'The Pantomimes: The Prince's Theatre', *Manchester Weekly Times*, 28 December 1867, p. 2.

60. 'Prince's Theatre', *Manchester Weekly Times*, 3 January 1874, p. 4.

61. 'The Pantomime at the Prince's Theatre', *Manchester Weekly Times*, 22 December 1877, p. 6.

62. 'Prince's Theatre', *Manchester Weekly Times*, 10 February 1877, p. 5.

63. The group was detailed in an extract from the Sidney Race diaries, cited in R. Illiffe and W. Baguley, *Victorian Nottingham: A Story in Pictures*, 20 vols (Nottingham, 1970–83), vol. xvi: *Photography in Nottingham, the Lambert Family Album, the Victorian Christmas*, p. 98.

64. *Manchester Weekly Times*, 3 January 1880, p. 5.

65. 'The Pantomimes: *Goody Two Shoes* at the Theatre Royal', *Birmingham Daily Mail*, 27 December 1887, p. 4; and BL: Brit. Mus. Add. Ms. 53489N: John Anderton, *Dick Whittington* (1891), book of words, p. 1.

66. Cited in Illiffe and Baguley, *Victorian Nottingham*, vol. xvi, pp. 95, 97.

2

'The best out of London': spectacle, status and tradition

Managers in all three towns had to attract audiences to the annual pantomimes by a deft combination of traditions and novelty. Audiences grew to expect certain features, especially in terms of spectacle and scale, which created additional financial and logistical pressures for each management. The first part of this chapter illustrates how, at the Theatre Royal in Birmingham and the Theatre Royal and Prince's Theatre in Manchester, managers aimed to create spectacular productions, in turn establishing specific local identities for their theatres, based on traditions of status and expenditure.

The Theatre Royal, Birmingham

The Theatre Royal, with its entrance on New Street in the town centre, was originally built in 1774 and rose from the ashes of two fires in 1792 and 1820, achieving a twenty-one year renewable licence by act of Parliament in 1806. The theatre had an auditorium capacity of between 2,000 and 2,500 by the 1890s, largely owing to an extension of the pit in 1876, which doubled its capacity. This move was indicative of the manager Mercer Simpson's commercial awareness; when giving evidence to the Parliamentary Select Committee on Theatres in 1892, he was to emphasise the importance of the pit as the 'mainstay' of provincial theatres.[1] Simpson and his father managed the Theatre Royal from the mid-1860s until the early 1890s and, in terms of the annual pantomime, this extended period of management enabled the creation and sustained emphasis of particular features, working relationships and standards of production that defined the identity of this theatre for its local and regional audiences.

The spectacular focus of Simpson's pantomimes in the 1860s was the transformation scene, but by the following decade the opening of each production incorporated increasing amounts of spectacular display in which painted backdrops alternated with 'heavy' or built sets. The large stage of the Royal enabled scenes comprising woodland glades with waterfalls and bridges, or palace ballrooms with sweeping staircases, terraces and chandeliers. Undoubtedly following the lead set by the Theatre Royal, Drury Lane, ornate and lengthy ballets, parades and themed processions featured several times in each pantomime, incorporating large numbers of adult and juvenile supernumeraries and dancers, and substantial mechanised stage props served to astonish audiences.

The annual pantomime did not of course stand alone in the provision of spectacle. The changes to the format of the genre and the emphasis on the visual splendours of productions reflected a contemporaneous cultural fascination with scale and spectacle, prompted by technological innovation in industry and the unprecedented output of goods enabled by mass production. As Thomas Richards has succinctly established, this increase in available goods together with a broadening sense of commercial awareness had led to the emergence of the commodity and the associated advertising that promoted desire over need for the expanding middle classes.[2] The instigation of the concept of the consumer and the growth of aspirational advertising engendered a cycle of desire and production, and the development of spectacular theatre linked directly into the promotion of the commodity. In the theatre, as Richards states,

> The primary result … was to instigate a continual escalation of representation. This escalation had its own logic of one-upmanship: everything had to outdo what had come before it, and in turn, everything had to be outdone by what came after it. The spectacles of the early Victorian stage conditioned their audiences always to expect more.[3]

An example of the technological and spectacular effect of this 'continual escalation' can be seen in the use of glass in pantomime sets. Whilst Boucicault's new water tank had enabled more realistic and effective uses of water on stage, the incorporation of glass linked the pantomime directly to the developments in urban spectacle. Isobel Armstrong, in *Victorian Glassworlds*, has established that the technologies of glass production, especially plate glass and its impact on the urban environment, led to a glass culture, a fascination with the practical and decorative possibilities of the transparent surface, epitomised by the building of the Crystal Palace in 1851. In writing of the urban experience of glass and, in particular, of the 'glazed shopfront', Armstrong states:

> Serving at once the needs of commerce and the cultural imaginary, the lyrical world of glass produced a landscape that conflated the real and imagined … the artificial lustre of consumer experience and urban pastoral, the spectacle as visual pleasure and reified commodity.[4]

Pantomime was both fantasy and commodity; whilst glass became an inherent part of the fairy-tale ballroom and palace scenes, it was an anticipated and therefore necessary economic investment by those managers who could afford it. Mirrors, with prismatic as well as reflective surfaces, recurred in pantomime sets in Birmingham and Manchester. The incorporation of glass enabled the play of light, the refractions of coloured lights and the multiple reflections of dancers and elaborate costumes. In December 1881, the *Birmingham Daily Mail* previewed the Theatre Royal production of *Beauty and the Beast*, and in particular the 'Hall of Splendour' on which not only had 'the scenic artist and stage carpenters … been engaged for several weeks past' but in its creation 'more money has already been spent than has sufficed to produce many a pantomime'.[5] The preview continued with a detailed description of the set:

> Then we are introduced to the great feature of the pantomime, the hall of splendour in the Beast's Castle.… Every inch of the stage is taken up with this gigantic set. The lights of hundreds of jets are reflected in plate glass pillars and beautiful mirrors; statues are arranged along the sides and in niches at every turn; the ceiling and walls are literally a blaze of rich colour; massive chandeliers hang in lavish profusion; and when everything is complete, and the gorgeously-attired nymphs come trooping down the sumptuously carpeted staircase, reaching from the middle of the stage to the bottom of the flies, we shall be certainly

surprised if it does not open the eyes of the audience a little to what can be accomplished.[6]

Sets such as the 'Hall of Splendour' defined the Birmingham Theatre Royal productions and the local newspapers revelled in long descriptions of the lavish provision of spectacle.

The previews and first-week reviews were not the only effective methods of defining and promoting productions at this house. Prior to the opening night, the Birmingham newspapers offered insights into individual pantomime productions in a selection of articles describing backstage visits to the Theatre Royal. In these articles the critic, as a guest of the theatre manager, wandered through the paint rooms, wardrobe and property man's rooms describing artefacts that attracted his attention and expressing constant amazement that a dazzling pantomime would, in only a few days time, rise out of the chaos that he saw. The articles acted as an additional promotional tool for the theatre; the items that the critic chose to describe were frequently those that featured in the later advertising and reviews. In the 1870s and 1880s, pieces such as 'Behind the Scenes at Pantomime Time', 'Pantomime in Plain Clothes', 'Christmas Stories: A Pantomimic Workshop' and 'Preparing the Pantomime' provided illuminating details about costumes and scenery, together with descriptions of the production processes of some of the properties.[7] For example, although by the 1870s most productions had ceased to use masks to mark the difference between the opening and harlequinade characters, they were still worn by supernumeraries in the crowd, comic and processional scenes of the opening.[8] In the 1874 pantomime *Ride a Cock Horse to Banbury Cross*, 'The stage [was] thronged in the various scenes with retainers and cooks of grotesque physiognomy – the art of the property-man', and in the 1876 pantomime of *Sinbad the Sailor*, the reviewer of the *Birmingham Daily Mail* drew attention to the 'red dwarfs … curiously masked' and to the 'masks of the sailors who are rushing about at the port' as being 'wonderfully comic'.[9] The article 'Behind the Scenes at Pantomime Time', which appeared in the *Birmingham Daily Mail* in 1873, included the following description of the process of making such masks:

The grotesque faces suggest that the designer supped heavily and dreamed hideously. The front face is modelled in clay, and on this cast the workman pastes his layers of paper, shapes, hardens, and dries them, until they are ready for the Munchausen-possessed brush of the artist.... A ... Sphynx too – a masterpiece of the property-man's' strange craft. The eyes work, the big mouth opens and grins, the hair lifts, and the fat cheeks rise.... On all sides great, goggling misshapen heads leer at us.... A most eccentric brass band has been devised. The unique performers are fashioned in quaint shapes of many instruments. One gifted being has a drum head, which he beats; another has ears which are large and brazen, and serve as cymbals; a third has a twisted body, and this walking trumpet blows his own dejected looking head out of the mouth of his instrument.[10]

This remarkable band featured in the subsequent newspaper reviews, which promoted the scene as amongst the 'spectacular effects' of the production and 'one of the most outrageously funny things we ever saw'.[11] The Birmingham articles are crucial in that they accentuated the importance of this particular provincial theatre and its ability to sustain inspection at close quarters. Such articles did not simply act as a promotion for the forthcoming production (although this was very effectively done in terms of foregrounding particular scenes and effects) but also celebrated the local artistic achievement and workmanship, intimating the ample resources available to the theatre. The London theatre managements also employed this practice of utilising 'behind the scenes' articles.[12] In encouraging such articles in the Birmingham newspapers, the management of the Theatre Royal was implicitly establishing the theatre both before and behind the scenes as a worthy equivalent to the metropolis.

Whilst Thomas Richards has acknowledged the incorporation of industrial technology into stage productions in terms of special effects and machinery (and nowhere more effective than in the machinery of the pantomime transformation scene), he does not class the theatre performance as a commodity (unlike Tracy C. Davis's transposition of the two).[13] However, Richards's concept of spectacular 'one-upmanship' was integral to pantomime production, both in terms of the whole performance as a commodity, purchased by the theatre-goer, and in relation to the overt display of the actual production processes evident in the 'behind the scenes' articles which promoted the Birmingham Theatre Royal. This latter emphasis on production in fact extends Richards's argument: whilst he presents the isolated and applauded commodity at the Great Exhibition as divorced in its presentation from the production processes, the pantomime producers in Birmingham actively encouraged those processes to be viewed as spectacle in their own right. The audience and critics did not necessarily want to see the mechanisation of the transformation scene obstructing parts of the stage in performance, but they were allowed to 'visit' backstage to applaud the creative skills responsible for it. The celebration of production processes was particularly relevant given the industrial context and local pride of Birmingham, and in Chapter 3 I will address how local trade and industry was further incorporated into the actual performances.

At the Theatre Royal, the overarching trajectory of production spectacle evinced increasingly expensive resources and display, which was evident by 1870. In that year the transformation scene was promoted alongside 'The Verdant Valley', 'sparkling with pendant jewels and coloured foil', and a Lord Mayor's show with 'gilded chariots [and] its cavalcade of richly attired attendants'.[14] As the theatre's resources were increasingly redistributed to create alternative features, the transformation scene became one of several spectacular features rather than the climax of the evening. The first sign of this shift, in terms of advertisements, was during the 1874 pantomime of *Ride a Cock Horse to Banbury Cross*, in which the 'GRAND PROCESSION OF THE MONARCHS OF ENGLAND' included 'Dresses from Authentic Drawings' and 'Armour and Regalia by Messrs. Kennedy of Birmingham'.[15] The reviewer of the *Birmingham Daily Mail* enthused that 'Nothing more costly or effective has ever been seen in Birmingham.... So far as the spectacular element is concerned this scene eclipses everything else in the pantomime.'[16] The scene became a feature of advertisements and by the beginning of January, an additional front-page advertisement offered 'A LESSON IN ENGLISH HISTORY FOR CHILDREN / THE MONARCHS OF ENGLAND / Correct and Magnificent Dresses and Regalia'.[17] For the 1878 pantomime of *Robinson Crusoe*, despite eleven scenes, including a wood with moving trees, and a warrior procession, the ship *The Lively Sally*, from which Crusoe was shipwrecked, was predominant in previews and reviews of the production.

It is an unusually fine stage property; an enormous amount of labour has been expended on it. We see the vessel in the block, as it were, with masts stretching as high as the top of the proscenium…. A chorus is given and we see the ship lurch and roll and at length move away across the stage…. The effect of the vessel moving in this way is exceedingly good, especially when taken in conjunction with the scenery at the back, which stretches nearly to the full length of the stage.[18]

The previews emphasised the fact that it had taken 'several men' five months to construct.[19] Again, the theatre management were promoting production efforts behind the scenes. A single team employed to construct a set was not unusual (see, for example, the records for the Theatre Royal at Nottingham, below) but for audiences used to their theatre simply being closed for a week's rehearsal prior to the pantomime opening, this emphasis on the months of construction on just one aspect of the pantomime inferred an overall effort of considerable proportions. By late January, this single prop had become the metonymic focus of advertisements; one on the front page of the *Birmingham Daily Post* announced that 'THE "LIVELY SALLY" SAILS AT 7.00'.[20] In addition to the inclusion of particular effects, scenes in all the Birmingham productions were augmented by numbers of elaborately costumed supers and dancers. In *Sinbad the Sailor* (1882), Scene 6 of the 'Rocky Serpents' Glen' not only featured 'a real waterfall 25 feet high' but also over 200 'red dwarfs' that 'throng[ed] down the sides of the glen like an army of ants'.[21] The densely populated scene provided what David Mayer has referred to as the 'necessary plasticity of the stage', creating a 'sculptural depth … and also mobility and malleability, the capacity of the *mise en scène* to periodically reshape itself to new depths and projections'.[22] This extension of the set by the incorporation of large numbers of supernumeraries and dancers was illustrated in the 1876 production of *Sinbad the Sailor* at the Birmingham Theatre Royal. The production included a scene entitled 'The Valley of Diamonds', in which 124 dancers in dresses of 'white satin fringed with gold and ornamented with stage gems' were incorporated into an illusion of perspective:

[They] start at a height above the gallery ... but when we look from the house to the point at which they first appear, and when the real distance is heightened by the tricks of the stage artist, the effect is bewildering. It appears as if we were looking at a picture through the wrong end of a telescope, but that it gradually came nearer until the actual reality was seen in all its force.[23]

Following the lead set by pantomimes at the major London theatres, each year productions were interspersed with grand ballets of sailors, flowers, precious stones, moonbeams, dolls, and powder-puffs, and revels, regal and ceremonial processions and celebratory scenes punctuated the stories. The human element of spectacle was complemented on occasions by the incorporation of live animals of varying degrees of co-operation. The trained 'TROUPE OF PONIES' from Sanger's Amphitheatre in London in the 1874 production of *Ride a Cock Horse to Banbury Cross* appears to have caused few problems, but the use of real lambs to accompany juvenile shepherdesses in the 'Highgate Hill' scene of *Dick Whittington and His Cat* (1884), and an inquisitive fawn for the transformation of the Princess into the *Fairy Fawn* of the 1872 pantomime, were a source of amusement for the critics. In *Cinderella*, the Theatre Royal pantomime of 1886, real fox hounds were used in the Royal hunt at the end of Scene 1, although at one point they strayed out of the theatre and Mr Simpson had to place an advertisement – 'STRAYED. – Two FOXHOUNDS. – Please Return them to Theatre Royal' – in the *Birmingham Daily Post* for their recovery.[24] Animals were also created by specialist performers, adept in what were termed 'skin parts' and provided in the scripts with sequences of comic business and interaction with other actors, for example the donkeys in the 1877 production of *The Forty Thieves*, 'styled Edward and Emma who ... make manifest their appreciation of humour by a series of kicks and lively jigs.'[25] Often the 'animals' on stage were examples of the property man's craft. In the aforementioned 1876 production of *Sinbad the Sailor*, an 'immense sea serpent' 'crawl[ed] along the floor of the stage – a wonderful piece of stage mechanism' and there was a 'life-sized elephant' that could 'move his trunk, his eyes, and legs in a way that is wonderful to see'.[26]

The ability to produce a selection of spectacular features in each production highlighted the financial and physical resources of the

Birmingham Theatre Royal, and because spectacular theatre as a whole was predicated on scale, its promotion at Birmingham was deeply indicative of the rising status and economic success of the town, which gained city status in 1889. Once again, this related to the broader concept of spectacle and, as Richards has emphasised, the persistent image of surplus in society suggested an inference of plenty, and thereby contentment.[27] The crowded stage with large sets and casts provided satisfaction for the audience in realising their expectations of scale and splendour, whilst also inferring the economic wealth of the theatre (and, by association, the new city) in being able to provide that level of spectacle.

The Theatre Royal, Manchester

The oldest theatre in Manchester was the Theatre Royal, the management of which had been granted a twenty-one-year licence by act of Parliament in 1775. The building was situated initially in Spring Gardens and then moved to a new site in Fountain Street in 1807, where it was run with varying degrees of success until fire destroyed the building in 1845. The 'patent rights' were sold to the then proprietor John Knowles, who had a new theatre built in Peter Street.[28] Pantomimes were produced there annually from 1845 and, as at the Birmingham theatre, the new proprietor influenced the style and identity of productions for much of the period to the 1870s. By 1859, that identity was established on the provision of expensive scenery and an assertion of status.

In the 1859 pantomime of *Blue Beard*, Scene 2 depicted '"A Fete Champetre a la Watteau," or the Elysian Grove' which had been 'painted and constructed by Mr. Wm. Beverley, after one that he produced last year at Drury Lane Theatre, and which in itself was the great attraction of the London pantomime season'.[29] Through the press, Knowles unashamedly advertised the London provenance of this scene, with its 'gilded and painted' trees and grouped figures, a number of which, 'diminishing in size according to the rule of perspective, are arranged on each side of the stage, running to its extreme length, and verging upon a picturesque fall of water – real water … which flashes and bubbles in the supposed sunshine'.[30] William Beverley, the acclaimed London scenic artist who had created the original transformation scene for Planché's *Island of Jewels*, had painted a new version of the pantomime scene specifically for the Manchester theatre. The promotional strategy was effective: in his comments, the *Manchester Weekly Times* reviewer established his own knowledge of the Drury Lane original and stated that 'Nothing at all approaching to this has previously been seen in a provincial theatre, and [in comparing it to the original] we must candidly give the preference to the present copy' which had been produced at a cost of 'full £500'. Similarly, the transformation scene 'The Happy Land' was painted by Mr Calcott, 'an artist of rising fame in the metropolis' who was re-commissioned to paint the transformation scene for the 1860 production. The remainder of the scenes were produced by the resident scenic artists Messrs Bickerstaff and Muir, and they too were praised in the press, albeit in a slightly more muted tone. The scene of 'Blue Beard's Chamber' was 'very cleverly painted by Mr. Muir', 'contrasting richly in tone and colour with the delicate hues of the preceding scene' and the third scene, of a 'Turkish Village', featured a combination of cottages, river and a well, with several bridges, the crossing of which was 'performed by cleverly constructed mechanical figures, with moving legs and heads and arms.… The procession consists of soldiers, slaves, grandees, camels, and a monster elephant' carrying the title character. The scenery – chiefly the second scene, the effects of the village scene and the transformation scene – drew on London and local talent and, according to the *Manchester Weekly Times*, was responded to in the first week of performance by 'cheers and the waving of hats and the cries of "Bravo"'.[31]

The pantomime of 1860 was *Cinderella* which included a coach drawn by 'six beautiful cream-coloured Arabian ponies' and an elaborate ballroom scene in which the

> walls and ceiling are draped in white Valenciennes lace, through which peep golden columns, whilst massive golden candelabra range down each side, running up into the extremity of the stage, where there is a large, supposed, mirror, in which the dancers, as they enter and form their various groups, are of course reflected.[32]

The detailed description of the sets continued in the first-week reviews and, as with those for the Theatre Royal at Birmingham, there is an inherent sense of significant expenditure on these productions. The pantomimes also promoted a sense of accumulated success. In the opening scene of the 1859 *Blue Beard*, the character of the 'Genius of Pantomime' had listed the past productions at the theatre. The self-referential speech created a sense of tradition – a method also utilised by Simpson at Birmingham – and it enhanced audience expectation with the list of assured productions. The technique was carried over into press reviews: at the start of the first main review of *Cinderella*, the *Manchester Express and Guardian* referred to the 'unparalleled success of *Bluebeard*' the previous year, underlined by a reference to 'our Royal', the inclusive nature of the title creating a sense of local ownership as well as shared pride in the consistent standards of production.[33] The reviewer did not merely provide a description of the scenes, but asserted the implicit status of the theatre and the skills of its manager, as well as engaging his readership (and potential audiences) in a united reflection on and expectation of past and future successes:

> Fairy scenes and caves, and grottoes must necessarily have much in common one with another; but he would be a bold manager who would now-a-days attempt a pantomime without freely having recourse to such things. Hence there is a great danger of sameness in the general character of the scenes year after year, which would be very damaging to the winter campaign at any Theatre, and especially at one like our Royal, the reputation of which for complete success in pantomimes is perhaps not exceeded by that of any metropolitan establishment, and certainly is not equalled by that of any one in the provinces… one of its chief merits will, we think, be admitted to be its perfect unlikeness in all its great features, to all that was great in 'Blue Beard.'[34]

Like yet unlike, traditional yet innovative: these concepts underscored the reviews of the Theatre Royal pantomimes. Even the opening dark scene – not usually a focal point of scene painting – was a source of admiration for the reviewer:

> There are two or three rows of massive pillars and arches, forming arcades across the stage. The style may be said to suggest the Moorish or Arabesque.… The pillars are covered with rich decorations; grotesque figures, grimly nodding, sit in rows in niches, along the lines of the

capitals and also above in the arches; and there are very fine contrasts of light and shade, real as well as painted.[35]

At Christmas 1861, the scene of the 'Garden of Roses' in *Beauty and the Beast* appealed to more than the visual senses when:

> to increase the pleasurable excitement, there is a perfume comes streaming from that single rose of gigantic size, placed in front of the footlights … and this delectable essence, flowing throughout the house, from pit and boxes, is wafted into the regions of the demi-gods in the sixpenny galleries. [36]

The scenery for the 1861 and 1862 pantomimes was created entirely by the resident artists, rather than buying or hiring in ex-London sets or engaging scenic artists from the metropolis. The early 1860s were years of economic depression in Manchester, following the impact of the American Civil War on cotton imports, and the reliance on local production staff at the theatre no doubt reflected a necessary drop in expenditure. However, the theatre management aimed to sustain its reputation for spectacles with the support of the local press. The scenery in *The House That Jack Built* (1862) included a panorama and, rather than the several spectacular scenes of earlier productions, the preview asserted the revised nature of the production, announcing that 'There is in every Christmas pantomime a speciality which is more particularly intended to be the main point of attraction', this time the 'building' of Jack's house. The production maintained the tradition of including a finale, this time incorporating Professor Wheeler's Fairy Fountain. This act had been seen in Manchester before, at the Mechanics Institute, and whilst it may have lacked novelty for local audiences, the preview reminded readers of how its success had drawn 'thousands weekly'.[37] In these few sentences the reviewer combined revised expectation with an assurance of tradition ('there is in every pantomime') and drew on favourable memories and possible missed opportunities in the chance to see once more Professor Wheeler's prismatic fountain.

In 1864, the Theatre Royal management presented *Puss in Boots* in which the opening scene of 'The Mill at Cloverdell Clough' featured mechanical swans on a lake and a revolving mill-wheel. An unusual spectacle was created in the scene of 'Whitehall in the King's Castle', in which, against a background of moonlit 'marble', bright foliage and a pale blue sky, a 'grand ballet luminaire' was performed by a number of dancers, men, women and children, whose 'graduated sizes … from men of six feet to children of two' made 'the effect quite novel'.[38] This concept was repeated in a later scene, in which the performers, grouped as 'Eastern Guards', wore costumes that were 'a combination of Assyrian, Egyptian and Turkish costume, with winged head-pieces' as they paraded across the stage.[39]

In an improved local economic clime, the Theatre Royal management resumed its policy of combining local artistic talent and bought-in scenery by London artists such as Telbin and Roberts, reinvigorating the theatre's reputation for pantomime scenery, which was emphasised in the local press. In 1866, the scenic effects included a dragon 'from the mouth of which flames of fire are constantly rushing' and a fourteen foot high giant, plus the transformation scene, 'The Pearl of the Ocean', by James Roberts (which had also been seen in Birmingham in 1865 at the conclusion of the Theatre Royal production of *Sinbad*).[40] In a preview for the 1866 production of *The Fair One with the Golden Locks*, the *Manchester Weekly Times* employed its earlier promotional tactics and began by establishing the traditions of the Theatre Royal and the fact that 'splendid pantomime has been an institution at this house'.[41] Conveniently forgetting those few years in which the scenery had attracted less fulsome praise, the reviewer here inferred an unbroken succession of high-quality productions, effectively – and no doubt intentionally – influencing the horizons of expectation of potential audiences.

Certainly, whatever limitations the economic depression of the early 1860s may have caused, it appears that the Theatre Royal had recovered by mid-decade, but by the early 1870s, despite the assertion that the Theatre Royal was 'in the front rank of the houses devoted to pantomime', the theatre management were clearly affected by the growing reputation of the Prince's Theatre pantomimes.[42] There were now three theatres in the city, the Theatre Royal, the Prince's and the Queen's, each attempting to supply spectacular pantomimes, and the particular emphasis on multiple spectacles in the annual production had clearly shifted to the Prince's Theatre, under the management of Charles Calvert. In reviewing the Theatre Royal pantomime of 1868, the *Manchester Guardian* chose to ignore the rival theatre and merely assert that 'Mr. Knowles's only competitor is his past reputation'.[43] However, by 1874, reviews in the same paper expressed concern that the scenery of the Theatre Royal pantomime was 'not very good', and the following year it was 'highly artistic without being too lavish'.[44] The *Manchester Weekly Times* was more encouraging and asserted that *Beauty and the Beast; or, Harlequin Prince Azor, and the Good Fairy of the Wedding Ring*, produced under the new management of Mr Sidney, was to be 'in every way an adequate revival of the traditional excellence of the Christmas entertainment at this house in former days.'[45]

By the late 1870s, the proprietors of the theatre, the Theatre Royal Company, also owned the Prince's Theatre and in 1879 they engaged new lessees, Mr Duffield and Captain Bainbridge, the latter of whom took on the general management of the theatre. Under the new management the advertisements for the Theatre Royal began to echo those for the Prince's Theatre in earlier years. The large inserts, placed centrally on the front pages of the newspapers, relied solely on puff: 'BEST AND ONLY GENUINE PANTOMIME' and 'UPROARIOUS MERRIMENT AND APPLAUSE'.[46] For the 1880 production of *Blue Beard*, the size of the advertisements increased again, to incorporate lengthy press reviews and regularly updated figures indicating the thousands of people who had paid to see the pantomime. The style of advertisements may have been influenced by the joint ownership of the two theatres or it may have been Bainbridge's decision in the face of competition. The notable difference in the advertisements lay in the selective incorporation of press quotes. In those for the Theatre Royal, all the quotes were from local and regional papers, rather than the London attention that the Prince's management highlighted in their advertisements. National reviews were available for the Theatre Royal: on 26 December and 1 January, the *Era* had included two reviews of the pantomime, each one containing eminently quotable praise. The crucial issue here was the choice of transformation scene, which that year was 'A Tribute to Lancashire', a focal point for regional celebration. It was also the central feature of the local press quotes cited in the advertisement and it appears therefore that Bainbridge, both with the subject matter of the transformation scene and in the choice of cited newspapers, was intending to create a specifically local appeal for his production. The insertion of local newspaper quotes continued in advertisements each year, with the exception of 1884 when two London papers, the *Stage* and the *Topical Times*, were quoted. Their inclusion, however, sat uncomfortably next to advertisements for the Prince's Theatre, which claimed success from the pages of arguably more influential papers, *The Times* and the *Telegraph*.

The shift to establishing a local identity in the visuals of production was not wholly sustained, however. Following the transformation scene of 1880, there were other, occasional locally themed scenes in the Theatre Royal pantomimes of the 1880s. For example, its 1883 production included a scene of Knott Mill Fair, but a later opportunity in the same pantomime to celebrate local achievement was missed. Just prior to the transformation scene there was a trade procession, but rather than taking the opportunity to celebrate local industry, this elaborate parade consisted of generic trades (butchers, clockmakers, poulterers, etc.) and was set against a London street. In contrast, the visual referencing of local places and events had been and continued to be effected on a much more regular basis by the managers of the Queen's Theatre and the Prince's. Bainbridge may well have experienced a managerial conflict between attempting to create productions that asserted local pride through sheer spectacle, glitter and quantity – in other words making an economic statement – and making specifically local appeals through themed scenery and local knowledge. Ultimately, in seeking a relevant promotional identity for his theatre, Bainbridge chose instead to try and rival the production values of the Prince's Theatre and reclaim a prominent reputation for spectacle. Certainly, the increasingly lavish scenery and costumes of productions in the 1880s were praised in the local papers. In the 1880 pantomime, the entrance of Blue Beard – always the occasion for scenic display at theatres – was here completed by a procession of 'brilliantly-attired soldiers and standard bearers' and the title character entered on a baby elephant, upstaged however by the 'artificial elephant' performed by two of the Lupinos.[47] Scenic effects included a Toy room collapsing to reveal a farmyard, a panorama and Blue Beard's courtyard: extravagantly lit terraces, fountain and waterfall, peopled by supers and variety acts, including a troupe of 'Baby Bicyclists'. Advertisements in early January claimed that over 126,000 people had 'PAID TO WITNESS' the pantomime, with large numbers of country visitors being turned away. Presumably to offset the Prince's Theatre tradition of running to Second Editions, advertisements at the end of January stated that due to the success of the Theatre Royal pantomime, 'NO IMPROVEMENT CAN BE MADE' and 'NO ALTERATION WILL BE MADE'.[48]

The principal scene for critics in the 1881 pantomime *Little Bo Peep* was the 'City of Lilliput', with the usual Lilliputian army, but the most interesting element was arguably the transformation scene. In the previous year's pantomime this scene had promoted local allegiance in its 'Tribute to Lancashire', but in the 1881 version the scene opened 'with a tableau illustrating the number of pantomimes played at the Royal since 1845'. As in the early 1860s, this device reiterated the role of the theatre as the most established house in the city, this time implicitly appealing to local allegiance in the face of the rival Prince's. The reviewer in the *Manchester Weekly Times* underscored this fact by stating that the ensuing scenes of the transformation were 'quite worthy of the past traditions of the theatre'.[49] The foregrounding of tradition was not sufficient to maintain audiences though, and, in contrast to the assertions of the previous year, this pantomime ran to a Second Edition at the end of February, with new scenery, costumes and dances, including a novel mirror ballet, music and songs, plus a new scene, 'The Gathering of Nations', symbolising, in scenery and staging, the 'friendly union of England and America'.[50]

In 1884, once again large and expensive newspaper advertisements contained extensive praise of the production of *Aladdin*, reiterating the reputation of the house for spectacle and scenery, despite the fact that 144 costumes had not been delivered in time for the first night. (Apparently this only affected three tableaux, which were consequently cut from the first few performances.) The incorporation of local press quotes also continued, with the *Examiner* in 1885 being quoted as writing of the 'great traditions of the house'.[51] The pantomime of 1886, *Blue Beard*, was heralded as Bainbridge's 'GRAND JUBILEE PANTOMIME'. The production, including 500 supers and 'The CHILDREN of the NATIONAL SCHOOL for DANCING', had been Augustus Harris's Drury Lane production, but was notably not advertised as a London pantomime, featuring instead a new, locally created scene illustrating the Building of the Manchester Royal Jubilee Exhibition. In not acknowledging the provenance of the overall production, Bainbridge was adopting similar tactics to the choice of press quotes in his advertisements, preferring to emphasise the local status of his theatre, achieved through extravagant spectacle and inferred financial capability. The *Manchester Weekly Times* reviewer appreciated the 'lavish expenditure of money' behind the production and Bainbridge evidently persevered in producing and promoting spectacular pantomimes, but the *Blue Beard* pantomime marked a turning point in his fortunes.

By 14 February 1887, the house receipts for the pantomime were £13,041 16s 9d, and under the terms of Bainbridge's agreement with Augustus Harris, he was to pay the Drury Lane manager a 'share of the receipts to be treated as profit under the agreement between the parties after the deduction of £10,000 for "reasonable working expenses"'. According to Harris, the Manchester manager had not paid the full amount, and the former consequently filed a suit in the Chancery Division, although an agreement seems to have been reached and the pantomime run continued without interruption. According to the report of this action, the profit at 14 February of £3,041 16s 9d was shared between Bainbridge and Harris, the latter receiving a one-third share.[52] However, Bainbridge had to pay another £500, indicating that Harris's share was closer to a half of the profits, leaving Bainbridge with about £1,500 profit at mid-February. The pantomime ran until 5 March so there would have been another three weeks' worth of income to draw on. Even so, this may have been less than Bainbridge had anticipated, especially if his initial outlay had exceeded the £10,000 spent on 'working expenses', but this outlay and the agreement with Harris clearly indicates the level of expense that Bainbridge sought to commit to his pantomime productions. A later report in the *Manchester Guardian* noted that the weekly running costs of the pantomime had been estimated at between £1,000 and £1,200, with the weekly profits varying from £69 to £1,121, very much depending, Bainbridge asserted, on the weather.[53]

In maintaining lavish productions and investing in elaborate and lengthy advertisements Bainbridge surely overstretched his resources and the following year the *Manchester Weekly Times* noted that the production of *Mother Goose* was less spectacular than former pantomimes at the Theatre Royal, relying more on fun and music and well-known company members such as Harriet Vernon and Ramsey Danvers. The advocacy of the local press could be depended on, however, and the *Manchester Weekly Times* reviewer quickly promoted the effectiveness of a simpler production, stating that 'There is generally admitted dulness in a purely spectacular pantomime, a ponderous machinery which moves heavily, and the weariness of excess is not unusually experienced.'[54] In 1888 Bainbridge returned to staging large spectacular pantomimes. *The Forty Thieves* featured 32 principals and 500 auxiliaries, the scenery using the full extent of the large stage at the Royal. The *Manchester Weekly Times* expected no less and, conveniently forgetting its approval of the simpler pantomime the previous year, stated that 'A successful pantomime at the Theatre Royal – and such is "The Forty Thieves" – must be rich in spectacle, and must be built upon a large scale. That which suits the little Vaudeville would never do for the big Drury Lane.'[55] Ironically invoking Drury Lane after the well-publicised financial problems of 1886–7, the intention perhaps was to set the Theatre Royal against the smaller and newer houses in Manchester, such as the Comedy Theatre, but Bainbridge could no longer sustain these levels of expenditure on the annual pantomime and by March 1889 he was bankrupt. With net liabilities of £32,380 4s 7d, Bainbridge claimed that 'bad business and failure of the pantomime of 1888, and competition of new theatres in outlying towns' were at the root of his failure; he also admitted to having been knowingly insolvent since 1884 but having relied on the pantomime profits to balance his theatre losses. At a later hearing, Bainbridge admitted that he had lost £8,000 on the production of *The Forty Thieves*.[56] He claimed that, largely owing to the local competition, fewer people came into Manchester to see the pantomimes at the major theatres there. Certainly the *Manchester Weekly Times* began reviewing pantomimes at Salford, Oldham, Stockport, Blackburn, Preston, Bury, Accrington and Rochdale in 1889, but the threat of competition and the recent financial history of the theatre did not prevent the new Theatre Royal lessee, Mr Thomas Ramsey, from staging *Dick Whittington* in 1889 'on a scale of splendour that should recall the palmy days of pantomimes at this old house', incorporating a combined ballet and chorus of 300.[57]

By the 1890s it was the stars rather than the spectacle who were dominating the pantomime expenditure. Lengthy spectacular scenes were becoming less popular and by the late 1880s, when variety and comedy were in the ascendance, Manchester audiences were not averse to shouting 'Time!' if tired of an overlong scenic display. At the Theatre Royal in Birmingham, 'behind the scenes' articles had effectively promoted the pantomimes when the vogue for spectacular productions there were in the ascendancy. In Manchester it was in 1893, at the point of decline in that style of production locally, that the *Manchester Weekly Times* featured a lengthy 'behind the scenes' article on the Theatre Royal. The illustrated, conversational piece described the journey undertaken by the journalist and Mr Ramsey to the various departments of the theatre as well as to a rehearsal. Ramsey himself explained that:

> The taste for the gorgeous ... has been dying for some time, and what the people of to-day undoubtedly want is a funny pantomime – something brisk and bright, that will make them laugh. Long ballets, which were at one time very acceptable, are now out of favour. The people tire of them if they last more than four or five minutes.[58]

The excesses of spectacle had largely ceased at the Theatre Royal, as they were so to do at most other regional theatres. However, the pinnacle of such display had been achieved by another theatre in Manchester in earlier decades: the Prince's Theatre, which opened in 1864 and which – as illustrated by the local career of Captain Bainbridge – provided the principal competition for the Royal.

The Prince's Theatre, Manchester

In 1863 the purpose-built Prince's Theatre opened, and in the *Manchester Weekly Times* review of the following year it was described as 'our pretty little theatre'.[59] Charles Calvert, who had been stage manager at the Theatre Royal, was appointed manager of the Prince's, and the theatre's proprietors allowed him far greater financial freedom than Knowles had at the Theatre Royal.[60] The impact of Calvert's expenditure and innovation was quickly apparent at the new theatre, and in the 1864 pantomime. In the opening scene of *Mother Goose; or, the Queen of Hearts, who Made the Tarts and the Knave of Hearts who Ate them*, the Fairy Queen descended from the clouds 'on the tip of a gigantic fern leaf'. The fairy scenery was noted for covering the full extent of the stage:

At the extreme back is a waterfall with an elevation of about twenty feet, the water rushing under a bridge close by, composed of rock and ornamented with jewels; while the centre of the stage, along its entire width is taken up with the 'rippling waters' ... increased by unseen supplies from each side of the stage. Here may be seen several nautilus shells revolving across the stream, each containing a fairy, who, as she sails along, amuses herself by catching up the water in an escallop shell, the scattered drops glittering in the artificial light like myriads of jewels. By the aid, too, of prismatic glasses, the reflection on the water gives it the appearance as though it were suddenly in a rainbow.[61]

The water contained gilded lilies and, at the end of the scene, the central one 'unfold[ed] and disclos[ed] a little child as "Cupid"'. A later scene of 'The Village of Fois-Gras' featured a working water wheel, smoke 'ascending from the cottage' and a series of bridges, over which morris dancers made their entrance. This scene was completed by '40 children, in proper costume, and with a real rush-cart executing the Morris dance'. In the same production, a scene of the 'The Grand Presence Chamber in Card Castle' was, according to the *Manchester Weekly Times* reviewer, 'one of the most prominent scenes in the pantomime', the scenery representing a huge pack of cards, with performers dressed as cards. The transformation scene was detailed, and culminated in the figure of the 'Genius of Peace' descending into the centre of the spectacle.[62] Calvert's reputation for the provision of spectacle had originated with his Shakespearean revivals whilst employed at the Theatre Royal, which he continued at the Prince's. Contemporaneous perceptions of high and low art forms were ignored as Calvert ran celebratory and crowd scenes from his Shakespearean productions on the same bills as the pantomimes. In March 1874 the pantomime was run with 'the celebrated NIGHT CAROUSEL SCENES from TWELFTH NIGHT', and in mid-February 1870 the pantomime of *Harlequin Blackbird; or, the Honey, the Money and the Dainty Dish* was preceded by Calvert's staging of *The Merchant of Venice*, complete with 'a "grand carnival" scene, which is to give a vivid representation of Venice in the sixteenth century'.[63]

Some of the more spectacular scenery for the 1865 pantomime was by Thomas Grieve. In *Little Bo Peep* the 'Butterfly's Haunt' by Grieve was described as 'one of the most delicious combinations of water, wood, rock, and cave we have ever seen upon the stage'.[64] The scenery and its artists, headed by Grieve, were the sole feature of advertisements for *Robin Hood* in 1866. Messrs T. and W. Grieve provided 'The entire New Scenery and Effects' for *Gulliver's Travels; or, Harlequin Billy Taylor and the Good Spirit Energy* at Christmas 1867, their contribution again forming the central element of advertisements. Both the Theatre Royal and the Prince's Theatre staged *Gulliver* that year but it is evident from the previews in the *Manchester Weekly Times* that there were more effects and evident expenditure in the Prince's production. The scenery was promoted in previews as 'entirely new' and Mr Grieve took a bow during the pantomime, for his scene of the ship at berth. Whilst Bainbridge at the Theatre Royal chose not to emphasise the London provenance of productions or quote the principal London press, Calvert actively promoted his metropolitan artists. The local identity that he sought to establish for the Prince's Theatre was as one that equalled the standards set by Drury Lane and Covent Garden, establishing his Manchester theatre as a first-rank provincial venue.

The level of spectacle, and the length of pantomime runs at the Prince's Theatre, suggest that Calvert's productions attracted large enough audiences to recoup such expenditure, but Second and occasional Third Editions (as in 1868), plus comments such as 'the changes which have been introduced are all improvements, and will well repay another visit from all those who saw the piece in its original magnificent garb', also suggest that competition in the city meant he could not be complacent in attracting audiences. Richard Foulkes has cited financial evidence from the theatre, which suggests that the 1870 pantomime *Harlequin Blackbird* was not successful[65], and according to press advertisements, elements of the production were indeed altered in early February to include new costumes and a shadow pantomime, thus enabling the production to run until Easter. In 1875, despite the evident success of *Aladdin* and the lack of a Second Edition, a January review recommended that 'The transformation scene must be seen more than once to be thoroughly appreciated, and the same may be said of all the grand spectacular scenes.'[66]

In 1871, previews of *Blue Beard* assured readers of the *Manchester Weekly Times* that 'in respect of spectacle and varied and comic interest, the production will be worthy of the reputation of the house'. Echoing words applied elsewhere to the Theatre Royal, the reviewer presented the theatre as an institution with established credentials. That year Calvert returned to the tradition of opening on Boxing Day, once again engaging locally produced scenery plus London scenery by Telbin. Blue Beard's grand procession was excessive, comprising 'troops of Spahis, a wonderful squadron of diminutive Zebra guards, a body of Arabian knights, warriors of the Black Mountains' and Himalayan horsemen on real horses, 'all clad in most gorgeous liveries or rich armour', headed by Blue Beard 'seated in a gigantic tandem drawn by giraffes'. The ballet was another important element of the Prince's pantomimes, which, in this production comprised 'an efficient body of French dancers, in addition to the well-trained home corps'.[67]

By the early 1870s the pantomime advertisements for all the Manchester theatres focused on the artistes in the production. However, the spectacles at the Prince's Theatre continued to impress its audiences, and the newspapers. For example, in the 1873 pantomime, the title character in *Cinderella* had not one but four fairy godmothers, the *Manchester Weekly Times* commenting that, 'it is characteristic of the generous prodigality which reigns at the Prince's that they have assigned her four'.[68] The reviews for *The Forty Thieves* (1872) went beyond simply describing the scenery to revel in a prose narrative, in which 'The Shore of Fairyland' incorporated 'soft moonlight' with the 'rising and falling of the waves breaking on the nearer beach, flashing and gleaming in the mysterious wonderful distance, or heaving and tossing in silver-crested billows, which furrow the surface of its silent green depths'. Another principal scene, 'The City of Falling Water',

occupies the entire stage. In the background is a cascade of real water, which gleams and glitters in the sunlight as it rushes down the steeps of its rock-bound bed. On either hand are the towers and minarets of the fairy city to which the falling waters give its name, and in the far distant perspective are Elysian plains and swelling hills, forming an enchanting landscape such as can only be seen in fairyland. In the foreground the view of the water-fall is broken by a rustic bridge of wonderful architecture and masonry of the soundest. The fairies of the waterfall troop upon the stage in myriads, and, after some clever evolutions, yield place to their Queen.... The ballet is closed by a review of the fairy troops, who march in companies from the city gates, and crossing the bridge in front of the waterfall, descend by a winding path cut through the rock to the stage. This review constitutes a scene which we speak within measure when we say has not been rivalled in this city within our recollection. The fairy soldiers are clad in the most picturesque uniforms conceivable – every imaginable cut and fashion has been laid under contribution to lend them variety, and every colour of the rainbow has been pressed into service to enrich their effect.[69]

After the procession and evolutions of the ballet – 'the plan of which has been patriotically patented by the proprietors of the Prince's' – the scene was concluded by the addition of outsized figures in grotesque masks, a military band and the fairy Commander-in-Chief riding on a white elephant. This scene was clearly the focal point of the pantomime.[70] To highlight the relative efforts at spectacle, compare this to the fairy scene at the Queen's Theatre that year, a simpler scene in which

[The fairies] are joined in their revels by a corps of cupids, and are attended by troops of the tiniest little fairy pages…. The ballet has been tastefully arranged and the dancing of the principals is much admired. The final grouping of the fairy legions at the close of their sports is extremely rich and picturesque in effect.[71]

Potential disaster was turned to promotional opportunity in December 1874 when the opening of the pantomime at the Prince's was delayed by the late arrival of 'some of the paraphernalia from Paris and a large portion of the principal costumes from London'.[72] The incident, detailed in the *Guardian*, permitted free advertising of the fact that the Prince's management could afford not only costumes from the metropolis but properties and effects from Paris. In the newspaper advertisements of January 1874, the quantity of spectacular features was awarded a timetable of when each would be featured during the three hour and forty minute performance. By February, advertisements for the theatre extravagantly announced that it was the 'MOST SUCCESSFUL PANTOMIME EVER PRODUCED IN ENGLAND' and claimed that '157,847 VISITORS HAVE PAID FOR ADMISSION', a promotional strategy that set a pattern for pantomime advertising for the

Prince's Theatre (and which was later copied by the management of the Theatre Royal, as discussed above). In December 1874, the advertisements and playbills primed an expectant public by listing all the spectacular features in that year's production, and the reviewer of the *Manchester Weekly Times* asserted Calvert's achievements:

> The Pantomime at the Prince's Theatre is always regarded, and justly, in theatrical circles the event of the Christmas season. This year Mr. Calvert has maintained, if he has not transcended, the reputation of the house which his well-directed enterprise and skilful management have elevated into the first rank in England.[73]

Later advertisements further presented an inclusive image of the temporary communities created by Calvert's pantomime:

WHEREVER YOU GO — IN HOTELS, RESTAURANTS,

... ON THE OMNIBUSES, IN THE PARLOUR,

THE COUNTING HOUSE, THE WORKSHOP, ON

THE RAILWAY, IN THE STREET, IN THE

HOUSE, IN THE CLUBROOM, IN THE

DOMESTIC CIRCLE — 'WHEREVER

PEOPLE MOST DO CONGRE-

GATE' YOU'LL HEAR THE

UNIVERSAL VERDICT

THE PANTOMIME AT THE PRINCE'S

IS THE BEST IN THE CITY

WHAT EVERYBODY SAYS MUST BE TRUE.[74]

This extension of the pantomime's appeal beyond the theatre and into everyday life recurred in advertisements in late January 1876; the series of features in the production were each headed by the question 'HAVE YOU SEEN ...', thus inferring both a sense of community among those who had seen the acts and a sense of exclusion for those who had not. The advertising strategy inferred a dominant theatre and confident management that continued to draw on Calvert's legacy after he had left the theatre in 1875:

The Prince's Theatre Manchester.

The reputation gained by the Prince's Theatre of late years for successful pantomime is one that it is difficult to enhance. Its former manager, Mr. Charles Calvert, who built up its reputation, was a master of pageant, and only required the unlimited resources which were placed at his disposal by the proprietor to produce a piece of fairy workmanship which should alike astonish, charm, and teach.[75]

And whilst advertisements for the Queen's Theatre modestly advocated the pantomime principals and Sanger's horses, and the Theatre Royal, even in its playbill-style newspaper advertisements, focused on the ballets, skaters and transformation scene, the lengthy Prince's Theatre advertisements detailed a succession of spectacular scenes and novel effects, including three trained adult elephants, twin baby elephants, trained ostriches, 250 performers, including a ballet of 100 dancers, a 'Dexterous Sword Combat', a 'Silver Cataract of REAL WATER', an American song and dance act, the Grand Barbaric Ballet, the comedy Polo Match and a company of actors and actresses all 'OF HIGH REPUTE'.

The tradition of liberality was successfully maintained by the new lessee and director Mr Bernard for the 1879 production of *The Forty Thieves*. '[I]n accordance with custom' Bernard produced a Second Edition of the pantomime in February, and although the *Manchester Weekly Times* reviewer found that it 'erred on the side of over-elaboration', such over-elaboration persisted in productions of the 1880s.[76] For the 1885 production of *Cinderella*, the advertisements invoked the theatre's prestigious past, likening the pantomime to those produced under the management of Charles Calvert. In the late 1880s, new theatre managements at the Prince's and the Theatre Royal instigated an era of competition in which the local status and identity of each theatre centred on personal ownership and reputation. Thomas W. Charles (the manager who had been responsible for developing scenic spectacle at the Theatre Royal in Nottingham) took over as manager of the Prince's Theatre in 1889, Thomas Ramsey was in charge of the Theatre Royal, and Pitt Hardacre took over the management of the Comedy Theatre the following year. All three men promoted their pantomimes as a series of personal achievements. Each advertisement and playbill was headed by 'Mr. Charles's third pantomime' or 'Mr. Ramsey's fifth pantomime' as occasion demanded, their names inferring the particular traditions of each house and their accumulated success. Charles's pantomimes featured some of the best-known and emerging names of the pantomime and music hall stage, including Little Tich, Witty Wattie Walton, Harry Fischer and Ada Blanche. The past reputation of the house for spectacle was not forgotten, however, and for his fifth pantomime in 1893 – the same year in which Mr Ramsey at the Theatre Royal claimed that scenic spectacle had become less important for audiences – reviewers of the Prince's Theatre noted that 'the pantomime will attract and prove a success chiefly from its splendour'. In particular reviewers focused on the 'Interior of the Cave', 'Aladdin's Palace and Grounds', 'Chinese Feast of Lanterns', 'The Quay and Market Place of Pekin' and, especially, 'The Palace in Egypt'. 'So successful was this portion of the entertainment that the "gallery" broke out into singing "For he's a jolly good fellow" in honour of the management.'[77]

The Prince's Theatre pantomimes did incorporate local visual and scripted references (to be discussed in Chapter 3) but the sustained reputation, reiterated in advertisements and reviews of the theatre, did not depend solely on a sense of specific localness, of the theatre reflecting Manchester tastes. Rather, it epitomised Manchester's civic and cultural standing in the country, by its national status among the first rank of provincial theatres. London papers as well as local, and sometimes instead of local papers, were cited in newspaper advertisements, but the Prince's Theatre managements did not attempt to present the theatre as a rival to or equivalent of Drury Lane or Covent Garden. There is no reference to the theatre being the 'Drury Lane' of the North West, the approach pursued by Andrew Melville, who owned the Grand Theatre at Birmingham. Whilst the work of nationally recognised artists (and writers) was used regularly at the Prince's Theatre, their names and reputations were assimilated into that of the theatre. In so doing, those managers sought to promote a very particular type of regional identity, one that depended on status. There was no inferred celebration of the fact that the theatre could afford to invest in work by Grieve and Telbin; instead there was an assumption that work of such quality would naturally find its place at the Prince's Theatre.

Whilst managers at theatres such as these sought to establish a local identity and reputation based on spectacle and status, other theatre managements struggled to follow the same national patterns of staging in the light of financial or logistical constraints. Their productions – at the Theatre Royal, Nottingham, the Prince of Wales Theatre, Birmingham and the Queen's Theatre, Manchester – therefore created alternative emphases, which could be promoted as specific and, importantly, local traditions.

Interior of the Theatre Royal, Nottingham in 1865.

The Theatre Royal, Nottingham

In Nottingham, the smallest of the three urban centres, there was only one theatre for much of the period: the Theatre Royal, which had been in existence in the town since 1760. The year 1865 marked the opening of the new purpose-built theatre, closer to the centre of the town and with an auditorium capacity of 2,200. Until 1886 and the building of the Grand Theatre in Hyson Green (a suburb a mile or so out of the town centre), only the Theatre Royal produced pantomime, and even after the second theatre opened, the managers of the Grand tended not to stage pantomime every year, instead hosting occasional short seasons of touring productions in January or February, rather than compete regularly and directly with the Theatre Royal.

As at the other centres, the management of the Theatre Royal promoted the spectacular features in their pantomimes, and the progression from an emphasis on the transformation scene in the 1860s and early 1870s to more varied spectacle was similar to the shifts at Birmingham. In line with such trends, the Nottingham theatre managements naturally also sought to maintain the cycle of 'escalation' in terms of spectacle and novelty. However, the smaller topography of potential audiences, and a fluctuating

local economy that at times could severely affect house takings, meant
that the scale and approach to staging spectacle differed, and the theatre
managers had to find alternative ways of impressing their audiences, of
maintaining standards of spectacle on a reduced budget. The financial
(and logistical) problems faced by managers were occasionally noted in
sympathetic press reviews, but they are more subtly evident through re-
readings of advertisements and previews. At Nottingham, not only do
such materials reveal the alternative strategies employed to encourage
potential audiences to visit their local pantomime, but extant financial
records reveal the underlying details of expenditure and savings made in
the annual production.[78]

The new Theatre Royal building opened in September 1865 and the
autumn season included a very successful run of the burlesque *Ixion, or
the Man at the Wheel* during the town's Goose Fair week in October. The
profits from the autumn, plus capital invested by the new owners Messrs
John and William Lambert, enabled preparations for the pantomime, *The
House That Jack Built*, to begin in November. The focus of the ensuing work
and expenditure was on creating the transformation scene, plus costumes
and masks, as well as enlarging the cast to include supernumeraries, ballet
and harlequinade performers. In creating the transformation scene, 'The
Jewelled Hall of the Amazonian Queen', the head carpenter engaged a
team of eight women to make and gild moulds with materials supplied by
Mr Long the property man.[79] This initial team was expanded in December
as construction work began on the scene, as well as on the harlequinade
tricks. By Christmas, the creation of the pantomime scenery and effects was
the responsibility of twenty-two people, plus an additional weekly team of
between ten and twenty carpenters. In *Economics of the British Stage* Tracy
C. Davis has argued that most provincial theatres bought their pantomimes
from London or other provincial centres and that those productions were
necessarily composite, including script, sets, costumes and effects.[80] To
some degree this was true, particularly in the later decades of the nineteenth
century, but there was greater variety across theatres, with productions
more frequently incorporating some bought-in elements alongside locally
produced sets and costumes. Such a pattern was evident in the production
of the 1865 pantomime at Nottingham. Local departments created the
scenery and properties, calling on the support of local businesses such as

Mr Brown, 'Dealer in paper hangings, painter, Glazier, &c' of Goldsmith Street, and Mr Thompson of Long Row, who provided the basket work for the properties, including the masks for the supernumeraries in the opening.[81] However, the wigs and some masks were hired from Willie Clarkson of Covent Garden and the theatre had a weekly hire contract with costumier Samuel May, also of Covent Garden, who also supplied the specialist harlequinade costumes, whilst the Nottingham wardrobe department took on extra staff to clean and repair the pantomime costumes during the run.[82] In terms of performers, a team of pantomimists was engaged in addition to the stock company, plus Miss Gilbert's locally trained dancing troupe of twelve girls to supplement the ballet of twenty dancers, which had been engaged at the start of the season. Supernumeraries were naturally also engaged and the total wages for them and Miss Gilbert's troupe increased the average total of weekly wages paid to performers from £80 to around £110.[83] The additional investments proved worthwhile: the pantomime ran for six weeks and concluded with a profit of £431, contributing significantly to the overall theatre season profit of £956.

However, 1866 witnessed poor trade and unemployment in the town and the new theatre struggled to maintain audiences. The autumn season failed to provide a profit comparable to that in 1865 – only £186 by November 1866 as compared to £743 the previous year – and it is unclear from the records whether the proprietors provided any capital for the pantomime production. The theatre managers were therefore faced with inadequate funds to provide a spectacular pantomime and the prospect of sparse audience income with which to recoup expenditure. The pantomime for 1866 was *Aladdin*, the script and music for which (plus a property 'pie') were purchased from the Theatre Royal, Manchester.[84] Advertisements promoted the traditional features of the production, the transformation scene and the harlequinade, but in comparison to 1865 there is little evidence amongst the financial records of extra time, labour or materials expended on the transformation scene. Fewer backstage staff had been engaged during the autumn season, and only a few extra joiners, flymen, stage men and cellar men were engaged for the pantomime.[85] The large teams of carpenters, glaziers, model makers and gilders employed in 1865 were conspicuous by their absence the following year. The reduced costs were evident in reviews of the pantomime, which identified more subdued scenery for this scene, 'a succession of tableaux' rather than the usual 'glitter and sparkle'.[86] To deflect attention from the less extravagant scenery, the production boasted an augmented cast of up to sixty people, largely supernumeraries. Rather than creating new scenery, masks and costumes for the larger cast were clearly the focus of expenditure, although even here some savings were made.[87] During the 1866–7 theatre season the Nottingham management changed their costume supplier from Samuel May to John Simmonds of London, who charged a lower weekly rate. The theatre wardrobe still had to hire extra dresses for the pantomime but there is greater evidence of locally made costumes using fabric from Nottingham suppliers.[88] In addition to the scenery and costumes, additional savings were sought by not engaging a ballet, simply re-booking Miss Gilbert's troupe for the Christmas season instead.[89] Not all of these attempts to save costs proved effective: an extended run, whilst intended to boost income, naturally increased the weekly cost of the dancers, and the additional London costumes increased expenditure in that department.

In simplifying the scenery and investing in a larger and cheaper number of supers, the theatre management at Nottingham established a pattern for their pantomimes which, with variations, was continued into the next decade. In the 1870s, the move from a creative emphasis on the transformation scene to other scenes in the opening did little to assuage a lack of financial investment. Promotional materials once again aimed to compensate for the disparities in the production. The Harvest Scene in the 1874 production of *Little Bo Peep*, for example, was described in the *Nottingham Daily Guardian* as 'the most artistic and successful scene in the pantomime' and front-page advertisements placed the scene above the transformation, drawing attention to the incorporation of 'A FLOCK OF SPLENDID SHEEP' and a 'CASCADE OF REAL WATER' not once but twice in the same advertisement.[90] Excess in the advertisement potentially distracted from a lack of excess on stage. In the 1876 production of *The Fair One with the Golden Locks*, 'the most successful scene of all' was 'one which represents the ice-bound regions "inside the moon"' and incorporated the 'novelty of a snow shower at the conclusion'.[91] Although the reviewers approved of novelties in the spectacular element of the pantomimes, there is little evidence in the advertisements and reviews that the Nottingham theatre staged 'heavy' sets or large, complex properties such as *The Lively Sally* of the Birmingham productions. In turn, it is clear from reviews of the transformation scene in those 1874 and 1876 pantomimes that the financial resources of the Nottingham theatre remained relatively limited. The transformation scene in 1876, for example, was prudently described in the *Nottingham Daily Guardian*: 'That this is the most beautiful production of its kind we have ever had in Nottingham we should hesitate to aver.'[92] The theatre management at Nottingham provided spectacular elements in each pantomime, but the limited descriptions in reviews and the repetitive nature of some of the advertisements suggest that the emphasis of production and expenditure was limited to one principal feature rather than several in each production.

In 1876 the theatre manager Thomas W. Charles instigated a new era at the theatre. Charles was an experienced manager, who was simultaneously responsible for the Grand Theatre in Glasgow. This dual management placed him at an advantage in terms of production resources, and the provenance of scenery and scenic artists in the books of words and reviews indicate that scenery was alternated between the two theatres. The *Nottingham Daily Guardian* referred uncritically to the '*quid pro quo* principle' in 1885; the Nottingham scenery of 1884 by Mr Potts was being used at Glasgow, whilst Mr McLennan of the Glasgow theatre was promoted in the Nottingham papers as the principal artist for the local production of *Little Red Riding Hood*.[93] Charles was aware of regional standards of pantomime – as mentioned above, he later managed the Prince's Theatre in Manchester – and the promotion of his pantomimes at Nottingham clearly displayed a desire to increase the spectacular element and the status of productions at the latter. In *Blue Beard* of 1877, the opening scene of 'Toyland' consisted of a central, large dolls' house and stage wings consisting of outsized toys. In Scene 3, the 'Grand Turkish Procession' marked Blue Beard's entry. There were

> children with red and white turbans, silver scimitars, and crescent-shaped shields.... After the procession of children came a train of women playing some very Oriental-looking bells ... followed by soldiers clothed in yellow jackets and steel armour and helmets. The children were then massed in the centre, the musicians and soldiers

flanking them, while behind the children were standards bearing the crescents and Bluebeard's bodyguard of misshapen gigantic monsters. Then seated on an elephant, in came Bluebeard to fetch Fatima.

This particular review also gave an extended description of the transformation scene, and concluded by praising the production, which 'redounds to the credit of Mr. Charles as a manager and an artist.'[94]

The years 1878 and 1879 were a time of bad trade and hardship in the town. However, during the 1878 9 season the *Nottingham Daily Express* commented that 'whatever may be the amount of distress in the town from insufficiency of work, there yet remains in the pockets of the people money enough to purchase seats in what is after all their favourite place of amusement – the Theatre'.[95] The effects of the economic downturn were evident in reviews of the pantomime, which only detailed the stage effects of the opening demon scene, emphasising instead the activities of the supernumeraries and dancers in the remainder of the production. For the next few years, critical descriptions of Charles's pantomime spectacles were very similar, praising the sets without really detailing them and instead highlighting the ballet and processional scenes. In 1884, Charles had the stage of the Theatre Royal enlarged, and that year the pantomime *The Forty Thieves* was previewed as being of a 'splendid and stupendous scale', the larger stage providing 'a scope for the arrangement of spectacles and effects that could never have been ventured upon a year ago'.[96] Charles also oversaw the installation of an electric room under the stage, which enabled the principal feature of the pantomime, the 'golden-jewelled, electric armour' for the forty thieves. This feature, comprising armour, dresses, batteries and appliances, apparently cost Charles in excess of £1,000.[97] The entire production cost £5,000, making it, according to the *Nottingham Daily Guardian*, 'the most costly pantomime … in the history of the Nottingham theatre'.[98] Significantly, that year saw the first 'behind the scenes' style article in the local press. In the *Nottingham Daily Guardian*, a reviewer presented a 'stroll' backstage, commenting on the technicalities of grooves, flies and gridiron, naming the scenic artists Mr Potts and Mr Camus, and stating that 'Upwards of fifty persons' were employed in the wardrobe. The emphasis in the article was on scale, stating that 'a modern pantomime is a huge "manufactured" piece of work', but the specifics of production, such as occurred in the Birmingham articles, were not provided.[99] In preparation for the following year's pantomime, *Little Red Riding Hood*, a second such article highlighted the work of the scene painters, ballet, wardrobe, property man and mask makers, but essentially the article created a sense of awe and mystery that shrouded any details of production: 'Everywhere things incomprehensible to the uninitiated are being done.'[100] Unlike the descriptions in Birmingham, this viewpoint exemplified the prevailing tone of the Nottingham reviews in the period, which contained an inference that the spectacle was not on such a scale as to warrant a closer inspection. For example, in a review of the 1889 production of *Sinbad the Sailor*, the *Nottingham Daily Guardian* praised the Palace Scene but simply drew attention to the fact that 'a vast amount of constructive skill and design has been lavished' on the scene 'and the stage is a mass of gleaming gold and silver, the effect of which can hardly be described'.[101] The larger stage was instead perceived as an opportunity for spectacular scenes in the sense of incorporating bigger processions and ballets, but not necessarily for an increased use of 'heavy' sets and spectacular scenery. Scale had always, and continued to be, achieved in the Nottingham pantomimes through the use of people. The *Guardian* observation, regarding the employment of fifty people in the wardrobe, highlighted the recurrent emphasis in Nottingham on quantities of elaborately dressed extras, in ballets, crowd groupings and processions; by the 1880s the large casts could incorporate 150 or 200 artistes.[102] In December 1882, the *Nottingham Daily Guardian* predicted that the forthcoming 'ball-scene' in *Cinderella* 'will, of course, be made by Mr. Charles one of his chief opportunities for display ... the opportunity for one of those elaborate processions without which no pantomime would be complete'.[103] The use of crowds of supernumeraries instead of large sets was not criticised by the Nottingham reviewers. Processions were an established feature of the London pantomimes and the existence of precedence – albeit on a very different scale to that provided at Nottingham – enabled critics to accept and promote the more modest local version.

However, if theatrical spectacle was predicated on the notion of surplus and satisfaction, then there is the suggestion of a palpable tension between cultural expectation and the amount of spectacle that the Nottingham Theatre Royal could realistically provide. The financial evidence from the mid-1860s, far from reflecting a unique situation in the economics of the town and theatre, defined a pattern that, despite the improvements and creative skills introduced by later managers, continued to influence pantomime production. The situation at Nottingham highlighted what Thomas Richards (drawing on the work of Baudrillard) describes as the 'myth of the abundant society', in other words the suggestion, through the promotion of quantity, of the notion of plenty.[104] Whilst the Birmingham Theatre Royal, for example, was located in a wealthy town and could partake of that wealth, expressing it in an excess of spectacle (that in turn mirrored the industrial success of the town), Nottingham, with its more defined economic fluctuations, could not, at times, uphold that cycle. Instead the sparser sets were filled with people and attention was deflected to other embellishments. The Nottingham theatre management, together with the newspaper promotions, was indeed partaking of the 'myth'; Baudrillard's definition of profusion as 'the magical, definitive negation of scarcity' was, albeit ironically, upheld.[105]

The Prince of Wales Theatre, Birmingham

Formerly the site of the Birmingham Music Hall, the Prince of Wales Theatre in Broad Street opened as such in 1863, with an auditorium capacity of 3,500. From the mid-1860s to the mid-1880s new theatres and theatre buildings were opened in all three towns and whilst the opportunity for audiences to see a greater range of productions is clear, managers of the recent additions to the local entertainment scene were faced with two related problems. Firstly, even with a large population of potential theatre-goers and competitive productions, audiences could not be guaranteed. Secondly, both audiences and local newspaper critics tended to have an intrinsic loyalty to the older theatres, usually the Theatres Royal, which had been established in the late eighteenth century. In 1886 the Grand Theatre opened in Nottingham, in Hyson Green, one of the town suburbs. Local newspaper reviewers regularly referred to the new theatre as 'the other place' or the 'Hyson Green House', firmly locating it in its suburban address and distance from the town centre, which was dominated by the Theatre Royal, the familiar 'old house'. In the 1860s, the recently opened Prince of Wales Theatre in Birmingham had also to contend with such demarcations. Whereas the Theatre Royal had become the well-known 'Royal', the younger theatre was referred to as 'the Broad

Street House', even though the two theatres were not very far apart in the town centre. Referring to the theatre by its address effectively distanced it in much the same way that the two Nottingham theatres were defined. Further, in 1865 a review in the *Birmingham Daily Post* claimed that, in relation to that year's pantomimes, 'Birmingham folks asserted that the minor house bore away the palm'.[106] Whilst according to this statement the Prince of Wales Theatre had provided the best pantomime in the town, its phrasing was less complimentary. The use of the word 'minor' intrinsically classed the theatre with the minor and illegitimate theatres of the pre-1843 period, whilst also inferring the building's heritage as a music hall.

Despite such comments, the Prince of Wales Theatre provided the sole legitimate competition for the Theatre Royal during the pantomime season, and the first manager at the new theatre sought to establish a distinct identity for his productions, focusing on the traditional elements of the genre. However, the opening dark scene of the 1863 pantomime, *The House That Jack Built*, failed to impress the reviewer of the *Birmingham Daily Post*, who claimed that 'what we mistook at first for a gigantic parrot cage of quaint construction … the playbill assured us was the "Dripping Well of Knaresborough and abode of Old Mother Shipton by moonlight"'.[107] In principle, W.H. Swanborough had bought the 1861 Drury Lane pantomime by E.L. Blanchard, but he had not purchased the entire production, due to either financial or logistical constraints (the Prince of Wales Theatre had a narrow stage). Certainly the 'Procession of Games' that had featured in the London version does not appear to have been reproduced at the Birmingham theatre, but the new manager expended considerable resources on the pantomime transformation scene, which was applauded by the critics. In reviews of the following year's pantomime, the 1863 production was declared retrospectively to have been unsuccessful and the manager, 'instructed by last year's failure, instead of concentrating his resources upon a single scene [the transformation scene], has recognised the necessity of providing a series of brilliant and varied spectacular effects, of which the transformation scene is but the culminating point'.[108] In responding to the expectations of his audiences, Swanborough's pantomimes of 1864 and 1865 were much more successful, each running for nearly three months. In 1866, James Rogers took over from Swanborough as manager and the quality of pantomimes improved, although for the first ten years of his management the provision of spectacle continued to be hindered by the small stage, and the level of spectacle, although good, appeared limited in comparison to the elaborate displays at the Theatre Royal.

At Nottingham, a fluctuating local economy and smaller local population dictated theatrical provision but in Birmingham a much larger population and better economic base would suggest that both the Theatre Royal and the Prince of Wales Theatre should have been able to attract sufficient income to maintain similarly spectacular pantomimes each year. However, later records suggest that multiple pantomimes in Birmingham could not always depend on an equal amount of attention from local audiences. In 1886, Andrew Melville, lessee of the Grand Theatre, applied for a dramatic licence for a fourth theatre in Birmingham. Messrs Simpson and Rogers, managers of the Theatre Royal and Prince of Wales Theatre respectively, opposed the application. Naturally they did not want additional competition in the town, but in the presented argument it was further stated that when the Prince of Wales Theatre opened in 1863 it had taken several years for it to become commercially successful.[109] The mid- to late 1860s was a period of national economic depression, and although the local economy was generally strong throughout the second half of the nineteenth century, a downturn in demand for some of the local trades may well have had an impact on the second theatre. It may, though, have simply been the case that the reputation of the Theatre Royal at the time, particularly for its pantomimes, was too well established, ensuring a loyal allegiance from public and press alike. The manager of the new theatre therefore had to contend with national and local economic factors but, while at Nottingham the initial lack of a second legitimate theatre and therefore direct competition permitted cost-saving exercises, in Birmingham any marked contrast with the productions at the Theatre Royal would have further discouraged audiences. Therefore, whilst the resources of the established theatre enabled lavish spectacle and backstage tours by the press, the Prince of Wales's management had to devise new methods of attracting audiences at Christmas time.

By 1868, Rogers had established a similar trend to that utilised at the Nottingham theatre, that of dependence on supernumeraries, but instead of engaging adult performers, his pantomimes became known for featuring groups, dances and processions by children. The engagement of children was another concept that had its precedent in the London pantomimes (and was copied at many provincial theatres). According to the *Times* reviews of the 1860s, large processions and themed groupings, including those by children, were one of the features of the pantomimes at 'Old Drury' and Covent Garden. The number of supernumeraries (adults and children) in those processions and ballets were between 150 and 200 for each pantomime, and those numbers rose steadily until by the 1890s pantomimes by Augustus Harris could boast 500 or more people in a single cast. The numbers at the Prince of Wales Theatre productions of the late 1860s were far smaller, the children engaged in each pantomime averaging around 80, but by the 1870s groups of juvenile performers numbered an average of 150, accompanied by large ballets. Whilst in principle the strategy echoed that at Nottingham, there the number of supernumeraries in the 1860s was even smaller (only sixty people), and it was another twenty years before the Nottingham pantomimes could include the sort of numbers seen in London in the 1860s, or in Birmingham by the early 1870s. The concept of the 'myth of plenty' can therefore be applied to a certain extent to the pantomime productions in Birmingham as well as Nottingham, but the manager at the former theatre was not only able to engage larger numbers of supers, but the subsequent savings on expenditure were diverted to create additional features several years before such a thing was possible at Nottingham. By the late 1870s, the Prince of Wales Theatre pantomimes were able to make a feature of both the transformation and one other major scene, although the incorporation of sets and large mechanical effects continued to be hindered by the narrow stage. The initial attempts by Mr Swanborough to limit expenditure on scenery had been unsuccessful, but Rogers, in adopting the use of children in his productions, deftly instigated a stylistic feature that both compensated for a lack of investment and logistical restrictions in the scenery and could be actively promoted as a defining feature in competitive advertising during the Christmas season. He effectively redefined the spectacle at his theatre, thereby creating a specific identity and, over time, tradition for his pantomimes.

In 1868, the juvenile 'army' in *Babes in the Wood; or, Harlequin Robin Hood and the Brave Little Soldiers of Lilliput* were promoted alongside the transformation scene as the principal feature of the production. The following year, reviews of the pantomime at the Theatre Royal emphasised the multitude of effects in the production, but in contrast, the chief features of *Little Red Riding Hood, or Harlequin Boy Blue and the Fairies of the Glow-worm Dell* at the Prince of Wales Theatre, aside from 'Glow-worm Dell' with a real waterfall, were the costumes and the performance of the eighty children. Despite the effective harvest scene with a mechanically moved wagon and real ponies in *Little Goody Two Shoes* (1871), the seventy children in the scene were again the focus of the production, in 'one of the children's scenes, which Mr. Rogers never forgets to provide'.[110] The incorporation of another miniature army of 100 children in the 1872 pantomime was complemented by a review in the *Birmingham Daily Mail*, which claimed that the Prince of Wales pantomimes were 'a favourite with the children'.[111] The *Birmingham Daily Post* reiterated the sense of tradition by stating that Scene 10, the castle scene, included 'one of those spectacular displays, in which children appear, for which the Prince of Wales Theatre is noted'.[112] Advertisements at the end of January appealed to the child's perspective, headed by 'Oh, Mama! Do take me to see Mr. Rogers's Pantomime; every-body says it is so very beautiful.'[113] Promoting a children's pantomime that children wanted to see, and the appeal to 'Mama', effectively conferred an air of respectability on the production for the scrupulous middle-class mother. It was an advertising strategy that Rogers repeated on occasions into the early 1880s.

In the 1874 pantomime *Little Bo Peep; or Harlequin Jack and Jill and Prince Truelove*, 180 children were the main feature of two scenes: the schoolroom, and the 'Hall of the Pelicans'. In the latter they were, once again, dressed as miniature, armoured knights, leading to the *Birmingham Daily Mail* commenting on the presumed expense of their costumes. The reviewer remarked that a 'strong point in the pantomimes at this theatre in former years has been the admirable manner in which the children have gone through their manoeuvres and this year … Mr. Rogers has eclipsed all his former efforts'.[114] Each year, children continued to populate the pantomime stage at the Prince of Wales Theatre. In 1876 Rogers invested in a new, extended stage, and the advertisement in the *Birmingham Daily Post* highlighted that 'The Pantomime this year, in consequence of the largely extended … New Stage, and improved Machinery, will be produced on a scale of magnificence never before attempted in Birmingham, and will constitute the whole Evening's Performances.'[115] However, the *Birmingham Daily Post* reviewer once again chose to focus on the tradition of 'transformation scenes, pretty spectacles with hundreds of children's characters, droll masquerades and comic dialogue' that defined productions.[116]

The first major stage property at the Birmingham Theatre Royal had been *The Lively Sally* in 1878; Nottingham too, under the management of Thomas Charles, began to include mechanised sets in the late 1870s, and in 1880 the Prince of Wales Theatre followed suit, with a village scene in *Little Red Riding Hood* that incorporated a mechanised windmill, waterwheel and mill, as well as a 'set' of the Squire's hall which took up the full depth of the stage. In 1882 Rogers's pantomime of *Sinbad the Sailor* included a mechanical Roc, whose 'huge wings flap all across the stage', plus Sinbad's ship which, according to the *Birmingham Daily Mail*, was 'no piece of pasteboard arrangement … it is a huge, substantial yet buoyant thing', plus a numerous crew on board: 'How this huge concern is moved about the stage … we do not pretend to be able to discover; the thing is done, and cleverly done.'[117] And again in 1887, the pantomime featured a 'full-rigged ship, which will sail from the back of the stage to the front', 'not seen before in Birmingham'.[118] In investing in these new features, Rogers had not forgotten the appeal of his juvenile performers and continued to include large numbers of children in his pantomimes. In the opening dark scene of the 1880 pantomime, the 'Wolf's Lair' included numerous children dressed as wolf cubs, and in 1881 an animated set of 'Toyland' featured over seventy-five children plus processions and ballets. In a review of the 1883 production of *Cinderella*, the *Birmingham Daily Post* commented that 'the liberal employment of children in the pantomime does much to win favour for it',[119] and another production, *Gulliver's Travels* in 1885, enabled a display of child Lilliputians in a parade of 'policemen and postmen and firemen and other developments of nineteenth-century civilisation, including the very latest on the list in the "newly enfranchised"'.[120]

By the late 1880s the Prince of Wales Theatre pantomimes began to exhibit regular set scenes and mechanical effects, and the emphasis on children's parades and ballets had largely ceased. Large casts continued to be engaged, but these tended to comprise adult performers. The signs of change had been witnessed in the 1881 pantomime, which also featured a selection of variety acts. These, along with real elephants and camels, had become the focus of advertisements later in the run. An incorporation of variety acts, and later of music-hall stars, reflected national production patterns and heralded the new emphasis of expenditure at the theatre. However, the shift in emphasis did not detract from the fact that the Prince of Wales Theatre under Rogers's management had become an established house in Birmingham alongside the Theatre Royal, a crucial development in the light of new competition in the town. Andrew Melville's theatre The Grand, which opened in 1883, also staged pantomime, initially opting for imported Drury Lane productions (and promoted as such), but the loyalties of press and audiences were defined in the *Birmingham Daily Post* review of the opening night. The reviewer commented that, although there would be a 'general desire' and curiosity to see Melville's first production at the new theatre,

> probably a large number of the patrons of pantomime living in or visiting Birmingham will feel inclined to take their first dose of the mirth that doeth good like a medicine at one of the establishments which have so long been regarded as reliable repositories of fun and scenic art.[121]

Queen's Theatre Manchester interior in 1880.

The Queen's Theatre, Manchester

The Queen's Theatre originally opened on the site of the old Theatre Royal in Spring Gardens when the latter was moved to Fountain Street in 1807. Initially simply known as the 'Minor Theatre', it acquired the title of Queen's Theatre in 1831.[122] In 1869 the building was sold and the venue moved to Bridge Street, north of the city centre and away from the more fashionable theatres, where it formally opened in November 1870 on the site of the old Amphitheatre. The new theatre was completed in six weeks and had an auditorium divided between a dress circle, pit and gallery, the last replacing the upper boxes. Despite the moves of more fashionable theatres, there was no accommodation for stalls, and the auditorium capacity, including standing room, was 2,750.

Unlike the Prince of Wales Theatre in Birmingham or the Prince's Theatre in Manchester, the Queen's Theatre had been in existence since the early years of the nineteenth century. At that point, under the dictates of the 1737 Licensing Act, only at the patent theatres (those which had been awarded the title 'Theatre Royal' by act of Parliament) could the spoken word be performed. Theatres such as the Queen's were classed as 'minor' theatres, where a more limited repertoire centred on music, dance and burlettas were necessarily staged. In her essay, 'Early Nineteenth-Century Theatre in Manchester', Katherine Newey has written of the Queen's Theatre's status in the period prior to the repeal of the Licensing Act in 1843. In particular, she highlights an 1847 article published in the *Dramatic and Musical Review*, in which the two Manchester theatres were still being defined in relation to what Newey terms the 'cultural capital' of the Theatre Royal, namely its former legal status allowing it to stage serious drama, as well as its greater size, which naturally enabled the staging of large spectacles. Arguing that 'a small theatre cannot compete with a large one', the critic of the *Review* suggested that in order to be commercially viable, each theatre should maintain a distinct repertoire. He allocated comedies, melodramas, operettas and farces to the Queen's Theatre, thus, as Newey notes, sustaining a differentiation of repertoire that was similar to that staged prior to 1843.[123] By the late 1850s, there is a sense that the Queen's was still hindered by its former status as a minor theatre. Its location was less auspicious than those of the Theatre Royal and the Prince's, and the theatre reputedly depended to a large extent on a mainly working-class audience (a point underscored by the exclusion of stalls in the auditorium). A brief survey of the Queen's pantomime advertisements, which frequently comprised only brief statements of the principal features, suggests a theatre that was unable to claim a substantial house income and a management that recognised a certain futility in employing extensive puff in the promotion of his productions.

Reviews of the Queen's Theatre pantomimes highlight the more modest emphasis of productions. Whilst the scenery in the Theatre Royal production of 1859 was extensively described in the *Manchester Weekly Times*, that of *Robin Redbreast and Prince Cock Sparrow* at the Queen's was simply described as 'first-rate'.[124] It was the harlequinade that commanded attention, and the comedy in the production – the 'Best Comic Business in the Provinces' – that featured most strongly in the advertisements after the opening night. The harlequinade featured five scenes, including old favourites: 'The rifle movement is not omitted, and the clown's rifle brigade is a capital scene.'[125] For the following year, the management of the Queen's Theatre adopted one of the Theatre Royal strategies: the latter theatre had promoted Mr Calcott's scenic work in their 1859 production of *Bluebeard*, and advertisements for the Queen's Theatre pantomime of *Aladdin* in 1860 promoted 'Mr. Calcott's Registered Scenic Effect' in the transformation scene.[126] In previewing the pantomime, the *Manchester Weekly Times* highlighted this scene, the '"Lake of Lilies and the Palm-tree Grove" in which is introduced Mr. Calcott's marvellous plan of scenic reflection, as first introduced by him with such immense success in the Lyceum Theatre, London'.[127] In 1864 the pantomime was *Humpty Dumpty, the Princess, the Peri and the Pearl Diver*. Once again, the only scene which merited a detailed response in the newspapers was the transformation scene, 'The Fairy Temple of the Golden Palms', in which 'The appliances of stage ingenuity have been called into service with unusual skill. The palm trees wave their branches in the air, the flowers open and disclose their sylph-like tenants' and 'Coloured lights diversify the picture.'[128] By mid-January 1865, the *Manchester Weekly Times* stated that all three theatres were continuing to attract good audiences and that none of the productions had gone to a Second Edition. The reviewer reiterated praise for the 'Home Brew'd' transformation scene at the Queen's, emphasising its creation by the resident artist Mr Brew, but with the emphasis in this brief review focused on the singing and comic business in the production, it is evident that scenic expenditure at the Queen's was centred once again on the transformation scene, in marked contrast to the various spectacles at the Prince's Theatre.[129] Similarly, in the 1865 pantomime *Whittington and His Cat*, the *Manchester Weekly Times* noted that 'the entire resources of the establishment have been concentrated upon the transformation scene, which is of a very elaborate and beautiful character'.[130] The sentiments were reiterated in early January, the reviewer remarking that there was 'less pretension in the matter of scenic display' but a 'lively enjoyable element' in the production as a whole.[131] Whereas the Prince of Wales Theatre management in Birmingham had been criticised by the press in the mid-1860s for limiting their resources to the transformation scene, at Manchester the newspaper reviewers appear to have clearly understood and sympathised with the financial situation at the Queen's. If the theatre did indeed rely on a working-class audience, their own fortunes in the depression years of the early 1860s would certainly have impacted on the theatre takings. As mentioned earlier, expenditure on spectacle in the Theatre Royal pantomimes had been reduced due to the adverse economic conditions, and in the opening scene of *Whittington and His Cat* at the Queen's the characters made an unusually frank admission of Manager Egan's battle for 'bigger houses'. Neither press nor public could be deceived. However, in this same scene the necessarily more restricted focus on spectacle was turned to good effect; the pantomime author created a local tradition out of limited expenditure. The good fairy announced that 'There's a spot in Manchester that's called the Queen's / famed for its glorious transformation scenes.'[132] At this particular theatre a perceived paucity of spectacular provision could be advantageously diverted into a celebration of production values. Nevertheless the Queen's pantomime closed several weeks before those at the Theatre Royal and the Prince's.

In the reviews of the following season's production of *Kafoozalum; or the Beau, the Beauty and the Babah*, the *Manchester Weekly Times* commented perhaps rather unkindly of the opening scene ('Bottom of the Atlantic Ocean') that 'it is probably as near to nature as we have any right to expect for sixpence'. It is unclear whether this comment referred to the lack of expenditure or to the popularity of the 6d gallery seats (or perhaps both, the one after all influenced the other). The usual advocacy of the press had only momentarily lapsed as the reviewer instead focused on the highlight of the production. Once again, this was the transformation scene, 'The Pagoda of Bliss' 'in which the strength and resources of the establishment are concentrated'.[133] By early January 1867 the *Manchester Weekly Times* was noting that in comparison to the Prince's where 'crowded houses' were a nightly feature, the Queen's was simply having 'a fair run', adding that 'If less pretentious in point of scenic display, it has compensating properties which are sure of popular recognition', chiefly the burlesque performers, the singing and dancing and the harlequinade, which, as always at that theatre, was 'really an important feature of the pantomime'.[134] It does appear that both prior to and after the opening of the Prince's Theatre, the Queen's management struggled to provide competitive spectacle, and audiences were not necessarily attracted by the concentrated focus on performers. In 1868 the theatre was alternately open and dark on regular occasions, but it also gained a new manager, Mr. J.P. Weston, from Bolton. At the close of a year he staged the pantomime *A Apple Pie, and Little Boy Blue; or, Harlequin Jack-in-the-Box and the World of Toys*. The production featured a 'triple transformation scene', a 'novel, complex, and necessarily costly production', plus an elaborate fairy scene on which 'the artist appears to have lavished his utmost resources', and a finale, 'The Grand Fairy Valentine', by local artist Mr Bickerstaff.[135] Weston had the theatre 'newly fitted up' for the pantomime of 1871, and in January a reviewer in the *Manchester Guardian* promoted the fact that the 'Queen's is doing very good service in providing a cheap healthy place of amusement for the masses'.[136]

For the 1872 pantomime, *Little Red Riding Hood*, the focus of attention was placed on the ballets and large groupings of supernumeraries in various scenes, including a 'review of Amazonian troops' in which 'Nearly a hundred amazons tread the stage, glittering in the sheen of brightly polished armour.'[137] The reviewer in the *Manchester Weekly Times* commented on the 'high merit' that the pantomime achieved as a spectacle, and on the 'growing reputation' of the new Queen's Theatre, and yet despite the full description of the transformation scene, the review focused much more on the burlesque performers and those scenes that involved large groupings of dancers and supernumeraries. The theatre was clearly still unable to fully compete with the spectacular productions at the Theatre Royal and the Prince's Theatre. The pattern of reviews was supportive but largely unchanging. The *Manchester Weekly Times* review of the 1873 pantomime *Little Jack Horner* focused on the artistic nature of the scene painting rather than spectacle, and in 1874 the reviewer of the *Guardian* stated that the scenery was 'in fact rather meagre' but assumed, sympathetically, that the damage from a recent fire may have contributed to the management's inability to provide a spectacular pantomime.[138]

The Queen's Theatre evidently received less house income than the Prince's Theatre, a comparison that was usually suggested rather than overtly stated in reviews and advertising phrases over the years, but by the mid-1870s the new theatre management, rather than trying to compete directly with the larger theatres, had settled on a distinctive and practical identity for the Queen's. In January 1876 all the theatres' managements were naturally advertising their pantomimes in the local newspapers. Underneath the lengthy advertisement for the Prince's pantomime, detailing all the scenic spectacles and special effects, and the London and local press quotes, the more modest Queen's advertisement for its 'COMIC CHRISTMAS PANTOMIME' instead promoted itself as 'The People's Pantomime at the People's Prices'.[139] Further, the new lessee and manager, Mr E. Edmonds, had adopted a very particular strategy for his pantomime *Twinkle, Twinkle Little Star*. In appealing to the 'people', the pantomime story was set in ancient Manchester, with local scenery and a script filled with local allusions. This in itself was not a new idea, but it served to crystallise the new approach to pantomimes and audiences at the theatre. In so doing Edmonds created a distinctive local identity whilst embracing the circumstances that defined the theatre. Once again the transformation scene was positively advertised as a distinctive tradition. The scene utilised an extended depth of stage and, according to the *Manchester Weekly Times*, 'quite sustained the reputation of the theatre for brilliant display in this respect', and the double harlequinade also supplied the traditional 'rollicking fun … which has become the special characteristic of the Queen's pantomimes'.[140] The traditional elements defined the pantomimes at this theatre, and whilst the transformation scene continued to be admired, the productions found their local niche in reflecting local identity together with fun and comic 'business' rather than extravagant spectacle.

Conclusion

Spectacle was clearly of import at all theatres and the response by the respective managers, in providing that spectacle in their pantomimes, shows that regional producers were alert to changes in taste and style. However, the practicalities of the theatres' logistical and financial resources meant that there were certain differences in the style and promotion of the pantomimes. In *The Economics of the British Stage*, Tracy C. Davis has argued that the smaller (non-West End) theatres felt a pressure to provide spectacle and that this economic pressure was part of the impetus behind the success and rise of spectacular theatre.[141] Theatre managers in all three towns felt that pressure incontrovertibly, but the presentation of necessary abundance took a slightly different form at each theatre.

At the larger centres of Manchester and Birmingham, the theatre managements all aimed to provide spectacle and novelty in their pantomimes, but it was the immediate competition for audiences that defined productions. In Manchester, the managers of the Queen's Theatre developed a very specific character for their theatre, but the various Theatre Royal managements, in their attempts to rival the Prince's Theatre, sometimes struggled to assert an independent identity. Competition between the two main houses was defined by the close of the century in the promotion of the individual managers, whose reputations held an inherent promise of success, whilst at the Queen's Theatre the promotion of local identity depended on recognising its audiences and their locale. For the Nottingham theatre, the use of supernumeraries suggests a compensatory rather than complementary gesture, but it was never criticised locally; instead it was applauded and formed part of the local pantomime tradition. The Prince of Wales Theatre management in Birmingham adopted a similar strategy in the formative years of the new venue, again using cheaper juvenile supernumeraries to create a pattern and tradition for its pantomimes. At all theatres in each town the appeal to audiences depended on providing the traditional elements of the genre along with developing trends of spectacle, but as each manager was forced to adapt that provision according to available income and the practicalities of staging, new traditions, features and reputations were formed.

Notes

1. *Report from the Select Committee* (1892), p. 195, in answer to question 2859. Booth also refers to the importance of the pit in the provincial theatres in *Theatre in the Victorian Age*, p. 17.
2. T. Richards, *The Commodity Culture of Victorian England: Advertising and Spectacle 1851–1914* (Stanford, CA, 1990).
3. *Ibid.*, p. 56.
4. I. Armstrong, *Victorian Glassworlds: Glass Culture and the Imagination 1830–1880* (Oxford, 2008), p. 133.
5. 'The Pantomimes', *Birmingham Daily Mail*, 23 December 1881, p. 3.
6. *Ibid.*
7. 'Behind the Scenes at Pantomime Time. By the "Odd Man Out"', *Birmingham Daily Mail*, 20 December 1873, p. 4; 'Pantomime in Plain Clothes [by the Odd Man Out]', *Birmingham Daily Mail*, 27 December 1875, p. 2; 'Christmas Stories: A Pantomimic Workshop', *Birmingham Daily Gazette*, 26 December 1876, p. 6; 'Preparing the Pantomime', *Birmingham Daily Mail*, 26 December 1888, p. 3.
8. Mander and Mitchenson, *Pantomime*, p. 30; and Frow, *'Oh Yes, It Is!'*, p. 105 (citing *Theatre*, 1883).
9. 'Christmas Amusements: The Pantomime at the Royal', *Birmingham Daily Mail*, 28 December 1874, p. 2; 'Boxing Day Amusements: The Theatre Royal Pantomime', *Birmingham Daily Mail*, 27 December 1876, p. 2.
10. 'Behind the Scenes at Pantomime Time. By the "Odd Man Out"', *Birmingham Daily Mail*, 20 December 1873, p. 4. See also M.J. Moynet, *French Theatrical Production in the Nineteenth Century* (1873), trans. and augmented A.S. Jackson with M.G. Wilson, ed. M.A. Carlson (New York, 1976), p. 156, for a brief description of mask-making using papier-mâché; the partly fictional account of a mask maker, reproduced from 'The Mask Maker' (1868), in Jackson, *Victorian Theatre*, pp. 178–82; and Booth, *English Plays*, Appendix C, 'Pantomime Production, Rehearsal and Performance', pp. 485–518.
11. 'Christmas Amusements: The Pantomime at the Royal', *Birmingham Daily Mail*, 27 December 1873, p. 2.
12. I am here referring to those London examples that have been cited in secondary sources, for example by Mander and Mitchenson, *Pantomime*, pp. 26–8 (citing the *Illustrated Sporting and Dramatic News* of December 1874); also by Booth in Appendix C of *English Plays* (citing Augustus Sala's article 'Getting up a Pantomime' from *Household Words*), pp. 487–97. See also contemporary reports such as 'The Reading of the Pantomime', in A. Halliday (ed.), *Comical Fellows; or, the History and Mystery of the Pantomime: With Some Curiosities and Droll Anecdotes Concerning Clown and Pantaloon, Harlequin and Columbine* (London, 1863), pp. 52–72; and Wagner, *Pantomimes and All About Them*, pp. 54–60.
13. T.C. Davis, *Economics of the British Stage*, p. 135. The concept also underlines much of her Chapter 10, 'Theatre as Cultural Capital'.
14. 'Christmas Amusements: The Pantomime at the Royal', *Birmingham Daily Mail*, 24 December 1870, p. 8.
15. Advertisement, *Birmingham Daily Post*, 24 December 1874, p. 1.
16. 'Christmas Amusements: The Pantomime at the Royal', *Birmingham Daily Mail*, 28 December 1874, p. 2.
17. Advertisement, *Birmingham Daily Post*, 7 January 1875, p. 1.
18. 'The Theatre Royal Pantomime', *Birmingham Daily Mail*, 27 December 1878, p. 2.

19. 'The Theatre Royal Pantomime', *Birmingham Daily Gazette*, 23 December 1878, p. 5. See also 'Amusements for Boxing-Day: Theatre Royal', *Birmingham Daily Gazette*, 26 December 1878, p. 5.

20. Advertisement, *Birmingham Daily Post*, 27 January 1879, p. 1.

21. 'Boxing Day in Birmingham: Theatre Royal', *Birmingham Daily Mail*, 27 December 1882, p. 2.

22. D. Mayer, 'Supernumeraries: Decorating the Late-Victorian Stage with Lots (& Lots & Lots) of Live Bodies', in Heinrich, Newey and Richards (eds.), *Ruskin*, p. 156.

23. 'Boxing Day Amusements: The Theatre Royal Pantomime', *Birmingham Daily Mail*, 27 December 1876, p. 2.

24. Advertisement, *Birmingham Daily Post*, 5 January 1887, p. 1. The advertisement remained in the paper for only a few days so presumably the scene was complete for the remainder of the run.

25. '*The Forty Thieves*', *Birmingham Daily Mail*, 27 December 1877, p. 2. See also the 1878 production of *Robinson Crusoe* in which 'the performance of the two sham bears … ke[pt] the whole house in roars of laughter' ('The Theatre Royal Pantomime', *Birmingham Daily Mail*, 27 December 1878, p. 2). The history of skin parts is outlined in Frow, '*Oh Yes, It Is!*', pp. 175–80.

26. 'Boxing Day Amusements: The Theatre Royal Pantomime', *Birmingham Daily Mail*, 27 December 1876, p. 2. See also reference to a 'property horse of most miraculous proportions' and 'a huge property lion' in a review of the 1881 pantomime, 'Christmas Amusements: *Beauty and the Beast* at the Theatre Royal', *Birmingham Daily Mail*, 27 December 1881, p. 2.

27. Richards, *Commodity Culture*, p. 28.

28. *Manchester Faces and Places: An Illustrated Record of the Social, Political and Commercial Life of the Cotton Metropolis and Its Environs*, 3 (1892), p. 58. Details of the license taken from Katherine Newey, 'Early Nineteenth-Century Theatre in Manchester', p. 1.

29. 'Theatre Royal – The Pantomime', *Manchester Weekly Times*, 31 December 1859, p. 5.

30. *Ibid*.

31. *Ibid*.

32. 'Theatre Royal – The Pantomime', *Manchester Weekly Times*, 22 December 1860, p. 5.

33. *Ibid*. See also the review of the 1862 pantomime, which again referred to 'our Theatre Royal', the manager of which 'for such a long succession of years has created for us spirit lands of his own.' ('Theatre Royal. The Christmas Pantomime', *Manchester Weekly Times*, 20 December 1862, p. 5).

34. 'The Christmas Pantomime at the Theatre Royal', *Manchester Weekly Times*, 29 December 1860, p. 3.

35. *Ibid*.

36. 'The Christmas Pantomimes. The Royal: "Beauty and the Beast"', *Manchester Weekly Times*, 28 December 1861, p. 3.

37. 'Theatre Royal. The Christmas Pantomime', *Manchester Weekly Times*, 20 December 1862, p. 5.

38. 'The Christmas Pantomimes. Theatre Royal – "Puss in Boots"', *Manchester Weekly Times*, 31 December 1864, p. 7.

39. *Ibid*.

40. 'Theatre Royal', *Manchester Weekly Times*, 22 December 1866, p. 5.

41. *Ibid*.

42. 'Theatre Royal', *Manchester Guardian*, 24 December 1870, p. 6.

43. '"Valentine and Orson" at the Theatre Royal', *Manchester Guardian*, 19 December 1868, p. 5.

44. 'The Pantomime at the Theatre Royal', *Manchester Guardian*, 21 December 1874, p. 6, and 'The Theatre Royal', 27 December 1875, p. 7.

45. 'The Christmas Pantomimes. The Theatre Royal – "Beauty and the Beast"', *Manchester Weekly Times*, 1 January 1876, p. 7.

46. Advertisement, *Manchester Weekly Times*, 10 January 1880, p. 1.

47. 'The Christmas Pantomimes. "Blue Beard" at the Theatre Royal', *Manchester Weekly Times*, 24 December 1880, p. 6.

48. Advertisement, *Manchester Weekly Times*, 29 January 1881, p. 1.

49. 'Little Bo Peep at the Royal', *Manchester Weekly Times*, 24 December 1881, p. 7.

50. 'Theatre Royal: "Second Edition" of Bo Peep', *Manchester Weekly Times*, 4 March 1882, p. 6.

51. Cited in an advertisement in the *Manchester Weekly Times*, 26 December 1885, p. 1.

52. *Manchester Weekly Times*, 26 February 1887, p. 3.

53. 'The Profits of "Blue Beard" Harris v Bainbridge', *Manchester Guardian*, 18 February 1887, p. 8.

54. 'The Manchester Pantomimes. Theatre Royal', *Manchester Weekly Times*, 31 December 1887, p. 3.

55. 'The Pantomimes. "The Forty Thieves" at the Theatre Royal', *Manchester Weekly Times*, 29 December 1888, p. 3.

56. 'A Theatrical Lessee's Bankruptcy', *Manchester Weekly Times*, 30 March 1889, p. 3, and 'The Affairs of Captain Bainbridge', *Manchester Weekly Times*, 6 April 1889, p. 3.

57. '"Dick Whittington" at the Royal', *Manchester Weekly Times*, 14 December 1889, p. 2.

58. 'The Secrets of Pantomime Production. By Our Special Commissioner', *Manchester Weekly Times*, 22 December 1893, p. 8.

59. 'Prince's Theatre – "Mother Goose"', *Manchester Weekly Times*, 31 December 1864, p. 7.

60. Louis M. Hayes, in *Reminiscences of Manchester* (London, 1905), went so far as to refer to Knowles's management policy as one that was run on a 'cheese-pairing principle' (p. 266). Cited in Foulkes, *The Calverts*, p. 37.

61. *Ibid*.

62. *Ibid*.

63. Advertisement, *Manchester Weekly Times*, 28 March 1874, p. 1, and 'Prince's Theatre', *Manchester Weekly Times*, 19 February 1871, p. 4.

64. 'Prince's Theatre', *Manchester Weekly Times*, 23 December 1865, p. 5.

65. Foulkes, *The Calverts*, p. 51.

66. 'Prince's Theatre', *Manchester Weekly Times*, 15 January 1876, p. 3.

67. 'Prince's Theatre – "Blue Beard"', *Manchester Weekly Times*, 23 December 1871, p. 4.

68. 'Prince's Theatre', *Manchester Weekly Times*, 3 January 1874, p. 4.

69. 'The Christmas Pantomimes. Prince's Theatre – "The Forty Thieves"', *Manchester Weekly Times*, 28 December 1872, p. 5.

70. *Ibid*.

71. 'The Christmas Pantomimes. New Queen's Theatre – "Little Red Riding Hood"', *Manchester Weekly Times*, 28 December 1872, p. 5.

72. Advertisement, *Manchester Weekly Times*, 28 February 1874, p. 1.

73. 'Prince's Theatre – The Christmas Pantomime', *Manchester Weekly Times*, 2 January 1875, p. 5.

74. Advertisement, *Manchester Weekly Times*, 9 January 1875, p. 1. Reviews cited in advertisement, *Manchester Weekly Times*, 23 January 1875, p. 1.

75. 'The Christmas Pantomimes. Prince's Theatre – "Aladdin"', *Manchester Weekly Times*, 1 January 1876, p. 7.

76. 'The Prince's Theatre', *Manchester Weekly Times*, 14 February 1880, p. 5.

77. 'Manchester Pantomimes. The Prince's', *Manchester Weekly Times*, 23 December 1893, p. 7.

78. A detailed survey of these financial records for the two theatre seasons 1865–6 and 1866–7 appears in J.A. Sullivan, 'The Business of Pantomime: Regional Productions 1865–1892', unpublished PhD thesis (University of Nottingham, 2005), Chapter 3, pp. 76–122. An earlier version of the section in the current chapter can be found in 'Managing the Pantomime: Productions at the Theatre Royal Nottingham in the 1860s', *Theatre Notebook*, 60/2 (2006), pp. 98–116.

79. Invoices for wages for this team are in NA: M8806: 'Receipted Bills, Mounted (September to December 1865)', pp. 71, 77, 83, 88, 98, 102, 109, 110, 119; the purchases by the Property man are at pp. 67, 80, 86.

80. T.C. Davis, *Economics of the British Stage*, Chapter 3, 'Labour and Labourers', pp. 309–33.

81. Invoices for the extended team of carpenters, etc., from the week ending 2 December 1865 to the week ending 6 January 1866, are in NA: M8806: pp. 97, 101, 107, 116, 120, and M8807: 'Receipted Bills Mounted December 1865 to August 1866', p. 1. Mr Brown's work is included in an invoice dated Christmas 1865 (M8807, p. 5). The basket-work invoice is in M8807, p. 28.

82. Receipts and invoices from Clarkson are detailed in NA: M8806, M8807, and in M8822/12 and 15: 'Collection of Loose Bills from 1865'; and deliveries were noted in M8817: 'Stage Door Book 1865–1867'. The May invoices and receipts are listed throughout M8806 and M8807.

83. Dated weekly expenditure for all performers is listed in NA: M8809, and M8812: 'Ledger of Accounts for Administration of Nottingham Theatre Royal, Sept to Dec 1865'.

84. NA: M8809 has the payment 'Chambers – for Pantomime 10.00' entered on 25 January 1866; receipt for payment and loan of music in M8808: 'Receipted Bills Mounted (September 1866 to April 1867)', p. 75; and an entry for postage/carriage – presumably the return of the loaned music in the 'Stage Door Book', M8817, p. 36.

85. Carpenters' invoices are entered weekly in NA: M8808.

86. 'The Christmas Pantomime', *Nottingham and Midland Counties Daily Express*, 24 December 1866, p. 3, and 'The New Pantomime', 26 December 1866, p. 2.

87. Cast numbers were promoted in 'The Christmas Pantomime at the Theatre Royal', *Nottingham Journal*, 24 December 1866, p. 3.

88. Simmonds's invoices are listed weekly in NA: M8808, and the hire of additional pantomime dresses in the invoice on p. 93. Invoices for locally purchased fabrics for the pantomime are in M8808, pp. 61, 68.

89. Miss Gilbert's payments are listed in NA: M8814, pp. 29, 30, 32, 34, 36, 38, 40, 42, 44.

90. 'The Pantomime', *Nottingham Daily Guardian*, 28 December 1874, p. 3; advertisement, *Nottingham Journal*, 30 December 1874, p. 2.

91. 'Christmas Amusements: The Pantomime', *Nottingham Daily Guardian*, 27 December 1876, p. 3. The snow shower featured in 'Theatre Royal', *Nottingham Journal*, 3 January 1877, p. 4.

92. 'Christmas Amusements: The Pantomime', *Nottingham Daily Guardian*, 27 December 1876, p. 3.

93. 'The Pantomime', *Nottingham Daily Guardian*, 26 December 1885, p. 8.

94. 'The Pantomime: *Blue Beard*', *Nottingham and Midland Counties Daily Express*, 27 December 1877, p. 4.

95. 'Theatre Royal', *Nottingham Daily Express*, 14 January 1879, p. 3.

96. 'The Nottingham Christmas Pantomime', *Nottingham Daily Express*, 22 December 1884, p. 8.

97. Advertisement, *Nottingham Daily Express*, 24 December 1884, p. 1.

98. 'The Pantomime', *Nottingham Daily Guardian*, 30 December 1884, p. 8.

99. '*The Forty Thieves*: Preparing the Pantomime', *Nottingham Daily Guardian*, 24 December 1884, p. 6.

100. 'Pantomime Preparations [By One Behind the Scenes]', *Nottingham Daily Express*, 23 December 1885, p. 6.

101. 'Theatre Royal', *Nottingham Daily Guardian*, 31 December 1889, p. 8.

102. See, for example, the promotion of 200 artistes in an advertisement, *Nottingham Daily Express*, 24 December 1883, p. 1, and 'over 150 artistes' in an advertisement, *Nottingham Daily Express*, 24 December 1884, p. 1.

103. 'The Approaching Pantomime at the Theatre Royal', *Nottingham Daily Guardian*, 18 December 1882, p. 3.

104. Richards, *Commodity Culture*, pp. 58–9.

105. J. Baudrillard, *The Consumer Society: Myths and Structures* (London, 1998), p. 26.

106. 'The British Drama in the Provinces [from the *London Standard*], The Prince of Wales Theatre', *Birmingham Daily Post*, 23 January 1865, p. 7.

107. 'Boxing Day in Birmingham', *Birmingham Daily Post*, 28 December 1863, p. 5. Swanborough had been manager of the venue when it was the Royal Music Hall Operetta House earlier in 1863 and had overseen the transition to legitimate theatre.

108. 'The Christmas Pantomimes: The Prince of Wales Theatre', *Birmingham Daily Post*, 29 December 1864, p. 4.

109. 'Mr. Melville's New Theatre: Application for a License', *Birmingham Daily Post*, 24 December 1886, p. 4.

110. 'Christmas Amusements: Prince of Wales Theatre. Pantomime of *Little Goody Two Shoes*', *Birmingham Daily Post*, 27 December 1871, p. 8.

111. '*Twinkle, Twinkle Little Star*', *Birmingham Daily Mail*, 27 December 1872, p. 2.

112. 'Christmas Amusements. "Twinkle, Twinkle, Little Star" at the Prince of Wales Theatre', *Birmingham Daily Post*, 27 December 1872, p. 8.

113. Advertisement, *Birmingham Daily Post*, 31 January 1873, p. 1.

114. 'The Pantomime at the Prince of Wales Theatre', *Birmingham Daily Mail*, 28 December 1874, p. 3.

115. Advertisement, *Birmingham Daily Post*, 23 December 1876, p. 1.

116. 'Boxing-Day Amusements', *Birmingham Daily Post*, 26 December 1876, p. 5.

117. 'Boxing Day in Birmingham: Prince of Wales Theatre', *Birmingham Daily Mail*, 27 December 1882, p. 2.

118. 'Prince of Wales Theatre', *Birmingham Daily Post*, 24 December 1887, p. 5.

119. 'The Pantomimes', *Birmingham Daily Post*, 21 January 1884, p. 6.

120. '*Gulliver's Travels* at the Prince of Wales Theatre', *Birmingham Daily Mail*, 26 December 1885, p. 3.

121. 'Boxing-day in Birmingham: the Grand Theatre', *Birmingham Daily Post*, 27 December 1883, p. 5.

122. Newey, 'Early Nineteenth-Century Theatre in Manchester', p. 10.

123. *Ibid.*, pp. 6–7, citing the *Dramatic and Musical Review*, 6 March 1847, p. 144.

124. 'The Queen's Theatre – The Pantomime', *Manchester Weekly Times*, 31 December 1859, p. 4.

125. Advertisement, *Manchester Weekly Times*, 5 January 1860, p. 1, and 'The Christmas Pantomime at the Queen's Theatre', *Manchester Weekly Times*, 24 December 1859, p. 5.
126. Advertisement, *Manchester Weekly Times*, 15 December 1860, p. 1.
127. 'The Queen's Theatre Pantomime – "Aladdin and the Wonderful Lamp"', *Manchester Weekly Times*, 22 December 1860, p. 5.
128. 'The Christmas Pantomimes. Queen's Theatre – "Humpty Dumpty"', *Manchester Weekly Times*, 31 December 1864, p. 7.
129. 'The Theatres', *Manchester Weekly Times*, 14 January 1865, p. 4.
130. 'Queen's Theatre: "Whittington and His Cat"', *Manchester Weekly Times*, 23 December 1865, p. 5.
131. 'Amusements in Manchester', *Manchester Weekly Times*, 6 January 1866, p. 5.
132. MA: Queen's Theatre, *Pantomime Books*, Spring Gardens Th792.094273 Ma80: *Whittington and His Cat* (1865), book of words, Scene 1, p. 4v.
133. 'Queen's Theatre', *Manchester Weekly Times*, 22 December 1866, p. 5.
134. 'The Pantomimes &c.', *Manchester Weekly Times*, 5 January 1867, p. 5.
135. 'The Pantomime at the Queen's Theatre', *Manchester Weekly Times*, 9 January 1869, p. 5.
136. 'Queen's Theatre', *Manchester Guardian*, 4 January 1872, p. 6.
137. 'The Christmas Pantomimes. New Queen's Theatre – "Little Red Riding Hood"', *Manchester Weekly Times*, 28 December 1872, p. 5.
138. 'Queen's Theatre', *Manchester Guardian*, 21 December 1874, p. 6.
139. Advertisement, *Manchester Weekly Times*, 8 January 1876, p. 1.
140. 'The Queen's – "Twinkle, Twinkle Little Star"', *Manchester Weekly Times*, 1 January 1876, p. 7.
141. T.C. Davis, *Economics of the British Stage*, p. 213.

Part Two

The Social Referencing of Pantomime

3

Local hits and topical allusions

In appealing to local and regional audiences, theatre managers incorporated traditional elements and spectacular novelties, variety acts and stars of the burlesque and music hall stage into their pantomimes. The promotion of these aspects enabled specific local identities to be adopted for each theatre, identities built on commercial status and reputation, legacy and locale. To attract and engage audiences, the managers and writers also employed more specific aspects of local and regional identity, with scenery, songs, dances and speeches reflecting and commenting on contemporaneous life and concerns. Incorporating commentaries on socio-economic and political issues in the *mise-en-scène* of productions was integral to the genre, inherited from the eighteenth- and early-nineteenth-century harlequinades. Historically, such referencing was ironically brought about by the restrictions of the 1737 Licensing Act on verbal satire; the repeal of that Act in 1843 and the development of the scripted pantomime opening allowed for far greater spoken referencing but it did not initiate a complete shift from the visual to the verbal. The spectacle of regional pantomimes regularly included visual references to local places and issues as well as celebrating aspects of local culture, trade and civic achievements. Those references sometimes stood alone in the production, for example to celebrate municipal achievements or well-known holiday locations, but the visual and performative aspects of local referencing also occurred alongside speeches about relevant and contemporaneous issues. In the 1860s the majority of these verbal references occurred in the opening scene. Characters provided an overview of the principal national, international and local events and people from the preceding year, the demons of the dark scene railing against improvements and peace or promoting electoral corruption and disease. In the second half of the nineteenth century, developments in urban life were also reflected in the pantomime texts, which incorporated an increasing number of references, not just in the first scene, but scattered throughout the scripts and interpolated topical songs. The sheer variety of the social referencing apparent in provincial pantomimes cannot be subsumed into any simple class or ideological distinctions. Nevertheless, it is clear that, at one level, there had to be an overarching appeal to local knowledge. Millie Taylor, in her discussion of modern British pantomime, refers to the community created between performers and audience in the recognition of local references, but she maintains a somewhat misleading model of a single audience community.[1] Whilst the importance of local and locally relevant issues being included in provincial pantomime lay (and indeed still lies) in them reflecting some shared interests, some sense of community, that 'community' will always contain a range of perspectives and different individual experiences.[2] Such references in nineteenth-century pantomimes included public holidays; the new responsibilities of municipal government and philanthropic ventures to improve public amenities; the survival of rural traditions and the celebration of modernity; iconic engineering projects and the state of the roads.

Local views

The depiction of local places, buildings and businesses had long been an element of harlequinade scenery. In *Illegitimate Theatre*, Jane Moody detailed some of the local scenes that were incorporated into the early-nineteenth-century harlequinades at Sadler's Wells, including particular inns and 'views of Lambeth Marsh, Vauxhall Bridge and the new penitentiary'.[3] In 1860, a *Times* reviewer was still able to comment on the 'number of local views familiar to the auditory' in the Sadler's Wells harlequinade.[4] This pattern of scenic referencing was echoed at all metropolitan and provincial theatres and by the second half of the century was a feature of the pantomime opening as well as the harlequinade. In the opening, places and buildings could be referenced both visually and verbally and clearly indicate the range of local knowledge of potential audiences. For example, Manchester pantomimes could include references to the port of Liverpool, with inferences about or direct comments on the rivalry created by the building of the Manchester Ship Canal in the 1890s, or friendlier references to the holiday destinations of Blackpool and the Isle of Man. In referring to Manchester itself, humorous references to the local weather were inferred by the fictional 'Mudcaster' in the pantomime of 1893 at the Comedy Theatre. The names of the city suburbs charted the growth of urban areas; the shifting middle-class preferences for localities beyond the commercial heart of Manchester and the growing urban working-class areas. In the naming of local places, certain references played on very specific local knowledge, precisely illustrating the issue of what might have signified topicality to whom in a local pantomime. For example, in the Comedy Theatre pantomime of 1886, one character aimed to build a 'fine new house' on Oxford Road (a middle-class suburb of Manchester)[5] whilst at the Nottingham Theatre Royal in 1880, Dick Whittington hailed from 'Mudslush in the Marsh', potentially recalling to many in the local audience the older, less salubrious parts of the town centre, Narrow Marsh and Broad Marsh. Characters could also be related to the urban environment in Manchester. In 1877, at the Prince's Theatre, the wicked Baron of *Babes in the Wood* had comic henchmen called 'Bill o' th' Irk' and 'Tommy o' Angel Meadow'.[6] The alignment of social significance to character type could be treated rather loosely in the broad comedy of a pantomime opening: the hero of *Jack and Jill* at the Comedy Theatre in 1894 hailed from 'darkest Salford'. The local rivalry between Salford and Manchester was well known, and such references potentially created a moment of unifying humour and shared knowledge amongst the audiences. However, 'Bill o' th' Irk' and 'Tommy o' Angel Meadow', as played at the Prince's Theatre, carried more specific connotations. Angel Meadow was a notorious slum area and the polluted River Irk was the subject of pantomime comment for many years. Aligning fictional wickedness with the reality of poverty and crime in these two characters surely created an uncomfortable illusion for some in the audience who could not distance their lives from such locations.

Scenery could effectively represent a combination of the historic and the modern urban environment. According to a reviewer in the *Manchester Guardian*, the opening of *Babes in the Wood* (1887) at the Queen's Theatre included a scene of 'our own Market Place, with the corner of the Cathedral pleasantly visible, and Old Trafford with the Ship Canal … and the forthcoming Exhibition'.[7] The past, present and future of

Manchester were encapsulated in this pantomime scenery. The distant past represented symbolically by just the 'corner' of the Cathedral is 'pleasantly visible', and 'our own Market Place' momentarily united an audience with varying experiences of the ancient yet still vibrant commercial centre of the city. Phrases such as 'our own Market Place' effectively encompassed the theatre and audience within the wider urban developments whilst implicitly marking the theatre as the focal point of reference in the changing city. In this production, the heritage of the city is displaced by ongoing engineering and industrial projects: the Manchester Ship Canal and the 1887 Jubilee Exhibition. The building of the latter had also been a focus of the Theatre Royal pantomime in 1886. Potentially highlighting a disparity in resources, the Queen's Theatre artists painted the image on a backdrop, whilst those at the Theatre Royal had included a scene wherein a troupe of juvenile builders helped to physically create a version of the exhibition hall on stage. The Theatre Royal management had devised a similar scene a few years earlier to celebrate the 1884 Health Exhibition in Manchester, a scene that had been the focus of a trip by characters in the pantomime, and provided 'a spacious, well-contrived, and animated sight'.[8]

Rural views were a regular feature of pantomime scenery, complementing the fairy-tale stories and providing idyllic country pictures, the picturesque nature of which could include streams, real animals and mechanised water- and windmills, as discussed in Chapter 2. More specific locations could provide a setting for local legends woven into the pantomime stories, such as that for the 1872 pantomime at the Queen's Theatre in Manchester. *Little Red Riding Hood and the Lancashire Witches; or, Harlequin Count Lothair, the Good Spirit Ariel, and the Demon Wolf of Boggart Hole Clough* included individual scenes depicting the 'Goblin Grove in Pendle Forest' and 'a plain near Pendle Hill – of which a pleasing sunset view is given' but which was the setting for a rather incongruous 'review of amazonian troops'.[9] Regional scenery might also represent both the historic past of the city and the surrounding region, creating a comparison – even tension – between a rural heritage and the modern world. The 1875 production of *Twinkle, Twinkle Little Star; or, Harlequin King Arthur, his Very Merry Knights of ye Days of Old, and ye Saxon Bold who in Mancestre was Sold* (also at the Queen's Theatre) relocated the setting for the court of King Arthur to the area around Manchester. The opening scene included a panorama of 'Manchester, representing in rapid succession the Infirmary, the Assize Courts, the Cathedral, the Exchange, and the Town Hall'. This was, according to the *Manchester Weekly Times*, 'a capital introduction and well kept up the local character which has been given to the plot'.[10] The *Guardian* reviewer also admired the panorama, with 'all the principal buildings of our city, with their windows illuminated'.[11] The inclusive 'our' in this sentence asserted civic pride; the lit windows – presumably achieved through dioramic effects – inferred life and activity in the modern city but the celebration of urban landmarks was not sustained. As the legend of King Arthur unfolded, existing villages and small towns beyond Manchester were referenced in scenery that depicted a picturesque rural past. For example, the village of Straightford in the pantomime story was recognised by a *Manchester Weekly Times* reviewer as Stretford, approximately four miles south-west of Manchester. In the pantomime the village was portrayed in a set scene with 'real water and the boatmen, the angler and the haymakers'. It must, continued the reviewer, 'have been an exceedingly pretty place in those days, and the arcadian simplicity of the spectacle was quite in harmony with the tradition of the plot'. The real village of Stretford was indeed attractive, but it was primarily a working, agricultural village, a fact ignored in this critic's interpretation. Other scenes were included: 'The woods of Bowden, the wastes of Chat Moss, the now familiar region of Campfield, and the historic groves of Canutesford, now sacred to picnic parties at Knutsford, are all made to do welcome duty.'[12] All these scenes were based on real places in the Lancashire region, mostly to the south and south-west of Manchester. The audience, this critic assumed, would be drawn in by the 'familiar' views of villages and small market towns, areas he associates with leisured activity, with the exception of Chat Moss, a former peat bog that by the mid-nineteenth century had been developed by the Liverpool and Manchester Railway Company. According to the reviewer, the audience would naturally recognise the rural retreats: 'as each familiar scene is unveiled to view the spectator feel[s] he is all the more thoroughly assisting at a spectacle from his familiarity with the terrain on which the rapidly evolving drama is being played'.[13] The concept of 'assisting at a spectacle' is crucial here in the active engagement of audiences through recognition and alignment of the scenes and places. The audience at the Queen's Theatre may have instantly identified the opening urban panorama, but with the rural scenes they needed to 'assist', to interpret the pictures displayed, even though – as with all social referencing – those interpretations would have differed. As mentioned in Chapter 2, the Queen's Theatre reputedly depended on a working-class audience, and certain aspects of the theatre, such as its repertoire (principally melodrama in the main theatre season), its promotion as the 'people's theatre' and its site on Bridge Street (nearer to a workhouse than the other more central theatres), do indeed suggest a large proportion of working-class audience members. The middle-class reviewer, however, irrespective of the actual and varied experiences of the audiences, superimposed his own reception and experience of leisured activities, of day trips and picnics, onto that of the larger audience.

Written in 1875, the pantomime *Twinkle, Twinkle Little Star* occurred on the cusp of changes in working hours which redefined leisure patterns for the working classes in the last quarter of the nineteenth century. Naturally, in this later period pantomime scenes reflected the newly available leisure time and holiday locations enjoyed by many more urban workers. The 1890 pantomime at the Prince of Wales Theatre, Birmingham included a scene of Llandudno in Wales, 'with the Great Ormes Head, the never-changing sea, and the terraces of hospitable houses dear to the hearts of Birmingham holiday-makers'.[14] For Nottingham workers, day trips could be made to locations closer to the town, especially in the wake of the introduction of half-day holidays for shop workers. In Scene 1 of the aptly titled *Robinson Crusoe; Or, the Good Friday Who Came on Thursday Half-Holiday* (1891), Crusoe asks his sweetheart Polly to be faithful to him while he is at sea:

> No flirtations whilst I am away. No picnics in Clifton Grove, no frolics at Beeston, no teas at Hazelford, and, mind, a trip to Colwick on the 'Sunbeam' will break off the engagement.[15]

These locations were close to the town, and trips on the 'Sunbeam' (a pleasure boat) were regularly advertised in the local papers during the summer. Manchester audiences were similarly presented with scenes set at Blackpool, more so in the 1890s, when 'approved summer holidays were officially extended to a week by industrial agreement in most of the cotton towns, and the exodus to the seaside could often be counted in tens of thousands'.[16] In 1892, the Theatre Royal management presented a scene 'which, perhaps, more than all the others astonishes and delights the audience'. It was 'a faithful reproduction of Blackpool, with its waves, piers, promenade, bands, sailing boats, bathing vans, donkeys, miscellaneous crowds, and other features of the great Lancashire pleasure resort'.[17] '[A] perfect picture of our Lancashire Brighton, taken from the north pier, which is certain to prove immensely attractive' formed the final scene in the Comedy Theatre production of *Aladdin* in 1888.[18] Within this known and popular locale, the site of annual holidays, the pantomime story was resolved, the wicked punished and the good rewarded. The idea was revived at the Comedy in 1896, when once again the characters of *Aladdin* were transposed from their Eastern story to a conclusion at Blackpool.

Working-class and rural traditions

Whilst modern holidays were celebrated, older holiday traditions of the fairground could also be featured. In the 1883 pantomime at the Manchester Theatre Royal, the local Knott Mill Fair was depicted as in 'the olden time', but with the 'shows and hawkers one knows as the features of a fair'.[19] Similarly, in Birmingham general references were made to the annual Cattle Show and fair, which had been established in 1849, in the pantomimes of 1873, 1874, 1883 and 1885.[20] In Nottingham the ancient Goose Fair, which had been established in the twelfth century, took place each October in the Market Square. It was an important occasion, bringing many visitors into the town from the surrounding rural and mining districts, and the theatre management always ensured that a popular burlesque or spectacular entertainment was programmed during that week. On several occasions in the second half of the nineteenth century, the fair was the disapproving focus of temperance reformers, and although they did not succeed in abolishing the event, it was reduced from a week to three days by the late 1870s. The fair was mentioned in the pantomimes of 1873, 1874 and 1877, and in the pantomimes of 1878, 1879, 1883 and 1891 the local pantomime authors F.R. Goodyer and Arthur Maddock evidently spoke for many in the audience by allotting their pantomime characters disgruntled comments against moves to shorten both the fair and the local races.[21] A magician in the pantomime *Jack and the Beanstalk* in 1879 conjured up a spectre who claimed:

I'm the departed spirit of Goose Fair,

Abr: Alas, poor ghost! no wonder you look pale,

They rob us now of all our cakes and ale;

You've only three days grace – your fame's receding,

They'll cook your goose – oh, what a foul proceeding.[22]

Whilst in Nottingham pantomime writers such as Goodyer and Maddock were aware of their rural and urban audiences, and in Birmingham the emphasis lay on the economic and political authority of the city (discussed later in this chapter and in Chapter 4), writers in Manchester reflected – more so than at the other centres – the close cultural relationship between a rural past and urban modernity. In particular, pantomimes in that city engaged with unique regional traditions such as rushbearing, as well as clog dancing and the Lancashire dialect. In these productions, it was a specifically working-class heritage that defined local identity in the pantomimes.

In the 1872 harlequinade at the Prince's Theatre, members of the corps de ballet gave a performance of 'Morris Dancing and Rushbearing'. It was previewed by the *Manchester Guardian* as a feature 'which will make its way at once to the breasts of Lancashire spectators'.[23] In rural communities of earlier centuries, rushbearing was a significant annual festival which celebrated the dedication of the local church. Rushes were gathered from surrounding villages and brought on decorated carts to the church, where they were used as floor covering for the ensuing year. The arrival of the carts was accompanied by music and morris dancers, and was an opportunity for 'hospitality, with houses being cleaned and whitewashed, and ale brewed to welcome relatives and friends from other villages.… For most people it lasted four or five days, but a few contrived to keep up the pace for a week.'[24] By the early nineteenth century, rushes were no longer used on the floors of churches, but the festival continued to be celebrated throughout the century, largely in 'south-east Lancashire and north Cheshire, though a less elaborate form of rushbearing survived elsewhere, especially in parts of rural Lancashire and Cheshire, north Derbyshire and the Lake District'.[25] Importantly, the building of the rushcarts was 'a collective enterprise', symbolising the rural communities of the region.[26] The balletic inclusion in the 1872 pantomime therefore drew on a very specific point of reference for the 'Lancashire spectators', demonstrating an awareness of rural traditions that potentially reflected actual attendance by visitors from the country to the pantomime, but also an acknowledgment of the inherited cultural knowledge of those workers whose families had migrated from rural areas to the city.

Whilst rushbearing and morris dancing had their origins in the hamlets and villages of the region, clog dancing was an urban tradition. It had 'developed in the 1820s and after in the cotton mill districts', and 'was an entertainment firmly confined to the industrial labouring class'.[27] It was a style of dance that had regional variants, and reviewers were quick to note differences in presentation. At the Manchester Theatre Royal in 1886, the pantomimic scene of the building of the proposed 1887 Jubilee Exhibition Hall concluded with a clog dance by the child performers, but one preview pointed out that it was in the Irish clog style not the Lancastrian. With this exception, the Lancashire clog dance was a feature of local pantomimes, primarily at the Theatre Royal or the Queen's Theatre. It could be performed by characters as a part of their individual regional identity, or as a set piece performed by the ballet or full company. In 1862, the pantomime at the Theatre Royal featured a Lancashire Clog Hornpipe at the end of the opening, which was danced by all the characters. The Queen's Theatre pantomime of 1881 included a clog-dance ballet, as did the Theatre Royal pantomime of 1887, and a group of twenty-four children performed a clog dance in the Comedy Theatre pantomime of 1893. At the Queen's Theatre in 1868, the character Fairy Thistledown performed a clog dance which 'appeal[ed] to the sympathies of Lancashire folk, and in acknowledging the enthusiastic encore with which it is invariably greeted, she had the good taste not to go back in the action'.[28] This comment by the *Manchester Guardian* is an interesting one. The dance was evidently well and accurately performed. It acknowledged and reflected the tradition of clog dancing in the locality and was assigned to the virtuous 'Fairy'. However, as a professional dancer, a repetition of the dance as an encore would have moved the performance beyond a staged yet, in the context of the pantomime story, 'impromptu' engagement with the local audience to a second performance where the dancer not the dance became the focal point.

Whilst such examples of dance and celebrations are expressions of regional identity, dialect is arguably a more integral form of personal and communal identity. However, an engagement with this aspect of regionality in the pantomimes is not evident in the reviews or books of words of pantomimes in Nottingham or Birmingham. In marked contrast, the Manchester pantomime writers and performers regularly featured local accents and dialect in their work. In performance the character most frequently allotted a Lancashire accent was the 'Dame', the comic yet essentially good-hearted maternal figure. The Lancashire Dame was a particular feature of productions at the Queen's Theatre, suggesting again a largely working-class audience, for whom the accent would have signified their shared and inherited regional identity, maintained in the urban environment. In 1883, the Queen's version of *Little Red Riding Hood* included Dame Durden, performed by Mr Bracewell, replete with a distinctive local accent, and in the Queen's pantomime of 1875, *Twinkle, Twinkle Little Star*, the linking of the rural landscape with modern Manchester, discussed above, was further achieved by the character of 'Leodegrance, King of Lancastre', who spoke with a heavy Lancashire accent. Pantomime performers and writers at the Theatre Royal and the Prince's Theatre utilised the regional accent on far fewer occasions. The Theatre Royal management engaged Mr Bracewell to provide a Lancashire-accented Ali Baba in the pantomime of 1888, and six years later Mr T.W. Rowley, who played Captain Hassan in the 1894 production of *Sinbad the Sailor*, gave 'a Lancashire twist to the character'.[29] The Dame character Mrs Angel Meadow in the Prince's Theatre pantomime *Mother Goose* (1864) gave, according to the *Manchester Guardian*, 'a capital imitation of the Lancashire dialect'.[30] In 1868, the Queen's Theatre pantomime of *Little Boy Blue* included the dialect character Dame Nursery, portrayed by Mr Elton and described in the *Manchester Weekly Times* as being 'an effective though somewhat harsh portrait of a Lancashire schoolmistress in the coarser days of old. Mr. Elton's best performance is the clog dance at the close of the first scene, arranged to the Breakdown air, "Skedaddle."'[31] The local writer J.J.B. Forsyth was praised by the *Manchester Guardian* for his 1877 pantomime *Jack and the Beanstalk* at the Queen's Theatre. In this production, the reviewer stated, 'the chief merit' was 'that its tone and colour throughout are local', chiefly in respect of its referencing, but also in the figure of Dame Daw, with her 'broad Lancashire dialect'.[32] And in *Sinbad* (1888) at the Prince's Theatre, characters were carried by a giant roc over Lancashire, 'Manchester being recognised by its rain and Widnes by its smells'. At the conclusion, the wicked Shipwreckeros was transformed into a good person, his improved qualities epitomised by the fact that he suddenly developed a 'strong Lancashire accent'.[33]

Much of the evidence for the use of accents emerges in the newspaper reviews, but there are also examples of dialect in the extant scripts and books of words. The Queen's Theatre production of *Little Red Riding Hood* in 1883 featured a secondary comic character, Sally in Our Alley, who was allocated the Lancashire dialect: 'I'm Lancashire, tha' knows … A gradely lass from Shudehill.'[34] Humphrey and his partner Dorothy in the Theatre Royal pantomime *The House That Jack Built* (1862) also both spoke in dialect: 'Know tho'! Oh, aye; aw see'd tho kissin' th' missis! Whau squire; yur rayley getting' wuss an' wuss.'[35]

Whilst there was an obvious appeal for local audiences in characters employing a regional accent, the creation in a script of a character speaking entirely in dialect can be linked to the established and re-emerging use of dialect in working-class literary culture. In *The Industrial Muse*, Martha Vicinus states that 'Before the middle of the century [dialect] was used almost exclusively for comic and satiric poems'[36] which fits well with its usage in pantomime. Vicinus has described how after mid-century, and particularly in the period 1860–85, there emerged a new generation of dialect writers, such as Ben Brierley and Edwin Waugh, both from Lancashire and two of the most prominent exponents of the genre.[37] They were two of the founder members of the Manchester Literary Club and Brierley had his own weekly journal, *Ben Brierley's Journal*, 'a Lancashire working man's *Punch*', which ran for sixteen years with a maximum circulation of 13,000.[38] Writers such as these, Vicinus notes, maintained the earlier comic and satiric potential of dialect, but revitalised the form through the combination of 'old traditions with the new industrial and urban values' to create 'a popular indigenous literature that spoke to and for the prosperous working class of the industrial North'.[39] The literary revival of dialect is reflected in the Manchester pantomimes and, in particular, the notable incorporation of work by Waugh and Brierley at the Prince's Theatre underscores the validity and effect of pantomime's role in the expression of local identity and local concerns. Vicinus states that 'Although the use of dialect meant speaking to a limited audience, it had the advantage of building upon local feeling – *my* region and its culture against the rest of the country.'[40] The growing popularity of dialect literature highlighted the requirement of accuracy in capturing the correct dialect, something that not all writers were competent to achieve.[41] Similarly, in pantomime, the performance of dialect had to be accurate. Local reviews were quick to criticise poor performance and delivery, particularly when it occurred at the Queen's Theatre. A reviewer in the *Guardian* was unconvinced by Mr Elton's portrayal of Dame Nursery in 1868, pointing up the difference between the written and spoken dialect: 'In reading the book, one character is a clever representation of an old Lancashire woman, and the part assigned to her is admirably written in the vernacular. But the exponent of the part does not possess the brogue, and what would have been a powerful aid in the success of the piece is thus lost.'[42] A similar complaint was voiced in 1889 when, although the local author T.F. Doyle had intended another variation of the Lancashire Dame in *Robinson Crusoe*, the actor interpreted the lines with a distinctly Irish brogue.[43]

Whilst dialect characters appeared more regularly in pantomimes at the Queen's Theatre, it was at the more fashionable Prince's Theatre that the management commissioned work by Brierley and Waugh for their pantomimes. In 1866, Waugh wrote the pantomime *Robin Hood* for the Prince's, in which he combined Standard English with Lancashire dialect, the latter reserved for the comic character of the Friar. In performance, the reviewer of the *Manchester Weekly Times* was able to pinpoint the accent to the region of 'Preston or Oldham'.[44] The balance of language evidently suited the audience at the Prince's and the pantomime was a success, but when Waugh was approached again a couple of years later to provide a topical song for the 1878 pantomime, the subject matter he offered was deemed unsuitable. In January 1879, he had been asked to write a dialect song for the Second Edition of *Puss in Boots*. Waugh's use of the Lancashire dialect was evidently not unknown at that theatre, but the 'voice' of the song touches on working-class poverty in a way that was normally avoided in local references, certainly at the Prince's Theatre. Usually in pantomimes, social references that highlighted harsh conditions rarely offered a solution and those particular speeches were often deflected into comic business or song (an issue I will return to in this chapter). In performance, it may have been too difficult for a performer to instil the usual comic tone into Waugh's song. A note in the supplement to the *Manchester Weekly Times* stated that it had been withdrawn 'simply because its character was too plaintive throughout for the occasion'.[45] The lyrics, as detailed in the *Weekly Times* report, are given in the Appendix to this chapter. Unlike the sustained engagement with dialect and, by association, a traditional working-class culture at the Queen's Theatre, it appears that the 1866 engagement of Edwin Waugh at the Prince's Theatre owed more to his fame than to the subject matter of his verse. In a similar manner to the engagement and promotion of London scenic artists, discussed in Chapter 2, the management of the Prince's Theatre appears to have preferred Waugh's reputation as a leading light of regional literary culture to the integral acknowledgement of working-class traditions in his work. When asked to provide a topical song (one that appears not to have been assigned to any one character or aspect of the pantomime plot), the theatre management were less comfortable with the harsh realities that he presented, although they were an accurate enough reflection of the reality of life for many.

The initial appeal to Waugh was undoubtedly made after a topical song was commissioned from Ben Brierley for the same pantomime, the 1878 *Puss in Boots*. Brierley's song had been accepted and was printed in a booklet, on sale in addition to the book of words. Accompanied by cartoons of the principal characters in *Puss in Boots*, and an outline of the pantomime story, the small, concertina-folded booklet had a selection of the pantomime songs, including that by Brierley (also given in full in the Appendix to this chapter), a song that, whilst it touched on contemporaneous hardship, focused on comically attacking the country's political leadership. In this verse, Brierley presents himself in his well-known persona 'Ab-o'th'-Yate', offering 'Ab' as not only a better political candidate, but one preferred by Queen Victoria herself:

But I'll tell Queen Vic-tory,
If hoo cares for her glory –
An' we know of a *good* name hoo's preciously fond –
Hoo should send Ab – o'th – Yate

To be th' yead man o' th' State,
Then that would be summat one's patience could stond.

Local issues and local authors

The occasional work by such distinctive regional authors as Brierley and Waugh highlights the issue of pantomime authorship, a subject often regarded as of little importance. Nineteenth-century critical works on pantomime in particular tended to be dismissive of the pantomime author, regarding his work as little more than a 'peg' on which to hang the comic business, songs and special effects.[46] Accordingly, in the period following the 1843 Licensing Act, a tension emerged in which the pantomime author was regarded as a necessity, whilst at the same time often treated as someone whose work was essentially dispensable, to be cut or altered as and when the producer or star performers required.[47] Twentieth-century critical works have done little to readdress those perceptions, and as a result only passing references have been made towards the work of the pantomime author in the provinces. However, the engagement by regional theatres of local authors, in addition to or in place of bought-in and adapted scripts, was significant. A reviewer for the *Western Morning News* in 1868 emphasised the importance of local authorship:

> It is a notable fact that among the most taking pantomimes recorded in the annals of the Plymouth Theatre, those which owe their origins strictly to local talent occupy a foremost place. Local points are appreciated by audiences everywhere, and these are always best 'got up' by writers on the spot. General allusions are all very well in their way; and often bring down the gallery. Indeed a pantomime opening would be terribly tame without them; but there must also be a seasoning of readily appreciable hits which will give the hearers a special interest in the performances.[48]

Amongst the various theatres in Birmingham, Nottingham and Manchester, there were managers who regularly engaged local writers, not simply to provide additional material for bought-in scripts, but to write the entire script. Several of these theatre managers had long-term working relationships with local authors, for example Thomas Charles with

F.R. Goodyer and George Dance (later Sir George Dance, the West End impressario) at Nottingham, Captain Rogers with John Anderton at the Prince of Wales Theatre in Birmingham, Mercer Simpson and James J. Blood at the Prince of Wales Theatre, Birmingham, and the partnership of Thomas Chambers and William Hyde at the Theatre Royal, Manchester. These writers offered a distinctive style of pantomime, employing social referencing that reflected a detailed local knowledge and at times intuitive understanding of local attitudes. Pantomime authors knew and understood their home town: they worked locally as professional journalists (such as Maddock in Nottingham and E.F. Fay and William Wade in Manchester), dramatic authors (for example, George Dance, James J. Blood, and T.F. Doyle in Manchester), poets (such as Edwin Waugh and Ben Brierley) and businessmen (Goodyer was a commission agent and John Anderton was an optician at Birmingham). These authors were therefore an integral part of the local cultural, political and business scene. The working relationship between the management of the Nottingham Theatre Royal and F.R. Goodyer was endorsed in September 1879 when he appeared at the Nottingham magistrates' court to support Thomas Charles's application for a renewal of the theatre licence.[49] Goodyer also provided evidence against a circus which had attempted to stage a play in the town, threatening the business of the legitimate theatre, and, similarly, John Anderton in Birmingham appeared for the prosecution in a case brought by the Prince of Wales Theatre against Day's Music Hall for staging a melodrama in 1891. Indeed, the circle of business associations in each town, often encompassing direct, working links with the local press, may offer further rationales for the supportive advocacy of press reviews.

The financial investment in the script and social referencing did not match that of the scenery or performers, which always dominated advertisements, and naming an author on playbills or in the book of words was not a legal requirement,[50] but the promotion of local authors, their provenance and œuvre was significant in establishing the relevance of their work. Authors such as Goodyer, Dance, Wade and Anderton had their local achievements listed on the frontispiece of the books of words: Goodyer, for example, was described in terms of his wider body of work in Nottingham; he was the 'AUTHOR OF "ONCE UPON A TIME", "FAIR MAID OF CLIFTON", "NOTTINGHAM CASTLE." &c., &c.'[51] By 1882 his credits in the book of words for *Cinderella* also included '*the pantomimes at the Theatre Royal, Nottingham and Grand Theatre, Glasgow*'.[52] In giving only abbreviated titles, there is a suggestion that his work was well known and that partial referencing would suffice to remind local readers of his writing; more importantly, the titles given reiterated his interest in local affairs: all the plays were based on local history and legends.

The pattern of Dance's promotion in Nottingham was similar to that of Goodyer. The books of words contained reference to Dance's earlier works: the book for 1887 cited *Oliver Grumble*, a burlesque he had written for the theatre in 1886, and '*Aladdin &c.*'[53] Whilst Goodyer had been writing in the town for the best part of thirty years, Dance's local achievements were written close to the start of his meteoric career and several of his pieces had already been written for London theatres. Irrespective of his work elsewhere, Charles, in promoting the pantomime, instead restricted Dance's œuvre to those items written locally, thus implicitly placing him alongside Goodyer as an established figure in the town. The *Nottingham Daily Guardian*, in previewing Dance's first pantomime, similarly selected his earlier work for the Nottingham theatre – 'Mr. George Dance, of Nottingham, author of "Oliver Grumble" and other pieces' – reiterating later that same week that Dance was 'a local writer'.[54] As with Goodyer, local reviewers recalled Dance's work and his localness; critics aligned him to the town: he was a 'townsman', a 'resident of Nottingham', and a 'local writer'. His engagement by the Theatre Royal highlighted the crucial tenet of many provincial productions: the importance of local knowledge, by the town of the author and by the author of the town.

Modern urban life

The minor irritants of everyday life: overcrowded tramcars, the attitude of tram drivers, dirty streets ('What's the scarcest thing in the world? / … A Nottingham street sweeper'[55]), taxes, rates and bills were a relatively easy target for the writers and comedians in all pantomimes, and reflected attitudes expressed in the correspondence columns of the local press throughout the period. Attitudes to the grand plans of council officials were neatly summarised in a song included in the 1869 pantomime *Frogee Would A-Wooing Go* at the Prince's Theatre in Manchester, to the tune of 'Oh Dear What Can the Matter Be?':

Improvements and plans they do nothing but hawk about,
Underground railways and tramways they talk about;
Whilst the 'buses so slow go you might as well walk about,
So long on their journeys they stray …[56]

The provision of public amenities in all three towns was charted in the pantomimes. For example, in Birmingham the founding of an art gallery and the donation of recreation grounds by Middlemore, a local philanthropist, in 1877 featured in the pantomime of that year and again in 1881.[57] By the mid-1870s not only the provision but also the financing and upkeep of public buildings and amenities in all the towns were under additional and sustained scrutiny by pantomime authors.

In Nottingham, the castle had been partly destroyed by fire during Chartist demonstrations in 1831; its owner the Earl of Newcastle had refused to rebuild the property and had left the area, and over time it became more of an eyesore than a reminder of the town's significant political past. In the 1870s, the municipal authorities planned to rebuild and open the site as a public building, and Goodyer, the author of the 1874 pantomime, applauded such moves. In Scene 1 of *Little Bo Peep*, King Arthur and his knights bemoan the lack of adventures in their lives. The king notes that they have met with no dragons or giants, and that

> Enchanted castles, too, are hard to find.
> SIR L.   They are, but I've a castle in my mind
>   Which, once with many a tower and battlement,
>   Proudly o'erlooked the peaceful vale of Trent,
>   A ruin now, an eyesore, and disgrace,
>   But yet I see arising in its place
>   A noble building, perfectly designed,
>   The home of literature and art combined …
>   Its purpose to supply an urgent want, meant,
>   Yes, this would be a castle of enchantment.[58]

The Castle was eventually reopened as an art gallery in 1878 ('Art now may aid the people's elevation'), although there were complaints that it was not open on Sundays.[59] In George Dance's 1889 pantomime, the Castle was the attraction for a half-day holiday, but other pantomimes in the 1880s and 1890s charted complaints about entrance prices and the occasional closure of the venue for council functions.[60] Such comments satirically expressed sentiments found in the correspondence columns of the local newspapers. In the pantomime of 1887 the admission charges to the Baron's castle in *Babes in the Wood* struck a chord with local audiences: 'You all are welcome who live in the town; / Come in thousands (*cheers*). Admission half-a-crown (*groans*).'[61] Later in the same production, in the schoolroom question and answer session, the teacher Miss Tabitha Bluestocking asked:

Tab.   History. When was Nottingham Castle closed to all outsiders?
Scar.   In Mortimer's time.
Tab.   Has it ever been closed since?
Lit. J.   Yes, whenever the Corporation have a soirée.[62]

Similar sentiments were expressed in the 1890 pantomime *The Babes in the Wood* at the Prince of Wales Theatre, Birmingham, in which the Baron outlined his generosity to the villains if they disposed of the babes. His reward would include 'a free admission to the Art Gallery when the Mayor doesn't want it'.[63]

In 1868 the character of the Baron in *Babes in the Wood* was indignant about the positive effects of government plans and local philanthropy in Nottingham. He and his henchmen argued that:

GROS.   Our rulers seek to educate the masses
CRUD.   Free libraries are given to the working classes
BARON.   And 'gainst us to cause further revolution
      They've built up the Mechanics Institution.
      Instruction with amusement is the plan
      They've formed to benefit the working man.

In late January 1869, this speech was extended to comment on the opening night of the Mechanics Hall, in particular the fact that the guest artiste Sims Reeves had cancelled at short notice. The *Nottingham and Midland Counties Daily Express* reported how the lines were 'received with great laughter and applause':

BARON. And 'gainst us to cause further revolution
    They've built up the Mechanics Institution.
    Instruction with amusement is the plan
    They've formed to benefit the working man.
LEAN.   Yet no one in a working man's condition
    Would like to pay a guinea for admission.
    But worth half twenty 'tis to hear them hum
GROS.   Why, how's that?
LEAN.   A good *tenor* didn't come.[64]

Whilst public pride could be reflected in the representation of new buildings and statues in the urban landscape (such as the New Town Hall in the Manchester harlequinades), speeches about the latest civic monuments were rarely untouched by satire. The structural problems that (literally) undermined the new university building in Nottingham were a source of amusement in the pantomimes of 1886, 1887 ('You're never satisfied, you're ever mumbling, / Like the University wall, he's *always crumbling*') and 1891.[65] In the aforementioned 1887 pantomime schoolroom scene, the Schoolmistress asked:

Tab.   U. What does U stand for , eh?
May.   U stands for University Museum; some wondrous things are
                                                           there;
    But six months out of every twelve, they close it for repair.[66]

A statue in memory of Sir Robert Clifton had been erected in Nottingham in the late 1870s, and references to its ugliness appeared in *Babes in the Wood* of 1878 and in all of George Dance's pantomimes from 1886 to 1889.[67] And in Birmingham, there was similar criticism of the statuary of local dignitaries, for example, that of George Dawson, a leading figure in the local council – 'Oh, it's vile, / It's something of the Dawson statue style' – in the pantomime *Sinbad the Sailor* in 1882.[68] At Manchester, a statue in honour of the former member of the influential Anti-Corn-Law League and local MP, Richard Cobden played an unusually active part in the Manchester Comedy Theatre pantomime of *Cinderella*. The character of the Baron, returning home from the ball in a state of intoxication, crossed the city's Albert Square where 'in the small hours of the morning' he 'sees the Cobden statue visibly shaking a solemn head at him'.[69]   Pantomimes at the Prince of Wales Theatre in Birmingham charted the sporadic efficiency of All Saint's Clock in the town centre. In the 1887 production of *Beauty and the Beast* the clock was noted as being 'nearly always wrong', and two years later the town hall clock and its timekeeping was the subject of extended comment in *Cinderella*. Here the ugly sisters Blothilda and Clothilda worried that the irregular striking of the clock interrupted 'Harrison's Popular Concerts', which were held at the Town Hall

> *Blo* –   It can't lose the time,
>   If there's a concert on it stops to strike and chime
> *Clo* –   To leave the Town Hall it won't move a finger
> *Blo* –   At Harrison's at times we've more clock than singer.[70]

Local police were traditionally and regularly a focus of comic business in pantomime, dating back to the night watchmen of the Georgian harlequinades. However, the heroism of real police officers was saluted in the Birmingham Theatre Royal pantomimes of the 1880s. Following the successful capture of a Fenian terrorist in 1883, the heroes of the hour, Inspector Black and Mr Farndale, the Chief of Police, were recalled in the pantomimes of 1883, 1884, 1888 and 1890. In the 1888 production of *Dick Whittington*, the hero escaped capture by the London police:

> DICK.   Escaped – and not a difficult affair.
>   London police are never anywhere.
>   We Brums can well afford a quiet smack at 'em
>   And only have to *look* Detective Black at 'em.[71]

By 1890, Farndale had been immortalised as 'Inspector Ferndale' who aided the good fairies in *The Forty Thieves*.[72] Epitomising justice, Farndale's name was changed to 'Ferndale' in the pantomime to correspond with the fairies' woodland scene and the pantomime tradition of the pastoral setting as the site for virtuous and protective spirits. Conversely, in the Nottingham version of *Aladdin* in 1886, the title character was supposed to have been one of those responsible for the local election riots that had occurred in central Nottingham that year. After being shut in a cave by the wicked magician, Aladdin regrets that he will not be able 'about election time, / To chase poor bobbies like in pantomime'.[73] This statement ingeniously references the riots but aligns them with the anarchic yet ultimately harmless police-chasing traditional in pantomime harlequinades. In so doing, the comment by Aladdin in approving the town-centre activities fits with the overarching characterisation of him in this production, whilst also appearing subtly to condone the actual riot. Similarly, whilst the Castle's destruction by Chartist rioters was conveniently forgotten in King Arthur's fantasy mentioned above, the 1874 pantomime *Little Bo Peep* at Nottingham included very specific references to 'Lambs', the nickname for militant political supporters in Nottingham. In Scene 3 Boy Blue enters with a minstrel troupe, and at the end of his speech he claims: 'The Cape Coast curly crops, a breed of quiet shams, / And wouldn't pass in Nottingham for Lambs.' Whilst visitors from further afield may not have recognised the significance, it allowed others in the audience to recognise a reference to political activity and riotous behaviour in the town.[74] In stark contrast, the Murphy Riots of June 1867, ignited by the anti-papal lecturer William Murphy, were condemned outright in the pantomime of that year at the Theatre Royal, Birmingham, although the Aston Riot of 1884 – in which a Conservative demonstration was disturbed by a group of Liberals – was treated rather more humorously ('Got at the fireworks "over the garden wall," / And mobbed the Tories in the Rink and Hall').[75]

Whilst Nottingham underwent a series of town improvements, including those connected with sanitation, ongoing concern regarding industrial pollution and the state of the Rivers Trent and Leen were sources of referencing in the pantomimes throughout the late 1870s, the 1880s and 1890s.[76] In the 1886 pantomime *Aladdin*, the Princess considers setting Aladdin a series of tasks to prove his love: 'Command him go and purify the Leen / Or sweep Saint Ann's Well Road and keep it clean.'[77] In the 1889 pantomime of *Sinbad*, the hero falls overboard and is rescued. The joke is unsubtle but reflects a genuine local problem:

Sin.   Aye, aye! … Oh, isn't the water nasty?

Hai   It is.

Hin   It's almost as bad as the river Trent, when the Manufacturers are emptying their paraffin on its troubled waters.[78]

The problems of the local tanneries polluting the river and the smells wafting from the nearby sewage works were a constant source of one-line jokes in the Nottingham pantomimes, reflecting a well-known problem. For most people, the smell and the state of the river were simply an inconvenience; the pantomime jokes did not require extended speeches or overly harsh admonitions. In Manchester, however, the state of the city's rivers for those living in the vicinity could not be so easily laughed off.

Living conditions

The Queen's Theatre had been refitted during late 1871 and, rather than the references to refinement and taste in the decorations that usually punctuated descriptions of similar work at the principal theatres, the *Manchester Guardian* commented that 'very warm and cheerful it looks'.[79] Such a description echoes reviews of the scenery in the pantomimes and yet the inferred homely qualities of the theatre fed into a certain ideology of intimacy, of engaging with audiences as an extended family rather than as objective visitors. In contrast to more prominent theatres, whose localness was promoted as part of a wider pursuit of status, the Queen's Theatre management maintained a local tradition that was little disrupted by grander concerns. The pantomimes reflected local character more regularly than the other theatres in the city, creating another level of tradition alongside that of the transformation scenes and 'rollicking' fun. In establishing a tradition of local identity, the theatre management and authors could be very specific in the issues addressed. The opening scene of *Cinderella* in 1871 was set 'Down, deep down, in a cave beneath the murky Irwell', where the 'plotters against human life and happiness' dwelt. The reviewer continued:

Greenfungus, king of that region; Dankyfume, his premier; and Slimy, whose name is legion, are there at work. You may call them Death, Disease, and Misery if you like; and the situation will only be the more veracious.[80]

The living conditions for many in the city near the Irwell River were notorious and had been exposed in the writings of Friedrich Engels thirty years earlier. Audiences were intended to be heartened by the swift and idealised solution offered in the pantomime, but the *Guardian* pointed up the irony:

> At the Queen's [the demons'] fell work is arrested, their power broken, and all these evil things and beings dispersed by the advent of Manchestrina and her attendant nymphs who watch over Salford, Rochdale, and other towns surrounding her own particular realm. Where these come, comes light and blessings and good news. But unfortunately 'tis but a play; and we would suggest that the mayor, the aldermen, the councillors, the clerks, the inspectors, and every functionary excepting the police should on a set day go in solemn state to the Queen's Theatre, and learn from Miss Lillian Graham there how to do their duty and carry out in real earnest the mimic change she works.[81]

A variation on this idea was presented at the Prince's Theatre in 1874, but here the councillors and inspectors who might not have attended the Queen's Theatre were directly implicated. The dark scene

> opens in Malaria's Laboratory – a dismal chamber.... It is stored with mysterious jars, which we learn are filled with the distilled essences of choice river and drain poisons supplied by the health committee from the Irwell, the Irk, and the Medlock, and bottled odours furnished by the gas committee from Rochdale Road and Gaythorn.[82]

In the concluding dark scene of this production, there was no representative and protective spirit of Manchester as at the Queen's Theatre. Instead the laboratory and its stored samples from the polluted rivers were magically transformed into a River of Glass, which reflected aesthetically pleasing groups of fairies and silver willow trees. The samples of poisons and named committees were an advance in assigning responsibility from the symbolic nymphs of the 1871 pantomime, and yet the mechanics of how polluted rivers could really be made pure and clean and who exactly was to take control of the situation were not provided.

This example points up in a particularly effective way the role of satire in Victorian pantomime and highlights the issue of whether it served to reflect society or actively urge change, even proposing resolutions. In *The Civilisation of the Crowd: Popular Culture 1750–1900*, Golby and Purdue briefly address the function of pantomime and melodrama in relation to authority figures, and argue for the inherently conservative nature of these genres; that it is 'not authority *per se* which is derided but the *wicked squire*' who has usurped and misused his power.[83] Certainly, pantomime satire did not attack English social or legal structures, but neither did they simply transpose wrongdoing onto the fictional demons and barons. In provincial pantomimes, real civic authorities and individuals were named and their faults pointed out, although the speeches and comments reflected what was already known by many in the towns and cities. In this sense the pantomimes could be critical, even outspoken, but they did not offer the kind of transgressive behaviour that Jane Moody suggests is potentially inherent in the genre. Indeed her discussion, centred on the harlequinade, is grounded in the mistaken alignment of pantomime with notions of carnival (a link also made by Golby and Purdue), which assumes that the satirical nature of the genre occurs within the boundaries of controlled anarchy.[84] Bakhtinian carnival, however, whilst providing a freedom to overturn 'oppressive social norms', traditionally belongs to the public spaces beyond the theatre. It is 'not a spectacle seen by the people, they live in it': it

> is by no means a purely artistic form nor a spectacle and does not, generally speaking, belong to the sphere of art. In fact, carnival does not know footlights, in the sense that it does not acknowledge any distinction between actors and spectators. Footlights would destroy a carnival as the absence of footlights would destroy a theatrical performance.[85]

Therefore, in the Bakhtinian sense, pantomime is not carnival and does not share its particular transgressive possibilities, but neither did the productions of the nineteenth century move beyond the satirical highlighting of local issues and the reflection of contemporaneous concerns to promote original solutions. Pantomime scripts and topical songs did not uncover previously unreported facts; the comments mirrored (occasionally using identical phrases) press articles and letters in the correspondence columns of newspapers. The problems were voiced but not resolved. In the Irwell example, perhaps comfortingly for middle-class audience members at the Prince's Theatre, the bottled gases and poisons are simply and efficiently transposed into pastoral perfection.

In 1878, the Queen's Theatre authors again provided a pantomime full of local references with representative characters. The dark scene foregrounded the Witch of Irwell, accompanied by her evil spirits Medlock, Irk, Tib and Blackbrook, all opposed by the good fairy Thirlmere (the improvements to the city's water supply during the second half of the century were crowned in 1894 with the completion of the Thirlmere Reservoir[86]). Adopting the same reference point of the Irwell, the Prince's Theatre pantomime, also in 1878, included a topical song during which Mr Doyle 'improves the occasion by displaying a map of the Irwell, and delivering from the deck of his ship a lecture on that dark and devious river in true professorial style – students might say quite Owenic'.[87] Again, the presentation at the Prince's Theatre offered a different perspective of the problem. Whilst the Queen's Theatre offered representative supernatural characters, the Prince's Theatre version was aligned with knowledge and education (Owens College in Manchester had been founded in 1851).

Education and the pantomime

Evidence from the extant books of words and manuscripts displays not only knowledge of local and locally relevant issues but also a pertinent awareness by authors of the impact of national issues on a provincial town. An illustration of this engagement can be found in relation to the effects of the 1870 Education Act, the local School Boards and related local concerns in the pantomimes by F.R. Goodyer at Nottingham.

After several years of campaigning by the National Education League, Forster's Education Act was passed in September 1870.[88] It was an attempt to provide schools in those areas that were under-represented by local voluntary schools, and it 'created a new type of local authority, the school board, directly elected by the ratepayers, to provide and run [the] new schools'.[89] Prior to 1870, the only reference to national policy in the Nottingham pantomimes was a brief explication in the 1868 production:

'Our rulers seek to educate the masses.'[90] Whilst fairly accurate, there was no sense of local engagement with the issue, although, as in many towns, there was a disparity of educational provision. On the contrary, this expression identified education as an external force, imposed upon the town, and between 1865 and 1873 the Nottingham pantomimes contained no further references to the national processes, nor to Nottingham's own branch of the Education League. Similarly, although the 'first Nottingham School Board was elected on 29 November 1870', the initial workings of the board and the funding difficulties its members faced were not addressed in the pantomimes.[91]

In 1873 the first thematic reference to education was made in F.R. Goodyer's version of *Little Red Riding Hood*, in his first pantomime for the theatre. The first intimation appeared on the playbill, in which it was stated that Red Riding Hood was 'no scholar (School Boards not then in existence)'.[92] In this pantomime, the heroine was a somewhat uncouth character whose Prince was constantly correcting her grammar and language. The repeated references to the importance of grammar, verb conjugation and nouns, together with correct speech style, continually highlighted the importance of education in order to succeed.

> R.R.H. ...
>   Indeed, you seem perticklar cross to-day.
> EDGAR. Particularly cross, you mean, my dear,
>   Your grammar seems particularly queer.
> R.R.H. Oh! bother grammar, we can love without it
>   I'm sorry that I don't know much about it.[93]

For Little Red Riding Hood, her improvement – applauded by the prince in her use of puns – gives her status and a royal wedding. However, in comparison to an emphasis on the value of education in a general sense, the critical references in the pantomime of the following year were far more specific.

Although the 1870 Act encouraged school-building and a greater number of places to be made available, no provision had been made to actually enforce attendance, nor was it to be a free provision.[94] Therefore, once local need had been identified and the schools built, one of the foremost problems facing the local authorities was that of truancy, although local School Boards did have the discretionary powers to create by-laws to enforce attendance.[95] The Nottingham School Board appears to have taken this option and established compulsory attendance for children for a period between the ages of five and thirteen.[96] However, even with the by-law in place, truancy remained a problem in Nottingham; the local historian Helen Meller has referred to a 'local standing tradition of child employment' in Nottingham that discouraged attendance.[97] In *Little Bo Peep* (1874), the wicked Giant hunted down children who were playing truant from school. This may be considered a positive attitude – insisting on a child's education – but the Giant was demonised in this particular pantomime. He promoted learning over food for children and spoke out against those who truanted to help out at home. Historian David Wardle, drawing on the results of an 1872 survey, has shown that whilst 'poverty was only given as the reason for absence in about twenty cases' (out of 1,232 children), 'it is very apparent that sheer indifference was the most common reason':

> Recalcitrant parents were prosecuted, but … the bench showed little interest in enforcing attendance. The usual fine for a first conviction was 2s 6d, which was quite inadequate in view of the earnings open to a truant. Since a child's income went into the parent's pocket it was well worth while for a parent to keep his children at work and risk the occasional fine, and it is quite clear that many did this.[98]

The issues that featured in the Nottingham pantomimes, of truancy and the problem of children being kept away from school to look after siblings, reflected real problems in the town that prevented children from being educated. How widely disseminated the 1872 report was is unclear, but the pantomime references promoted the issue of poverty rather than indifference as the main cause of truancy. It is noticeable that a reviewer in the *Nottingham Daily Gazette* commented that of the Giant's speech in *Little Bo Peep*, 'The local points were well made by Mr. Collard.'[99] The character of King Arthur, who presided over the rewards and punishments at the end of the opening, decried the Giant as a 'School Board Blockhead', suggesting that he be made 'Minister of Education, / There's scope for harshness in that situation; / As when a starving urchin's craving bread, /

He'll cram his maw with A B C instead.'[100] The Giant's lack of empathy and direct character-linking to the School Board and government suggest that the pantomime was criticising the education system rather than education *per se*. As presented at the Theatre Royal, the Giant was deaf to the underlying – and local – problems behind truancy. The Education Act of 1876 (more commonly known as Sandon's Act, after Lord Sandon, its instigator), was an attempt to resolve the issue of attendance. The Act 'declared that it was the duty of parents to send their children to school', but again provision was not uniformly applied.[101] The problem remained in Nottingham as evinced in a brief reference in the 1877 pantomime: 'I never played the truant like a fool, / Because they never let me go to school.'[102] Board school attendance did rise slowly in the town, but by 1883 the issue of poverty and attendance once again featured in the Theatre Royal pantomime.

The 1880 Education Act (Mundella's Act) made school attendance compulsory between five and twelve, 'with partial or full exemptions from the age of ten, dependent on the attendance record of the child and his or her educational attainment'.[103] Not many boards actually took up the option of making attendance compulsory, 'but pressure was increasingly exerted on parents to make their children attend' and a School Attendance Officer could check on suspected truants.[104] Parents who allowed their children to truant, or who did not pay the fees, could be taken to court, and whilst school fees 'could be excused on account of poverty … recourse to the Guardians could be a humiliating experience and forfeited the right to vote'.[105] The Education Department was well aware that 'if many parents refused to send their children to school, local authorities were dilatory about prosecuting them'.[106] Particular problems were faced by poorer parents during the depression years of the 1880s, and in the pantomime of 1883 the schoolroom examination session included the following question set by the schoolmistress Dame Gamp:

> [*Gamp*] If a widow woman has a family of five small children, and her income is only four shillings and sixpence per week, what amount of education would be necessary to keep them from starving? You surely ought to have an answer, pat.
> *Simon*. Mister Mundella couldn't answer that![107]

At the end of the scene a truant child, Johnny Stout, was brought in by Ben Boosey the Beadle, representative of the Poor Law Guardians. The latter remarked that the child 'says he's forced to stop at home and nuss, / Because his mother's got a job o'washin'. At this Dame Gamp retorted:

> You can't expect the law to give you bread,
> It kindly gives you A B C instead.
> Poor people's brats are shockingly neglected
> *Boos.*   I'll hunt them up – the law must be respected.[108]

The first speech in particular attracts attention by its use of prose rather than couplets (the traditional form for pantomime speech, as seen in the second example) and appears to be very directly attacking the inadequacies of the system. By referring to the conflicts of education and work, in speeches that are not intended to amuse (Dame Gamp is often drunk in other scenes, but not in this one), Goodyer again sought to address issues that were extremely relevant to Nottingham. The irony of Simon's answer in the first extract lay in the fact that Mundella – the instigator of the 1880 Education Act – was also a Nottingham MP. Once again, pantomime satire foregrounded an immediate and important problem but, again, the writer did not intervene to propose a solution. Who, for example, was responsible for the children being 'shockingly neglected', their parents or the authorities? The issue is deflected into a more general comic scene, ending with a song. Suggestive evidence of the relevance to Nottingham people of the above speeches lies in the fact that Goodyer's script (and probably the rest of the production) was re-used at Thomas Charles's theatre in Glasgow the following year, but the introduction of Johnny Stout and the reason for his truancy are cut from the scene.[109]

The concerns regarding enforced attendance and educational provision were replaced in pantomimes after the mid-1880s by references to the increase in school-building. By the late 1870s there still remained a deficiency of school places in Nottingham and from 1877 there was a concerted effort by the authorities to build more Board schools.[110] The increased number of building projects in Nottingham lasted until the early 1890s[111] and the related costs and the effect on local rates became the focus of comments in the annual pantomimes. The 1877 pantomime *Blue Beard* featured a number of dolls in the first scene who complained at the excess of educational provision in the town. It was a humorous yet backhanded compliment to municipal achievements, which encompassed further and technical as well as primary education. A less than subtle approach to the subject occurred in George Dance's 1887 pantomime *Babes in the Wood*:

Tab.   Well, sir, I've been
    To our school board meeting – there *was* a scene!
    They're going to build a school in every street,
    You'll have a thumping District Rate to meet.[112]

At Birmingham, the focus of references regarding education was apparent in pantomimes from a much earlier date and effectively charted the development of educational provision in the late 1860s. The necessity for improved provision was reflected in the pantomime of *Aladdin* in 1866. In this production the Widow Chow-Chow appeared as the schoolmistress of a ragged school, and exchanges between her and her pupils underlined the low standard of teaching available to poorer children from unqualified teachers:

[WIDOW]   First class in front, for lesson number one.
    C-A-T?
CHILDREN.   Dog!
WIDOW.   D.O.G?
CHILDREN.   Cat!
WIDOW.   Well done!
    If thus, *unsiezingly*, they grasp at knowledge,
    I soon may raise the charges at this college.[113]

The Birmingham Education League was the dominant force in the move to establish a national elementary education scheme and to provide education beyond the poor provision of ragged schools. Furthermore, the League fought for school places to be free (unlike Widow Chow-Chow's 'college'), although that was not a feature of the 1870 Act. By 1869, the proposed Education Bill (Forster's Bill) became the focus for references in the pantomime *Blue Beard*. In Scene 7 a topical song sung by Blue Beard's fiancée Fatima and her sister, envisioned the future, including:

ANNE.   And can I believe my eyes –
FATIMA. Say, what is this new surprise?
ANNE.   An *education scheme* – and not too late.[114]

More specifically, in Scene 9 Oberon insists that 'this scheme for *education* / Must first be *forstered* by good legislation'.[115] In 1873, the same year that the Nottingham pantomime expressed concern at attendance issues, the Birmingham Theatre Royal pantomime applauded the work of the School Board system and the role of local men:

> Well, there's no denial,
> That modern notion now is on its trial!
> We've had a fight – a popular election,
> A move I fancy, in the right direction.
> The men we've sent to do the work, I guess
> Will do their utmost to achieve success.[116]

Following the enactment of the 1870 Act and the establishment of School Boards, the curriculum and methods of teaching in the 1880s became a focus of attention in the pantomimes. Two of the Nottingham productions, in 1877 and 1884, included brief yet humorous references to cramming; in the latter a talking donkey was compared to a School Board pupil ('all his standards won – / They'll turn out lots like him before they've done').[117] This method of teaching was criticised more fully in the Birmingham pantomimes and followed national concerns. Sophia Jex-Blake had written to *The Times* in 1880 complaining about the system of cramming (a style of rote learning) and the number of subjects taught in Board schools.[118] In 1883, the opening scene of the pantomime *The Queen of Hearts* at the Theatre Royal, Birmingham, featured a witches' brew that contained ''mongst other ills / The code of "cram" the School Board child that kills'.[119] Two years later, the theme recurred in *Robinson Crusoe* (also at Birmingham). In a portrayal inviting comparison with the ragged school mistress of 1866, the 1885 pantomime contained a similarly disparaging picture of teaching. Dame Crusoe was described in the book of words as a 'School Board Mistress (Certified) who knocks Knowledge into her Pupils, and takes it out of them also'. Knowledge with a capital 'K' epitomised the contemporaneous debate, and Mrs Crusoe lamented her responsibilities in Scene 3:

DAME.　A School Board Mistress! What a lot – to teach
The young idea to shoot – beyond their reach;
To pass examinations 'ere they toddle,
And cram with knowledge every little noddle;
Until so closely packed, their little brains
Resemble crowded cheap excursion trains.
For little baby *buntings* can't be lagging,
But pass their *standards* with a zeal un-*flagging* …
Besides my troubles thick and threefold flurrying,
For my opinion folks are always worrying.[120]

This speech represented the schoolmistress as an acknowledged figure in the local community, respected for her views but who at the same time holds deep reservations about what she does. The emphasis that Mrs Crusoe places on the quantity of information is interlinked in her speech with infant ability, a concern also related to contemporaneous debates regarding the negligence of the physical health of children in favour of academic work. Those debates led to the instigation of exercise in schools, but as Gretchen R. Galbraith has stated, there was an associated concern in the mid-1880s regarding illness amongst London Board school pupils: that illness and fatigue were due to the fact that the brains of working-class children were not capable of excessive learning.[121] From the sentiments expressed by Mrs Crusoe, it is evident that belief was not confined to London. As late as 1895, similar concerns were being addressed by John Anderton in his script of *Goody Two Shoes*, written for the Prince of Wales Theatre in Birmingham. In this pantomime, 'Goody' was a schoolmistress and in Scene 6 she was confronted by a demon who attempted to frighten her. She responded:

I am quite used to trying examinations; and as for your horrifying sights – can your friends shew me anything more agonising than half clothed, wholly starved shoeless little ones striving to stock their ill-nurtured brains with knowledge? I have seen such through many a winter, and wept.[122]

In the original draft, the phrase 'half clothed' is crossed through, with a handwritten amendment 'ill clad'. Similarly, 'wholly' starved is amended to 'half' starved, but even with these changes, Anderton's prose lines have considerable impact. His script therefore provides another view of life in Birmingham, indicating an audience with different experiences and perspectives on the education issue.

Trade issues: Manchester

During the 1860s, the Theatre Royal pantomimes at Manchester were written by the manager, Thomas Chambers, sometimes in collaboration with another local author, W.S. Hyde. Their scripts reflected knowledge of the town whilst also evincing a subtle understanding of the difficult trade issues in the first part of that decade. In 1860 the opening dark scene of *Cinderella* was set in the 'Hall of the Gnomes', into which the Prince and Dandini accidently wander. Appealing to the prominent trade of the region, their conversation is littered with puns on cotton and spinning:

DANDINI. To *thread* this gloomy place we have no *clue*,
  I *reel* with terror, *really*, now – don't you?
PRINCE.   How curious! well, the *winding* of the chase
  Has sent us *bobbin* to a funny place.[123]

In the Theatre Royal pantomime of 1861, *Beauty and the Beast*, Beauty's father was an 'honest merchant' ruined by speculation:

Quick, quick, get on, we can't one moment stop,
For cotton specs have caught me on the hop.
And sell I must; but where's the buyer found –
Who'll take Orleans at thirteenpence a pound?
'Invest!' cried all, until smash'd, ruin'd, diddl'd,
The *Brokers broke* me, and my profits mizzl'd.[124]

The American Civil War of the early 1860s halted the supply of raw cotton to Britain, paralysing the Lancashire mills. What became known as the Lancashire Cotton Famine led to extremes of deprivation for many people in the region. A local historian George Saintsbury wrote retrospectively in

1887 that by 1862 'the distress reached its height. It being estimated that in September 1862 one in every twenty-five persons (more than a hundred and sixty thousand in all) throughout the manufacturing district of Lancashire was in receipt of parish relief.'[125] The Manchester pantomimes, whose social referencing reflected the fluctuations of trade, naturally remarked on both the war and the local impact on employment. However, the worst effects were not commented on; the *Manchester Guardian* remarked in 1862 that recent events were too serious to be included in a pantomime and approved of the 'childlike' escapist quality of that year's pantomime story, *The House That Jack Built*.[126] There remains, however, a speech in the book of words that did engage with the subject of under-employment. Although it may have been cut from the performance (as suggested by the *Guardian* comment), it praised the attitudes of local people. The speech occurred in the opening overview of the year by the character of 'Time':

> In England, *short time* to our working bees
> Has brought, this *long time*, hunger and disease.
> But they, unlike their looms, have ne'er run rusty;
> And, short of *bread* have never once looked *crusty*![127]

Direct reference to the famine may well have been potentially injudicious, but it may also have reflected the action that was being taken to help the unemployed operatives. Saintsbury highlighted the fact that by 1862

> Measures … had already been taken to cope with this gigantic disaster. A Cotton Famine Relief was started by Lord Derby in London, and a great county meeting being held at Manchester in September, 130,000*l*. was subscribed. Even this great sum was but a small proportion of what was raised and distributed by the Relief Fund managers, whose headquarters were in Manchester; while a special Act of Parliament was passed enabling the unions to borrow money for expenditure on public works, and an extraordinary Poor Law Commission was established for the regulation of this and other methods of directing public as distinguished from private relief. By the end of 1865, the famine had practically ceased, and by that time considerably more than a million had been raised and expended.[128]

The Theatre Royal pantomime of 1863 was *Sleeping Beauty*, which, with its motifs of spinning and spindles, would have had resonance in the city. After three years of affected trade, more detailed discussion was no doubt unnecessary, and the verbal references to trade are only to be inferred from the opening demon scene, in which Fairy Spiteful proclaims how ''Tis delightful web and woof of war to twine.' The *Manchester Guardian* reviewer instead focused on the visual setting of this scene, 'The Factory of Spite', and the presumed response from certain sections of the audience:

> The machinery is in rapid motion, if not with the regularity of which our factory operatives would approve in a spinning mill. They will be greatly amused, and doubtless we shall hear many droll observations from the galleries, on the clumsy inefficiency of the demons as weavers and spinners. They are weaving discord and misery for mankind, and we all know that however awkward their manner may seem to be, they are sadly too successful in producing a substantial web.[129]

These comments acknowledged both those in Manchester who were earning and able to attend the theatre and those still affected by under- and unemployment. Importantly, the reviewer recognised the inferred praise for the expertise and skill of the local factory operatives that the scene, with its incompetent demons, foregrounded.

However, at the Prince's Theatre the wealth of speculators was instead the focus of comment in the 1864 pantomime of *Mother Goose*:

BARON. ...
>I've lots of shares in mines, in banks, in rails;
>And as to cotton I've two thousand bales.

COLINETTE.   Don't stuff them in your ears like men of station;
>And then lament the rage for speculation;
>But spin 'em, weave 'em, work 'em up in mills,
>Don't let our *drawing frames* be *drawing bills*.[130]

In 1865 the American war was nearly at an end and supplies of cotton had started to resume. The opening dark scene of *Whittington and His Cat* at the Queen's Theatre featured the characters of 'Discord', 'Famine' and 'War', who plot to go to Manchester to spoil Christmas. 'Famine', however, is reluctant:

> Stay! you go to Lancashire there I can't follow
> Their pluck and independence beats me hollow
> When in America the War began
> I thought that I should have them to a man
> And when I heard that cotton was so deare,
> I stalked abroad and sought to inspire feare,
> But they naught daunted, Sire, got up a fund
> And fed the people, till I fairly stunned …[131]

By 1866, the dominant local industry was concisely represented by the figure of a bale of cotton symbolising 'trade' in the opening scene of the Prince's pantomime. The bale was one of the items, along with a pen, a press, a steam engine, a plough and a ship ('Commerce') that the Good Fairies Energy and Knowledge summoned to fight the demons of Sloth, Ignorance, Drunkenness and Poverty. But generally, by the late 1860s, cotton and fabric production were not dominating pantomime trade references to the extent that might be imagined; the financial dealings of the Manchester Exchange featured in a range of puns on 'bulls' and 'bears', but the emerging chemical and engineering industries were not reflected until the proposed and actual building of the Ship Canal, discussed below. Indeed, even references after the 1860s to cotton tended to occur in visual inclusions of the finished product or more general representations of trade. As mentioned in Chapter 2, the 1880 production of *Blue Beard* at the Theatre Royal included the unusual transformation scene tableau of 'A Tribute to Lancashire'. In this 'the central figure represents Manchester, whilst the bannerets or flowers held by the surrounding figures show, when reversed, the names and coats of arms of the principal if not all the Lancashire towns and in the background appear the words "Success to Lancashire"'.[132] Neither the newspaper reports nor the book of words give further details about this scene and it does appear that it was a static but symbolic salute to Lancashire that depended on audience interpretation rather than overt representations of trade. More effective perhaps in promoting local industry and commerce were inclusions of the finished product. In the 1881 pantomime at the Prince's Theatre, the scene of 'The Golden Island' included a ballet in which the turbans and dresses of the dancers were made of 'Manchester printed and dyed goods' suggesting, offered the *Manchester Guardian*, a region ruled by free rather than fair trade.[133] The feature was obviously a success as the management repeated the idea in the following year's pantomime *Robin Hood* in which 'a special feature' was 'the costumes of the ladies of the ballet, who are arrayed in Manchester prints made up according to special designs'.[134] In 1882 the Queen's Theatre adopted the same device and in the concluding wedding scene of *Beauty and the Beast* the event included 'a grand calico ball (the dresses from Messrs. Kendal, Milne, and Co., being representative of various designs in Manchester printing)'.[135] Such inclusions represented and celebrated both the range and quality of fabrics produced by local industry and the influential and up-market department store and production centre of Kendal, Milne & Co, in Deansgate. The celebration of output rather than process mirrors the visual referencing in Birmingham (discussed below) and the very occasional references at Nottingham (such as a Lace Ballet). In emphasising displays of the finished product, the Manchester pantomime references emphasised the city's role in commerce and, in visibly producing a range of designs, can be aligned to Thomas Richards's concept of the aspirational qualities of the commodity. However, the references also emphasise the issue of locating regional identity: writers and theatre managers did not solely site identity within references to 'Cottonopolis', but responded to the wider range of civic, political and social issues that occurred each year and over time.

Trade issues: Nottingham

Whilst farm and rural scenes populated all pantomimes, usually providing an opportunity for spectacle, these particular pantomime settings and references at Nottingham held a more pertinent interpretation for local audiences. Unlike the industrial centres of Birmingham and Manchester, where theatre managements advertised to a principally urban audience, the theatre at Nottingham depended on audiences from the town and also from the large farming regions of South Nottinghamshire and Derbyshire.

It was important, therefore, that the pantomimes reflected rural as well as urban issues.

The rages of Cattle Plague were bemoaned by the Fairy Queen in the production of *Aladdin* in 1866, and the farming depressions of the late 1870s and early 1880s were similarly reflected in the pantomimes of 1879 and 1883.[136] In the 1879 pantomime *Jack and the Beanstalk*, the effects of American competition were remarked upon by Jack's mother:

> In poor old England it's all up wi' farmin';
> Ploughing and sowing's all a waste o' seed,
> It's downright harrowing – it is indeed,
> And all because those meddling Yankees, spiteful,
> keep sending weather positively frightful,
> Spoiling our crops with endless floods of rain,
> That we must buy their corn against our grain.[137]

In more successful years, the local impact of good fortune in agriculture was celebrated. In the 1868 version of *Babes in the Wood* the good fairy Welcome was given an extended comment on the recent harvests:

> Well, as I came I saw a harvest field,
> Which this year seemed a double crop to yield,
> Rich, ripe, and full, the wavy corn there gleaming,
> Declared our land with prosperous plenty teeming…

And later, in a scene entitled 'Harvest Landscape', the character of Farmer Marrowphat exclaimed: 'Great was the crop of dear old sixty eight, / And now our harvest home we celebrate.'[138]

As outlined earlier, the principal industries in Nottingham for much of the nineteenth century were lace and hosiery making. Poor trade and unemployment in these industries were also acknowledged and discussed; the only surviving portion of the 1867 pantomime is an extended speech advocating new business practices:

> But ere I go a word or two I'd say,
> Which is not part of this our Christmas play;

I'd speak a word for Nottingham, if you'll allow,
A rare good town to live in, all avow;
I'd wish trade better th', all hands employed,
For without work, there's naught can be enjoyed,
There's one thing, th', to me seems rather strange,
If hose and lace won't pay, then why not change
To other manufactures more in 'quest,
Machinery, jewels, boots, or cloth? invest
Your surplus capital, and labour too,
Then fickle Fortune, swift again to woo,
And joyous faces happy homes will tell
That Nottingham once more is thriving well.[139]

The speech did not dwell on the difficulties of trade or the inherent criticism of the manufacturers, and indeed, the suggestions of alternative trade do not seem realistic, given the lack of suitable infrastructures in the town. Aware of its audiences, the speech was instead deflected to acknowledge charitable and civic assistance:

Your many charities to aid distress,
Bring comfort to the sick and penniless;
The Ragged School, where oft an erring lad
By Virtue's precepts has escaped the bad.
Your General Hospital's a blessing too,
For aid, no suff'rer there need vainly sue.
The Free Dispensary much comfort brings,
With medicines and other useful things.
The Midland Institution for the Blind,
Where the poor sightless some relief may find
To ease their grief and cheer their dull career,
Deserves indeed a special mention here.

In the 1880s, the local lace trade was faced with competition from Germany as a result of free trade policies, and from Derbyshire (principally the town of Long Eaton) as a result of strikes in Nottingham, both centres provoking antagonistic comments in the pantomimes of the period. Whilst the theatre managers advertised in Derbyshire and frequently depended on audiences from further afield to maintain the pantomime run, strong local opinion in Nottingham proved more persuasive for the author. In the 1886 production of *Aladdin*, the Widow Twankey commented on the Emperor's laundry:

> And if to pay fair prices he ain't sweet on,
> Why let him send his orders to Long Eaton,
> (*She throws shirt at Vizier*)
> Their price is less than ours is – very true,
> You know the adage – cheap and nasty too.[140]

The directness in these lines was typical of George Dance's scripts. In marked contrast to the subtleties of local businessman F.R. Goodyer's pantomimes, Dance, who was establishing himself as a professional author, directed his satire with a scattergun approach, attacking each and every available local target. In 1887, bitterness about foreign and regional competition had not subsided. In the schoolroom scene of *Babes in the Wood*, the pupils responded thus:

> *Tab*.   Commerce. What does 'free trade' mean?
> *Ned*.   It means starvation for British workmen.
> *Tab*.   Where is Nottingham hosiery made?
> *Ned*.   Germany
> *Tab*.   Where is Nottingham lace made?
> *Dick*.   Long Eaton.[141]

The issues were unresolved two years later, as inferred by an exchange in the 1889 pantomime *Sinbad the Sailor*. In this, Hinbad challenged Tinbad to accept the 'new card', or working terms. The latter refused, at which point the exchanges disintegrated:

> *Hin*.   Then I'll go to Long Eaton
> *Tin*.   You can go to Trent if you like
> *Hin*.   I give you notice, I'm going to strike
> *Tin*.   I give you notice (*strikes him*) I have struck.[142]

The setting of the scene was uncontroversial: 'The Sea Shore'. Similarly, the opening of the scene started humorously with Hinbad pushing Tinbad on stage in a perambulator, but the characters were firmly assigned in the book of words and the playbills. In the former Tinbad is 'the Tailor – The originator of the Sweating System / The Oppressor of the *Pore*' and Hinbad, 'the Apprentice'. Therefore the opening action signified the roles of parent and child, as well as those of the domineering employer and poorly paid employee. The exchange was concluded by a physical action and, rather than allowing for comic business, Tinbad simply exited. The pantomime once again, although not offering a solution – and indeed with free trade relating to national policy this would have been difficult at local level – clearly reflected the feeling amongst Nottingham lace and hosiery workers. Dance's script had been used at Manchester the year before, at the Prince's Theatre, managed, as at Nottingham, by Thomas Charles. The character descriptions of Hinbad and Tinbad in that version were identical, but the exchanges there centred on accusations of shoddy homespuns and tweeds bought from Rochdale.[143] The overarching trade references concerning employer and employee could be applied in both cities, but Dance clearly understood the different concerns and the exchange at Manchester was implicitly more humorous than those at Nottingham.

Unemployment

Although the effects of free trade, poor harvests and war on local and regional trade could be commented on in pantomimes, the issue of the individual unemployed worker was more problematic for pantomime writers and performers. Representative figures were occasionally included in the stories, but pantomime's role in reflecting social issues could not easily be extended to provide or instigate social remedies. The Manchester Theatre Royal pantomime in 1887 included a character of 'The Unemployed', played by lead comedian Ramsey Danvers. Reviewers complained about his aesthetically unpleasing costume, but there seems little in the script to infer serious engagement with local issues. The *Guardian* reviewer disliked the general idea and thought that 'topical allusions to political events might easily have been worked in more kindly and indirectly'.[144] However, by mid-February, reviews in that paper approved of the character, although chiefly of the manner in which Danvers had turned it into an opportunity for visual, knockabout comedy.

Although periods of bad trade in the national economy were not comprehensively experienced in Birmingham, the pantomime authors there did not ignore those who were affected. Unemployment in the late 1870s and mid-1880s, as well as trade unrest in certain branches of local industry, did feature amongst the local referencing in productions at the Theatre Royal. Brief, somewhat general references were made to 'hard times' in *Robinson Crusoe* (1878) and to the unemployed in the version of 1885.[145] More specific, although again brief references were made to unemployment in the nail-making industry as related to free trade competition in *Goody Two Shoes* (1887), plus the local bedstead-makers' lockout in *Aladdin* (1889).[146]

In 1883, the poverty of farm workers and their treatment by landowners were voiced by the hero 'Boy Blue' in the Nottingham production of *Little Bo Peep*:

> *Boy B.* Farm lab'ring's not a lively occupation.
>   A trifle, merely, better than starvation;
>   Tyrants like him can do just as they like.
>   He knows full well we are too poor to strike;
>   We have no Union, such sharks to torture,
>   Except the parish one, and that's a scorcher!
>   The army, sometimes, I have thought the cheese,
>   A soldier, now and then, can stand at ease;
>   Again I thought 'twere better than enlisting
>   To go to Nottingham and learn the 'twisting,'
>   I'd earn enough to be a downright dasher,
>   Then all the girls would cry – 'There goes a masher.'[147]

The alternatives that Boy Blue considers set up the urban environment as an enviable option, in particular employment in the lace trade (one of the production methods of which was known as 'twisting'). The speech is interesting in that it does consider the role played by unions, but – delivered by the Principal Boy – it resolves in a fantasy in which he/she becomes a 'masher'. The tyrant farmer, Farmer Grump, assumes the villainous role of the pantomime, also opposing the local Goose Fair, and in the final reconciliation scene he is made to pay for his bad treatment of the hero and heroine. Bo Peep suggests that 'In these hard times, when farming's so adverse / *Double* his rent – he can't be punished worse.'[148] Here, the farmer is held responsible for the way he has overworked and underpaid Boy Blue but the proposed punishment is offered within the confines of the story and by the childlike 'Bo Peep'. Further, any inferred extended comment to real farmers and landowners in the audience is reversed in the following scene by the 'Farmer' appealing to the audience for sympathy and applause: the pantomime concludes by focusing on the overarching issue of agricultural depression rather than seeking to resolve the specifics of the employment of farm labourers.

> A luckless farmer, I appear before you.
> And for some slight assistance now implore you;
> My crops have turned out profitless for years,
> Will you reward me with a crop of cheers?[149]

A more general example of socio-economic struggle featured in the 1868 pantomime *Babes in the Wood* in Nottingham. Here the hero Charley discovered his royal birthright and highlighted social hypocrisy:

> Now I'm a prince, all treat me with respect;
> When but an orphan foundling, folks would spurn.
> Now they crawl after me at every turn.
> So runs the world, the great have all that's needed,
> While struggling merit toils and dies unheeded.[150]

The heartfelt outburst was not sustained; instead in the next line Charley suddenly commented on his favourite seasons. The lines were not remarked on in previews or reviews and the appeal for 'struggling merit' hangs curiously in the air, the author apparently unable to satisfactorily conclude the argument.

Civic culture, the pantomime and processions

The increased use of supernumeraries, referred to in Chapter 2, not only provided opportunities for displays of fairy-tale and supernatural characters. Themed processions and parades also featured in the pantomimes. Regional pantomime producers were no doubt influenced by those staged at Drury Lane, and staged similar processions with themes such as historical figures, fashions through the ages, packs of cards and monarchs. In terms of regional identity, the London theatre invoked symbolic representations of England or Britain. The counties of England or the countries of the Kingdom could initiate or conclude a story, but these motifs related to overarching themes of national identity. Such representations effected the image of London as the centre (and Drury Lane as the theatrical centre) of the nation. Similarly, images of London or, for example, of the engineering project of the Thames Tunnel (in the Drury Lane pantomime of 1869) illustrated London as the epitome of the modern city. In *Reflecting the Audience* Davis and Emeljanow discuss the production of Andrew Halliday's play *The Great City* at Drury Lane in 1867, and cite the *Spectator*'s interpretation of the appeal of the play: 'a new-born desire to idealize the unique metropolis in which we live and work'.[151] Further, Davis and Emeljanow argue, the audiences who attended the West End theatres comprised people 'with few geographic or spatial ties'.[152] The processions, therefore, were not intended to engage with a localised sense of identity, certainly not in terms of trade or industry. Conversely, the pantomimes at the transpontine and provincial theatres were more easily able to engage with such a concept. The reliance on a core topography of potential audiences permitted direct referencing to local communities and the iconography of local and regional identities.

In the larger provincial centres such as Birmingham, the incorporation of processions was an effective and assertive mode of referencing regional status and success. Such processions did not simply originate in the pantomime traditions established at Drury Lane; their combined grandeur and regional celebration reflected real processions that celebrated civic and industrial achievements beyond the theatre. Simon Gunn has written of the civic culture of the urban metropolises of Birmingham, Manchester and Leeds, and of the civic and political importance of processions which were increasingly used to celebrate local achievement and the local engagement with national occasions. Such 'public pageants', he writes, were occasioned by 'Royal coronations and visits, the opening of public buildings, the unveiling of statues and monuments, and the funerals of civic worthies'.[153] George Saintsbury, writing in 1887, commented on the reputation of Manchester regarding processions and public occasions: 'Manchester has what is called in the trade slang of the day a "speciality" in processions, demonstrations, and general organisation of a popular character.'[154] Gunn offers a more detailed analysis of the potential of such displays, stating that

> The parades and processions that formed an essential part of these events represented the urban population to itself in a collective act of identification and celebration. As David Cannadine has observed, such spectacles did not so much serve as the expression of urban community, as its actualisation.[155]

Gunn adds: 'At the same time as representing community, however, the highly visible nature of ceremonial occasions offered special opportunity for the symbolic display of leadership and authority.'[156] He highlights the royal visit to Manchester in 1851 and the pageant of civic leaders who adopted specially created 'robes of scarlet and purple' for the occasion.[157] Importantly, he further suggests that

> There was no single overarching meaning to civic ceremonial and pageantry. Rather, civic ritual had multiple overlapping meanings, depending on context and the position of the observer. First and foremost, it was intended to project the corporation itself as an elected public body representing the town … civic ritual worked to merge the identity of the corporation with the city, so that the city, its trades and institutions, were the subject of simultaneous celebration.[158]

The spectacle of specific processions in the civic environment of the city was not reproduced in the pantomimes; references could be made to such events but to try and reproduce with exactitude what many in the audience had already experienced would have lacked originality and, even with the use of 'lots and lots' of supernumeraries, would have been unable to reflect a fraction of the crowds at the original event. At Manchester, for example, the opening of the New Town Hall in 1877 was marked by a trade procession of some 40,000 local people, and the agreement to start the Ship Canal project in 1885 was celebrated by a similarly large procession. The former occasion included

> Filesmiths, boilermakers, lath cleavers, plasterers, meat cutters, power loom overlookers, fine and coarse cotton spinners, beamers, twisters and drawers.… Many of the workers' organisations marched in time to their own bands. The glass cutters were armed with glass swords while several carried a huge glass cask filled with beer. The printers carried a large banner with the motto 'Let there be light'. The umbrella makers carried a banner with the motto 'Self Protection' as well as a gigantic sample of their work made from the finest gingham. The tailors were dressed stylishly and had flowers in their buttonholes. The bakers carried a loaf of bread weighing 164 pounds …[159]

Reality outshone the pantomimes and there was no attempt to emulate the civic processions in the pantomimes of those particular years; instead parades featured the British army and a history of dress. Further, it may have been considered impolitic to risk any sense of disruption of the demarcated and political ordering of local parades by trying to present them on stage. However, there were occasions in the Birmingham pantomimes when the celebration of trade with inferences of civic (and political) authority could be effected.

Birmingham trade and civic status

In the 1865 pantomime *Little Bo Peep* at the Prince of Wales Theatre, the hero of the story, 'Bois Bleu', was initially a miner. The theme of mining provided a framework only and was not maintained for the whole pantomime story, but in the opening and concluding scenes tributes were paid to this crucial regional industry. In the first scene, the 'Iron King' praised 'Bois Bleu':

> And you shall see Aston's true heir Bois Bleu,
> Toiling on bravely as our miners do,

Far from the light of day, carving the name
Dear Birmingham upon the scroll of fame.

A symbolic tableau was then revealed of 'THE WORKERS IN THE CRIMSON MINES'. At the conclusion of the pantomime the Fairy Queen rewarded Bois Bleu:

and I have contrived
That Bois Bleu shall be aided by the town
Of Birmingham, his happiness to crown.
See now where comes his army –
I declare
An army made of Birmingham hardware![160]

The stage was then filled with a 'PERSONATION ARMY OF BIRMINGHAM WARE'. The two scenes managed to reflect, perhaps not very deftly, the interdependence of the Birmingham metalwork trades and the mining industry of the Black Country. It was the only example of such a procession at the Prince of Wales Theatre; regional trade processions were used to greater and more symbolic effect at the Theatre Royal.

The Theatre Royal at Birmingham had a reputation for scenic spectacle; large and 'heavy' sets, and mechanical effects reflected certain national developments and influences in the genre whilst asserting the status of the theatre and, by implication, the town. In particular, the incorporation of elaborate processions was adopted and adapted in the pantomimes to symbolically express the economic power of Birmingham. The town's reputation as the 'Workshop of the World' was a contemporaneous, not historically retrospective appellation (as was Manchester's identity as 'Cottonopolis'). The wide range of finished metalware products in Birmingham created greater possibilities for the staged spectacle of numerous and individual objects. In 1879, the entire first scene of *The Fair One with the Golden Locks* depicted Birmingham as 'Workshop of the World', with supers dressed in pasteboard versions of local products. The *Birmingham Daily Gazette* previewed the parade which consisted of 'a teapot, pins, pans, cannon, gun, bell, needles, buttons, bayonet, and coins'.[161] The *Birmingham Daily Mail* expanded the description: 'great imitations of … almost every article of Birmingham manufacture are brought on by active youngsters, who must be well nigh smothered in their pasteboard prisons'.[162]

In the 1887 pantomime *Little Goody Two Shoes*, the micro-economic successes of the town were epitomised by the presentation of a coin press in 'King Gold's Mint'. The coin press featured in the production was a stage property, but it warranted particular attention from the local newspapers as it had evidently 'been suggested by a visit to Messrs. Ralph Heaton & Son's famous local establishment' and was 'an exact facsimile of one of Mr. Heaton's Presses'.[163] On a larger scale, in the 1884 production of *Dick Whittington and His Cat*, the Lord Mayor's celebrations included a 'GRAND PROCESSION OF KNIGHTS Bearing the Arms of the various Towns of the Midlands and Workmen with the Emblems of their Manufactures'.[164] The *Birmingham Daily Gazette* described this scene:

> A grand procession of knights takes place, each knight bearing a banner on which are the arms of some town in the Midlands and accompanied by a juvenile representing the workmen of the town, and carrying emblems of the local manufacture. Among the towns thus represented are Wolverhampton, Walsall, Willenhall, Leamington, Coventry (with a tricycle as an emblem), Droitwich (with a square of salt), Worcester (a bottle of sauce), Redditch (with a huge needle), Dudley, Tipton, Northampton, Tamworth, Burton-on-Trent (with a barrel of beer), Derby, Gloucester, Nottingham, Stafford (with a pair of boots), Kidderminster, Shrewsbury, Crewe, Rugby, Stratford-on-Avon (with a Shakespeare bust), Hereford, Birmingham, Sheffield (knife and fork), &c. The idea is very good and well carried out.[165]

The procession celebrated the whole of the Midlands, but it was significant that the celebration took place at the Birmingham theatre. That theatre by implication had the resources and was representative, as the Theatre Royal, of the regional capital. Furthermore, the procession was celebrated in 'London' but the national capital was a static setting for regional spectacle, underlined by the inclusion of 'a highly successful parody on the well-known song of "Old England," the chorus beginning with the words, "Honour old Brum"'.[166] Birmingham was here celebrated as a metropolis, drawing the other towns beneath its spectacular wing. In 1888, another version of *Dick Whittington* also culminated in a magnificent scene, this time set in 'London in the Olden Times', in which a 'Procession of Emblems of the Industries of the Midlands' celebrated Birmingham's newly acquired status as a city.[167] The *Birmingham Daily Gazette* expanded on this, its description appropriately noting 'the modern Midlands' and the shift in representative trades:

> Here takes place a grand procession of beefeaters, knights, and trumpeters, and an emblematic processional tableaux of all the trades of the modern Midlands. A series of banners bearing the names of the different towns are brought on one after the other, in each case followed by a model representing the trade of the town introduced. Burton, for instance, is symbolised by a huge barrel, Coventry by a watch, Banbury by a cake, Redditch by a case of needles, the Potteries by a teapot, Cradley by an anvil, Crewe by a locomotive, and Northampton by a boot.[168]

In Chapter 2 I discussed the concept of spectacle and the way in which the production processes of the Birmingham pantomimes were celebrated in local newspaper articles. In performance, although all of the above items were stage props, their relationship to actual production (whether by linking products to towns or reproducing a coin mint with exactitude) again extends the idea of spectacle and the commodity. As I mentioned in Chapter 2, in his discussion of products at the Great Exhibition, Thomas Richards has identified that the status of the commodity as spectacle is one that is necessarily divorced from production[169] but his theory is overturned in evidence from the Birmingham pantomimes, in which the very celebration and admiration of the commodity depended upon its correlation with labour: the coin press, for example, was set in motion, albeit pantomimically, to produce 'coins' as part of the action of the first scene.

The regional trade processions at the Birmingham Theatre Royal were symbolic of the importance of both the town and the theatre. The variety of industries in the Midlands enabled such a display, but theatres in Nottingham did not try to emulate such motifs and only one example occurred at Manchester. Nottingham arguably lacked the national impact of Birmingham economically and politically, but the relative lack of Manchester- and Lancashire-related processions seems a strange omission. In the 1881 pantomime at the Manchester Theatre Royal, the promoted 'Hive of Industry' spilled forth children dressed, for example, as bricklayers, shoemakers and bakers. The advertisements for the feature introduced it with 'Hurrah for the loom and the lathe / Hurrah for the spade and the plough'.[170] The range of items suggests urban as well as rural workers and the first reference to the loom is specifically representative of Manchester and Lancashire trade, but there is no other evidence that particularly localised references were made, in terms of banners or spoken lines, in the same way that they were at Birmingham. Similarly, in the 1893 pantomime of *Babes in the Wood* at the Manchester Theatre Royal, Scene 11 was set in a London street and presented an elaborate trade procession. The trades, however, were generic, such as butchers, fishmongers and tallow chandlers, and the accompanying banners were instead international flags. The procession was certainly a show-stopping spectacle as the variously costumed representatives paraded down a large central staircase, but it bore no immediate relevance to Manchester. The pantomime *Dick Whittington* was regularly produced at the Theatre Royal in Birmingham, where the final scene of the Lord Mayor's procession provided an ideal opportunity to promote both the economic and the political power of the town (discussed in Chapter 4). However, this potential was only once realised at Manchester, where the staged event tended to draw instead on the traditions of the original London parade, national contexts and, again, generic trades, (for example, at the Theatre Royal in 1870 and 1885 and the Comedy Theatre in 1888). In 1889, the Theatre Royal in Manchester did present a regional trade procession during the final scene of *Dick Whittington*. In that year, the municipal borough had become a county borough, as part of the creation of county councils in England. The new distinction gave the city greater autonomy in the running of its affairs and, in the pantomime, a distinctive display of the 'Procession of the Trades of Lancashire and Yorkshire', staged prior to the London-related elements of the Lord Mayor's Procession, prioritised (as at Birmingham) local achievements over the heritage of the metropolis.

The Manchester Ship Canal

In the late nineteenth century, the most significant development for local trade was undoubtedly the building of the Ship Canal. It was proposed in order 'to lower the costs of transporting goods between [Manchester] and Liverpool, which was in effect Manchester's harbour' and thereby to counteract the threats of foreign competition instigated by free trade policies.[171] Initially opposed in London and Liverpool, it took many years for the project to become a reality and succeeded largely due to the initiating actions of local engineer and entrepreneur Daniel Adamson. Parliament passed the Canal Act in August 1885 and eventually the Ship Canal was opened on 1 January 1894.[172]

The planning, financing, building and completion of the canal were monitored closely by pantomime authors at all the city's theatres; the project was talked about, illustrated on scenery and even partially reproduced in stage properties each Christmas. Pantomime barons and merchants all had access to ships, and heroes travelled to distant lands in a range of spectacular stage-property ships. Whether stationary in port, effectively shipwrecked, sailing across or downstage or seen in perspective, property ships provided both stage spectacle and, in their journeys and symbolic distance, an opportunity for characters to objectively view places and events. The motif of ships and journeys was embraced by pantomime writers and performers in the 1880s and early 1890s as an obvious opportunity to comment on Manchester's latest achievement. In the 1882 version of *Beauty and the Beast* at the Queen's Theatre, Sir Gooseberry received news that his last ship had been sunk in Salford Bay. The characters chartered a tug to rescue the cargo, 'travelling' via Stalybridge, Salford and Flixton. The journey provided sufficient excuse to mention the Ship Canal, but as the *Manchester Weekly Times* suggested, 'the author's geographical ideas of the ship canal and certain bays [were] a little complicated'.[173] The reviewer made allowance for the necessity of imagination in pantomime on this occasion, but as the actual project progressed, the pantomime writers and producers charted it more accurately. In that same year (1882), the Theatre Royal had aimed at a more realistic demonstration, and a drop scene showed a practical 'map of the district through which it is proposed to carry the Ship Canal, with the canal itself'.

The concept of the canal had been discussed for many years, but the influential initial meeting between Adamson and prominent local men had only taken place in 1882. The pantomime responses were therefore very quick and did not fail to take account of the political issues involved: in this pantomime the Demon King 'Obstruction' was opposed by the Fairy Enterprise, who sent the hero in his ship to the 'port of Manchester *via* the Ship Canal'. The *Guardian* added that 'it is perhaps significant that the party did not reach their destination'.[174] Whilst this comment no doubt referred to the fact that the project had yet to be undertaken and completed, the character reference to obstruction was pointed: the railway companies and the Port of Liverpool authorities were opposed to the canal scheme and delayed the parliamentary process for two years, from 1883 to 1885. The same point was made in the 1884 pantomime at the Queen's Theatre in the following exchanges:

Prince of D.	Haw! Really! When will you be mine sweet gal;
Princess	When Manchester obtains its Ship Canal!
King C.	I think that will be soon
Lubin.	I hope it will
	It's cost some brass to try and pass the bill
Prince of C.	Talk of obstruction (*sarcastically*) Oh Yes! what a pity!
Queen.	The true obstructive's a Select Committee.[175]

The Ship Canal was mentioned in the 1883 pantomime at the Theatre Royal, and was applauded by the audience, as it also was at the Queen's Theatre in 1884. However, the pantomime writers and artists were eager to celebrate the completed canal. At the Theatre Royal in 1884, a group of characters set out to the Ship Canal 'where we see a pretty nautical ballet "by the crew of the good ship Adamson"'.[176] And, despite the fact that it would be another ten years before the project was completed, one scene was actually set at the Ship Canal:

Emp.	Oh the canal can I believe my eyes
Hymen	Behold the fruit of noble enterprise
	Our pluck and energy have won the day
	Manchester has her will and water way

Honour to *Adamson* is justly due
Oppressive tariffs are numbered with the past
And Manchester's good time has come at last.[177]

And in the Queen's Theatre pantomime *Babes in the Wood* in 1886 a scaled-down version of the Ship Canal was represented by a long water tank set horizontally across the stage, populated by swans, canoes and pleasure boats, with the opportune and perhaps inevitable comic moment of a tumble into the water.[178] The Prince's Theatre pantomime *Blue Beard* in 1887 included a Ship Canal song which showed 'an intimate knowledge of Manchester topography'.[179] In 1891 it was referenced at the Comedy Theatre, and there were numerous references in the Queen's pantomime of 1893. The *Manchester Weekly Times* printed a sample chorus from one of the production songs at the Queen's, which celebrated the completed project:

Cheer, boys, cheer, for in spite of long delay,
There's water all the way from Salford to the Say;
Cheer, boys, cheer, for our grand new waterway,
Good old Manchester has won the day.[180]

Although the pantomime comments were generally celebratory, the Ship Canal project also highlighted regional rivalries between Manchester and Liverpool, especially following the attempts to block the project in its early stages. These were initially highlighted in the schoolroom scene of *Cinderella* in 1893 at the Prince's Theatre: 'Dame. Where is Liverpool? / A. Liverpool is a deserted seaport near the Ship Canal.'[181] At the Theatre Royal, characters continued the theme:

Sir M.   That great work has now been accomplished,
    Despite what all the envious croakers said.
Ted.   Then Manchester's a seaport now.
Sir M.   That's right
    Of Liverpool she's independent, quite.[182]

The antagonistic attitude to Liverpool was more explicit the following year. In *Little Red Riding Hood* at the Prince's Theatre the traditional fairy scene

159

was set in Thirlmeria, ruled by the Queen of Lakeland. Her attendants included Canalmia, Hydraulica, and Electricia, signifying 'the spirit and enterprise of Manchester', and they were opposed by Jealoustina, Enviesta and Malicia, 'three bad fairies who hail from Liverpool, who, after abusing the Thirlmere Works and the Ship Canal, confess that they are jealous because they "haven't the pluck to do the same"'.[183]

Conclusion

The range and style of references in provincial pantomimes reflected the changing world of provincial life and the immediate concerns of audiences. In turn, the subtle differences of approach and emphasis reflected the trusted work of specific authors engaged by the various theatre managements, and established the role of the local writer as a crucial part of the production of successful pantomimes. At the Prince of Wales Theatre in Birmingham, the local businessman and writer John Anderton was engaged to write the pantomimes from 1887 to the end of the century. In his work he was sensible of the preferences of local audiences and the nuances of local matters but he could also demonstrate a keen understanding of the changing requirements of the genre. He was noted for the way in which his scripts allowed for the later inclusion of 'gag' and improvised business by the performers. The local press applauded the way in which 'he has no difficulty in confining his book within reasonable limits, and so leaving plenty of room for the variety show which gets to be more and more an element of successful pantomime'.[184] In turn, the performers appear to have respected Anderton's scripts. In 1888 they 'displayed little of that vicious disposition to ignore and supplement the book, which is the besetting sin of so many pantomime favourites'.[185] At provincial theatres, pantomime authorship was determined not by convenience but by affiliation and reputation, and their promotion was based on more than a desire by local theatre-goers for recognisable authors. The choice of particular authors drew once again on an acute commercial awareness by the theatre managers of the relevance of localness and status.

Notes

1. Taylor, *British Pantomime Production*, pp. 135–8.
2. The London transpontine theatres also contained a range of local subject matter, reflecting a variety of interest groups in the community. Some of those referenced at the Sadler's Wells Theatre are detailed in Davis and Emeljanow, *Reflecting the Audience*, pp. 120–1.
3. Moody, *Illegitimate Theatre*, p. 171.
4. 'Sadler's Wells', *The Times*, 27 December 1860, p. 7.
5. *Little Red Riding Hood* (1886), book of words, Scene 11, p. 41.
6. 'The Pantomime at the Prince's Theatre', *Manchester Weekly Times*, 22 December 1877, p. 6.
7. 'Queen's Theatre', *Manchester Guardian*, 28 December 1886, p. 8.
8. '"Aladdin" at the Theatre Royal', *Manchester Weekly Times*, 27 December 1884, p. 7.
9. 'New Queen's Theatre "Little Red Riding Hood"', *Manchester Weekly Times*, 28 December 1872, p. 5.
10. 'The Queen's – "Twinkle, Twinkle, Little Star"', *Manchester Weekly Times*, 1 January 1876, p. 7.
11. 'The Queen's Theatre', *Manchester Guardian*, 27 December 1875, p. 8.
12. 'Queen's Theatre', *Manchester Weekly Times*, 22 January 1876, p. 5.
13. 'The Queen's – "Twinkle, Twinkle, Little Star"', *Manchester Weekly Times*, 1 January 1875, p. 7.
14. 'Prince of Wales Theatre. "The Babes in the Wood"', *Birmingham Daily Post*, 27 December 1890, p. 5.
15. NLSL: L79.8: Arthur L. Maddock, *Robinson Crusoe* (1891), book of words, Scene 1, p. 10.
16. J.K. Walton and R. Poole, 'The Lancashire Wakes in the Nineteenth Century', in R.D. Storch (ed.), *Popular Culture and Custom in Nineteenth-Century England* (London and New York, 1982), p. 114.
17. 'Theatre Royal Pantomime', *Manchester Weekly Times*, 30 December 1892, p. 5.
18. '"Aladdin" at the Comedy Theatre', *Manchester Weekly Times*, 29 December 1888, p. 3.
19. 'The Pantomimes: Theatre Royal', *Manchester Weekly Times*, 27 December 1883, p. 7.
20. BCL: L28.1.64589: Charles Millward, *Beauty and the Beast* (1873), book of words, Scene 1, p. 5; L28.1.314833: Charles Millward, *Ride a Cock Horse* (1874), book of words, Scene 4, p. 11; L28.1.64595: Frank Hall and J.J. Blood, *Queen of Hearts* (1883), book of words, Scene 7, p. 18; F/1 243679: J.J. Blood, *Robinson Crusoe* (1885), book of words, character list inside front page, and Scene 9, p. 8.
21. References to Goose Fair in NLSL: L79.8: F.R. Goodyer, *Little Red Riding Hood* (1873), book of words, Scene 6, p. 20; F.R.Goodyer, *Little Bo Peep* (1874), book of words, Scene 2, p. 9; BL: Brit. Mus. Add. Ms. 53197R: F.R. Goodyer and Hain Uthermann, *Blue Beard* (1877), Scene 1, p. 3; Brit. Mus. Add. Ms. 53229D: F.R. Goodyer and Hain Uthermann, *Jack and the Beanstalk* (1879), Scene 5, p. 22. For comments about the curtailment (proposed and actual) of Goose Fair, see Brit. Mus. Add. Ms. 53212R: F.R. Goodyer and Hain Uthermann, *Babes in the Wood* (1878), Scene 8, p. 44; Brit. Mus. Add. Ms. 53229D: F.R. Goodyer and Hain Uthermann, *Jack and the Beanstalk* (1879), Scene 1, p. 5; NLSL: L79.8: F.R. Goodyer, *Little Bo Peep* (1883), book of words, Scene 2, p. 6; and Arthur L. Maddock, *Robinson Crusoe* (1891), book of words, Scene 8, p. 31 (both Goose Fair and the races). For letters regarding temperance and Goose Fair,

see *Nottingham Daily Express*, 17 February 1880, p. 3 and also a letter regarding the race course on 6 January 1881, p. 3.

22. BL: Brit. Mus. Add. Ms. 53229D: F.R. Goodyer and Hain Uthermann, *Jack and the Beanstalk* (1879), Scene 1, p. 5.

23. 'Prince's Theatre', *Manchester Guardian*, 26 December 1872, p. 8.

24. Walton and Poole, 'Lancashire Wakes', p. 100.

25. *Ibid.*, p. 107.

26. *Ibid.*

27. C. Kershaw, 'Dan Leno: New Evidence on Early Influences and Style', *Nineteenth Century Theatre*, 22/1 (1994), p. 50.

28. 'The Pantomime at the Queen's Theatre', *Manchester Guardian*, 4 February 1868, p. 6.

29. 'Sinbad the Sailor at the Royal', *Manchester Weekly Times*, 28 December 1894, p. 3.

30. 'Prince's Theatre', *Manchester Guardian*, 24 December 1864, p. 5.

31. 'The Pantomime at the Queen's Theatre', *Manchester Weekly Times*, 9 January 1869, p. 5.

32. 'Queen's Theatre', *Manchester Guardian*, 27 December 1877, p. 5.

33. '"Sinbad the Sailor" at the Prince's Theatre', *Manchester Weekly Times*, 29 December 1888, p. 3.

34. BL: Brit. Mus. Add. Ms. 264: J. Wilton-Jones, *Little Red Riding Hood* (1883), p. 10r. 'Gradely' = proper or decent.

35. MA: Th792.094273 Ma86: Theatre Royal, Manchester, *Pantomime Books*, vol. i, Thos. Chambers, *The House That Jack Built* (1862), book of words, p. 7 (no scene numbers). 'Rayley' = really; 'wuss' = worse.

36. M. Vicinus, *The Industrial Muse: A Study of Nineteenth Century British Working-class Literature* (London, 1974), p. 185.

37. *Ibid.*, pp. 185, 192.

38. *Ibid.*, pp. 201–2.

39. *Ibid.*, p. 185.

40. *Ibid.*, p. 190.

41. *Ibid.*

42. 'The Pantomime at the Queen's Theatre', *Manchester Guardian*, 26 December 1868, p. 5.

43. 'The Christmas Pantomimes: "Robinson Crusoe" at the Queen's Theatre', *Manchester Guardian*, 26 December 1889, p. 8.

44. 'Prince's Theatre', *Manchester Weekly Times*, 22 December 1866, p. 5.

45. 'Song for the Times', supplement to the *Manchester Weekly Times*, 25 January 1879, p. 27.

46. Booth, *English Plays*, p. 51, n. 1, citing Wagner, *Pantomimes and All About Them*, p. 11. See also Booth, *Victorian Spectacular Theatre*, pp. 75–6.

47. In *English Plays*, Booth addresses the collaborative nature of the production of the pantomime opening, between the 'dramatist, manager, scene painter, machinist, and gasman', whilst at the same time acknowledging the infringement on the author's work (pp. 50–1).

48. *Western Morning News*, 23 December 1868, p. 3.

49. 'Local and General: Renewal of the Theatre License', *Nottingham Journal*, 17 December 1873, p. 3.

50. John Palgrave Simpson of the Dramatic Authors' Society stated that he wanted theatre managers to be legally obliged to list the author's name on playbills ('Report of the Royal Commission on Copyright', p. 122). As J.R. Stephens states in *The Profession of the Playwright: British Theatre 1800–1900* (Cambridge, 1992), p. 100, none of the recommendations of the Committee were carried out.

51. See, for example, NLSL: L79.8: F.R. Goodyer, *Little Red Riding Hood* (1873), book of words; and *Little Bo Peep* (1874), book of words.

52. NLSL: L79.8: F.R. Goodyer, *Cinderella* (1882), book of words, title page.

53. NLSL: L79.8: George Dance, *Aladdin* (1886), book of words, front cover and title page.

54. 'The Pantomime', *Nottingham Daily Guardian*, 24 December 1886, p. 8; and 'Bank Holiday: The Pantomime', *Nottingham Daily Guardian*, 28 December 1886, p. 8. See also 'Music and Drama', *Nottingham Daily Guardian*, 20 December 1886, p. 6.

55. NLSL: L79.8: George Dance, *The Babes in the Wood* (1887), book of words, Scene 4, p. 24.

56. MA: Th792.094273 Ma83 and Ma83/A: Prince's Theatre, Manchester, *Pantomime Books*, vol. i, *Frogee Would A-Wooing Go* (1869), book of words, Scene 5, p. 35.

57. For the founding of the art gallery, see BCL: L28.1.64594: Charles Millward and T.C. Clay, *Beauty and the Beast* (1881), book of words, Scene 2, p. 8. Middlemore's gift is detailed in BCL: L28.1.202317: Charles Millward, *The Forty Thieves* (1877), Scene 1, p. 4. Supporting evidence for the art gallery is in *Showell's Dictionary of Birmingham* (Birmingham, 1885), pp. 10–11.

58. NLSL: L79.8: F.R. Goodyer, *Little Bo Peep* (1874), book of words, Scene 1, pp. 9–10.

59. BL: Brit. Mus. Add. Ms. 53212R: F.R. Goodyer and Hain Uthermann, *Babes in the Wood* (1878), Scene 8, p. 44.

60. For comments on visiting the Castle, see NLSL: L79.8: George Dance, *Sinbad the Sailor* (1889), book of words, Scene 1, p. 9; for Sunday closing of the Art Gallery, see *ibid.*, Scene 1, p. 14; BL: Brit. Mus. Add. Ms. 53212R: F.R. Goodyer and Hain Uthermann, *Babes in the Wood* (1878), Scene 10, p. 65; and NLSL: L79.8: George Dance, *Aladdin* (1886), book of words, Scene 4, p. 30. For comments on the Castle being closed to the public because of it being used by the Corporation, see *Aladdin* (1886), Scene 3, p. 18. See also the letters regarding the Sunday opening of the Museum in *Nottingham Daily Guardian*, 5 January 1880, p. 2 and *Nottingham Daily Express*, 29 December 1879, p. 2.

61. NLSL: L79.8: George Dance, *Babes in the Wood* (1887), book of words, Scene 2, p. 12, and references also in Scene 4, p. 23.

62. *Babes in the Wood* (1887), book of words, Scene 4, p. 23.

63. BL: Brit. Mus. Add. Ms. 53465E: John Anderton, *The Babes in the Wood* (1890), book of words, Scene 2, p. 9.

64. *Babes in the Wood* (1868), book of words, Scene 7, p. 33. The additional lines are reported in *Nottingham and Midland Counties Daily Express*, 23 January 1869, p. 2.

65. NLSL: L79.8: George Dance, *Babes in the Wood* (1887), book of words, Scene 8, p. 38, see also Scene 3, p. 16. Also NLSL: L79.8: George Dance, *Aladdin* (1886), book of words, Scene 2, p. 12, and Arthur L. Maddock, *Robinson Crusoe* (1891), book of words, Scene 12, p. 47. There are two copies (an extant book of words and a photocopy of a separate book of words) of *Babes in the Wood*, and in general both copies match in terms of referencing. However, these speeches regarding the university only appear in the photocopied version, hence one of the copies must have been a reprint for an altered performance later in the run. It is more likely that the excised copy is the later print, reflecting a revised and perhaps shorter performance. For supplementary evidence regarding the university, see a letter on the state of the building in *Nottingham Daily Express*, 26 December 1882, p. 2.

66. NLSL: L79.8: George Dance, *Babes in the Wood* (1887), book of words, Scene 4, p. 22. As mentioned above, there are two versions of this book of words in the collection, one of which does not contain the section with the question and answer session; similarly, they are not included in the version sent to the Examiner of Plays.

These lines are hardly scurrilous so presumably this version of the book of words simply presents another example of a reprinted book of words produced later in the pantomime run.

67. References in BL: Brit. Mus. Add. Ms. 53212R: F.R. Goodyer and Hain Uthermann, *Babes in the Wood* (1878), verse 15 of a topical song in Scene 4, p. 31; NLSL: L79.8: George Dance, *Aladdin* (1886), book of words, Scene 3, p. 18; *Babes in the Wood* (1887), book of words, Scene 4, p. 24, and *Sinbad the Sailor* (1889), book of words, Scene 10, p. 44.

68. BCL: L28.1.69240: F.W. Green, *Sinbad the Sailor* (1882), book of words, Scene 4, p. 12. Details of the statue are in *Showell's Dictionary*, p. 292. Dawson was a leading figure in the local council; see C. Upton, *A History of Birmingham* (Chichester, 1993), p. 149. For criticism and lampooning of statuary in the Birmingham pantomimes, see BCL: L28.1.64594: Charles Millward and T.C. Clay, *Beauty and the Beast* (1881), book of words, Scene 6, p. 16; and L28.1.64595: Frank Hall and J.J. Blood, *The Queen of Hearts* (1883), book of words, Scene 1, p. 3.

69. 'The Christmas Pantomimes: "Cinderella" at the Comedy', *Manchester Guardian*, 21 December 1895, p. 8.

70. *Cinderella* (1889), book of words, Brit. Mus. Add. Ms. 53443E, Scene 8, p. 28. Harrison's concert seasons were held in the spring and autumn and ran from 1853 until 1916.

71. BCL: L28.1.243338: J.J. Blood, *Whittington and his Cat* (1888), book of words, Scene 4, p. 12.

72. See also praise for Black in BCL: L28.1.64595: Frank Hall and J.J. Blood, *The Queen of Hearts* (1883), book of words, Scene 1, p. 3; and for Farndale in L28.1.92007: J.J. Blood, *Dick Whittington* (1884), book of words, Scene 10, p. 30. Supporting evidence regarding Black and Farndale is in *Showell's Dictionary*, p. 168.

73. NLSL: L79.8: George Dance, *Aladdin* (1886), book of words, Scene 4, p. 22. See reports on the 1886 election riots in *Nottingham Daily Guardian*, 15 February 1886, p. 6, and 17 February 1886, p. 6.

74. NLSL: L79.8: F.R. Goodyer, *Little Bo Peep* (1874), book of words, Scene 3, p. 15.

75. For the Murphy Riots, see BCL: L28.1.243337: Charles Millward, *Robinson Crusoe* (1867), book of words, Scene 1, pp. 4–5; and for the Aston Riots, L28.1.92007: J.J. Blood, *Dick Whittington* (1884), book of words, Scene 1, p. 3. The latter took place at Aston Lower Grounds on 13 October 1884. According to *Showell's Dictionary*, the Liberals 'breached the walls, spoilt the fireworks' (p. 272), which echoes the lines in the pantomime.

76. See, for example, BL: Brit. Mus. Add. Ms. 53197R: F.R. Goodyer and Hain Uthermann, *Blue Beard* (1877), in verse 3 of a topical song in Scene 7, p. 46; NLSL: L79.8: George Dance, *Aladdin* (1886), book of words, Scene 3, p. 18, and Scene 6, p. 30; *Babes in the Wood* (1887), book of words, Scene 4, p. 22; *Sinbad the Sailor* (1889), book of words, Scene 4, p. 21; and Arthur L. Maddock, *Robinson Crusoe* (1891), book of words, Scene 3, p. 17.

77. NLSL: L79.8: George Dance, *Aladdin* (1886), book of words, Scene 6, p. 27.

78. NLSL: L79.8: George Dance, *Sinbad the Sailor* (1889), book of words, Scene 4, p. 21.

79. '"Cinderella" – Queen's Theatre', *Manchester Guardian*, 4 January 1872, p. 6.

80. *Ibid.*

81. *Ibid.*

82. 'Prince's Theatre – The Christmas Pantomime', *Manchester Weekly Times*, 2 January 1875, p. 5.

83. J.M. Golby and A.W. Purdue, *The Civilisation of the Crowd: Popular Culture 1750–1900*, 2nd edn (Stroud, 1999), p. 71.

84. Moody, *Illegitimate Theatre*, pp. 106–8.
85. M. Bakhtin, *Rabelais and His World*, trans. H. Iswolsky (Cambridge, MA, 1968), p. 7, cited in G.S. Morson and C. Emerson, *Bakhtin: Creation of a Prosaics* (Stanford, CA, 1990), p. 92.
86. Kidd, *Manchester*, pp. 127, 155.
87. 'Prince's Theatre', *Manchester Guardian*, 24 December 1878, p. 5.
88. The historical details for this discussion have been drawn from G. Sutherland, *Elementary Education in the Nineteenth Century* (London, 1971), E. Hopkins, *Childhood Transformed: Working-Class Children in Nineteenth-Century England* (Manchester, 1994); D. Wardle, *Education and Society in Nineteenth-Century Nottingham* (London, 1971); and G.R. Galbraith, *Reading Lives: Reconstructing Childhood, Books, and Schools in Britain 1870–1920* (New York, 1997).
89. Sutherland, *Elementary Education*, p. 28.
90. *Babes in the Wood* (1868), book of words, Scene 3, p. 7.
91. Wardle, *Education and Society*, p. 82. Historian Roy Church claims that the first Board school was not built until 1874 (*Economic and Social Change*, pp. 317, 357), but evidence from Wardle as well as evidence from the pantomime texts suggests that Board schools were already up and running by that date.
92. NLSL: RL79.8: Loose collection of playbills: playbill dated 26 December 1873.
93. NLSL: L79.8: F.R. Goodyer, *Little Red Riding Hood* (1873), book of words, Scene 3, p. 10.
94. Sutherland, *Elementary Education*, pp. 33–4.
95. This instigated a mixed provision: 'there were areas with no boards and no by-laws; areas with boards but without by-laws; areas with boards and by-laws, but also considerable variety in the standards set for exemption' (*Ibid.*, p. 34).
96. *Ibid.*, p. 34, although Hopkins states twelve 'with exceptions (full or part time) from the age of ten, dependent on the child's educational attainment' (*Childhood Transformed*, p. 235).
97. Meller (ed.), *Nottingham in the Eighteen Eighties*, p. 38.
98. Wardle, *Education and Society*, p. 89.
99. 'The Pantomime', *Nottingham Daily Guardian*, 28 December 1874, p. 3.
100. NLSL: L79.8: F.R. Goodyer, *Little Bo Peep* (1874), book of words, Scene 9, p. 29.
101. Hopkins, *Childhood Transformed*, pp. 238–9.
102. BL: Brit. Mus. Add. Ms. 53197R: F.R. Goodyer and Hain Uthermann, *Blue Beard* (1877), Scene 5, p. 34.
103. Hopkins, *Childhood Transformed*, p. 239.
104. *Ibid.*, p. 237.
105. *Ibid.* The Poor Law Guardians had taken over this aspect of administration from the School Boards as a result of the 1876 Act.
106. Sutherland, *Elementary Education*, pp. 39–40.
107. NLSL: L79.8: F.R. Goodyer, *Little Bo Peep* (1883), book of words, Scene 3, p. 15.
108. *Ibid.*, Scene 3, p. 16.
109. *Little Bo Peep* (1884), book of words pasted within F.R. Goodyer, *Odds and Ends* (unpublished) NLSL: L80.2 GOO D1.
110. Wardle, *Education and Society*, p. 87. Sutherland states that the Boards had the authority to draw on the local rates for the money to provide schools, but that they could also be financed by grants and fees paid by the families of those children who attended (*Elementary Education*, pp. 28–9).
111. Wardle, *Education and Society*, p. 87.
112. NLSL: L79.8: George Dance, *Babes in the Wood* (1887), book of words, Scene 2, p. 15.

113. BCL: L28.1.64584: Charles Millward, *Aladdin* (1866), book of words, Scene 5, p. 14.

114. BCL: L28.1.64585: Charles Millward, *Blue Beard* (1869), book of words, Scene 7, p. 20.

115. *Ibid.*, Scene 9, p. 22.

116. Previewed in 'The Birmingham Pantomimes: Theatre Royal', *Birmingham Daily Post*, 22 December 1873, p. 8.

117. NLSL: L79.8: F.R. Goodyer, *The Forty Thieves* (1884), book of words, Scene 5, p. 17.

118. J.S. Hurt, *Elementary Schooling and the Working Classes 1860–1918* (London and Buffalo, 1979), p. 106. For an earlier expression of concern regarding cramming, see J. Morley, 'The Struggle for National Education', *The Fortnightly Review*, New Series 14 (July–December 1873). His argument is printed in three parts, and the issue of standards and cramming occurs in Part III, pp. 411–33.

119. BCL: L28.1.64595: Frank Hall and J.J. Blood, *The Queen of Hearts* (1883), book of words, Scene 1, p. 3.

120. BCL: F/1 243679: J.J. Blood, *Robinson Crusoe* (1885), book of words, Scene 3, p. 3.

121. Galbraith, *Reading Lives*. For her discussion of exercise in schools, see pp. 94–6, and Chapter 7, 'Overpressure in London's Board Schools, 1883–1884', for a full discussion of the health issues that concerned the authorities in London.

122. BL: Brit. Mus. Add. Ms. 53587: John Anderton, *Little Goody Two Shoes* (1895), Scene 6 (no page numbers).

123. MA: Th792.094273 Ma86: Theatre Royal, Manchester, *Pantomime Books*, vol. i, Thos. Chambers, *Cinderella* (1860), book of words, Scene 1, p. 4.

124. MA: Th792.094273 Ma86: Theatre Royal, Manchester, *Pantomime Books*, vol. i, Thos. Chambers, *Beauty and the Beast* (1861), book of words, Scene 1, p. 5.

125. G. Saintsbury, *Manchester* (London, 1887), pp. 183–4.

126. 'Christmas Pantomimes: The Theatre Royal', *Manchester Guardian*, 20 December 1862, p. 2.

127. MA: Th792.094273 Ma86: Theatre Royal, Manchester, *Pantomime Books*, vol. i, Thos. Chambers, *The House That Jack Built* (1862), book of words, Scene 1, p. 3.

128. Saintsbury, *Manchester*, p. 184.

129. 'The Pantomimes: "Sleeping Beauty"', *Manchester Guardian*, 26 December 1863, p. 5.

130. MA: Th792.094273 Ma83 and Ma83/A: Prince's Theatre, Manchester, *Pantomime Books*, vol. i, Pyngle Lane, *Mother Goose; or, Ye Queene of Heartes that Made ye Tartes, and ye Knave of Heartes who Ate 'em* (1864), book of words, p. 11 (no scene divisions).

131. MA: Th792.094273 Ma80: Queen's Theatre, Spring Gardens, *Pantomime Books*, *Whittington and His Cat* (1865), book of words, Scene 1, p. 4.

132. 'The Christmas Pantomimes: "Blue Beard" at the Theatre Royal', *Manchester Weekly Times*, 24 December 1880, p. 6.

133. 'Prince's Theatre', *Manchester Guardian*, 19 December 1881, p. 5.

134. 'Prince's Theatre: "Robin Hood"', *Manchester Guardian*, 27 December 1882, p. 5.

135. 'Queen's Theatre', *Manchester Weekly Times*, 23 December 1882, p. 7.

136. Cattle Plague in NLSL: L79.8: *Aladdin* (1866), book of words, Scene 2, p. 9. See also the issue of the poverty of farm workers in F.R. Goodyer, *Little Bo Peep* (1883), book of words, Scene 2, p. 9 and Scene 13, p. 44, and in BL: Brit. Mus. Add. Ms. 53229D: F.R. Goodyer and Hain Uthermann, *Jack and the Beanstalk* (1879), Scene 2, p. 8.

137. BL: Brit. Mus. Add. Ms. 53229D: F.R. Goodyer and Hain Uthermann, *Jack and the Beanstalk* (1879), Scene 2, p. 8.

138. *Babes in the Wood* (1868), book of words, Scene 2, p. 9 and Scene 4, p. 21.

139. 'The Grand Comic, Christmas Pantomime', *Nottingham and Midland Counties Daily Express*, 27 December 1867, p. 3. It is also quoted in R. Benyon (ed.), *The Theatre Royal Nottingham 1865–1978: A Theatrical and Architectural History* (Nottingham, n.d.), p. 8.

140. NLSL: L79.8: George Dance, *Aladdin* (1886), book of words, Scene 3, p. 19. Comments about competition from Germany and Long Eaton also feature in *Sinbad the Sailor* (1889), book of words, Scene 6, p. 26, and *Babes in the Wood* (1887), book of words, Scene 4, p. 23. For further evidence of the issue of trade competition, see letters regarding free trade in the *Nottingham Daily Guardian*, 21 December 1887, p. 3, 22 December 1887, p. 6, 24 December 1887, p. 8, and 27 December 1887, p. 6.

141. NLSL: L79.8: George Dance, *Babes in the Wood* (1887), book of words, Scene 4, p. 23.

142. NLSL: L79.8: George Dance, *Sinbad the Sailor* (1889), book of words, Scene 6, p. 26.

143. '"Sinbad the Sailor" at the Prince's Theatre', *Manchester Weekly Times*, 29 December 1888, p. 3.

144. 'The Christmas Pantomimes', *Manchester Guardian*, 23 December 1887, p. 5.

145. BCL: L28.1.98582: Charles Millward, *Robinson Crusoe* (1878), book of words, Scene 3, p. 9; and F/1 243679: J.J. Blood, *Robinson Crusoe* (1885), book of words, Scene 2, p. 3.

146. Reference to the nail-makers and foreign competition in BCL: L28.1.125961: J.J. Blood, *Goody Two Shoes* (1887), book of words, Scene 2, pp. 5, 7, and to the bedstead-makers in L28.1.243339: J.J. Blood, *Aladdin* (1889), book of words, Scene 4, p. 16. See also references to foreign competition in L28.1.243340: Geoffrey Thorn, *Sinbad the Sailor* (1891), book of words, Scene 2, p. 5.

147. NLSL: L79.8: F.R. Goodyer, *Little Bo Peep* (1883), book of words, Scene 2, p. 9.

148. *Ibid.*, Scene 13, p. 44.

149. *Ibid.*, Scene 14, p. 45.

150. *Babes in the Wood* (1868), book of words, Scene 7, p. 32.

151. 'The Fortunes of Nigel at Drury Lane', *Spectator*, 3 October 1868, p. 1153, cited in Davis and Emeljanow, *Reflecting the Audience*, p. 207.

152. Davis and Emeljanow, *Reflecting the Audience*, p. 225.

153. Gunn, *Public Culture*, p. 163.

154. Saintsbury, *Manchester*, p. 181.

155. Gunn, p. 163, citing D. Cannadine, 'The Transformation of Civic Ritual in Modern Britain: the Colchester Oyster Feast', *Past and Present*, 94 (1982), p. 129.

156. Gunn, *Public Culture*, p. 163.

157. *Ibid.*, p. 165.

158. *Ibid.*, pp. 168–9.

159. G.S. Messinger, *Manchester in the Victorian Age: The Half-known City* (Manchester, 1985), pp. 157–8.

160. BL: Brit. Mus. Add. Ms. 53047: Martin Duttnall, *Little Bo Peep* (1865), book of words, Scene 5, p. 20.

161. 'The Theatre Royal Pantomime', *Birmingham Daily Gazette*, 24 December 1879, p. 5.

162. 'Christmas Amusements: The Theatre Royal', *Birmingham Daily Mail*, 27 December 1879, p. 3.

163. 'The Christmas Amusements: *Goody Two Shoes* at the Theatre Royal', *Birmingham Daily Post*, 24 December 1887, p. 5. Heaton's Mint was in Warstone Lane, Birmingham (*Showell's Dictionary*, p. 314).

164. BCL: L28.1.92007: J.J. Blood, *Dick Whittington* (1884), book of words, Scene 9, p. 29.

165. 'Theatre Royal Pantomime', *Birmingham Daily Gazette*, 27 December 1884, p. 5.

166. 'Theatre Royal', *Birmingham Daily Post*, 27 December 1884, p. 5.

167. BCL: L28.1.243338: J.J. Blood, *Whittington and His Cat* (1888), book of words, Scene 9, p. 29.

168. '*Dick Whittington* at the Theatre Royal', *Birmingham Daily Gazette*, 27 December 1888, p. 5.

169. Richards, *Commodity Culture*, p. 57.

170. 'The Pantomimes: Theatre Royal', *Manchester Guardian*, 19 December 1881, p. 5.

171. Messinger, *Manchester in the Victorian Age*, p. 160.

172. *Ibid.*, pp. 161–5; and additional information on Adamson and the project in *Oxford Dictionary of National Biography*, vol. i, pp. 282–3.

173. 'Queen's Theatre', *Manchester Weekly Times*, 23 December 1882, p. 7.

174. 'The Christmas Pantomimes: Theatre Royal', *Manchester Guardian*, 18 December 1882, p. 8.

175. BL: Brit. Mus. Add. Ms. [1884]: J. Wilton-Jones, *The Queen of Hearts* (1884), book of words, Scene 8, p. 15.

176. '"Aladdin" at the Theatre Royal', *Manchester Weekly Times*, 27 December 1884, p. 7.

177. BL: Brit. Mus. Add. Ms. 53329B: T.F. Doyle, *Aladdin* (1884), Scene 14, p. 70.

178. 'The "Babes in the Wood" at the Queen's Theatre', *Manchester Guardian*, 25 January 1887, p. 8.

179. 'Prince's Theatre', *Manchester Guardian*, 23 December 1887, p. 5.

180. 'The Stage', *Manchester Weekly Times*, 22 December 1893, p. 5.

181. Cited in '"Cinderella" at the Prince's', *Manchester Weekly Times*, 29 December 1893, p. 7.

182. MA: Th792.094273 Ma86: Theatre Royal, Manchester, *Pantomime Books*, vol. ii, Fred Locke, *Babes in the Wood* (1893), book of words, Scene 3, p. 35.

183. 'Little Red Riding Hood at the Prince's', *Manchester Weekly Times*, 28 December 1894, p. 3.

184. 'Boxing-Day in Birmingham', *Birmingham Daily Post*, 27 December 1888, p. 5.

185. *Ibid*.

3 Appendix

The topical song

The phrase 'TOPICAL SONG' or 'TOPICAL DUET' could appear in stage directions and books of words, or, very occasionally, 'NEW TOPICAL SONGS' might feature in an advertisement as one of the attractions in a second or revised edition, such as appeared in the *Manchester Weekly Times* in January 1881.[1] From the 1870s, the theatre managements increasingly engaged prominent comedians from the burlesque stage and music hall for the pantomime opening, and the topical song became their domain during the run. Songs such as 'Don't Let It Go Any Further', 'Would You Be Surprised to Hear' and 'In the Time to Come' provided ample opportunity for an immediate response to recent events that was reflected in encore verses being added in performance. A pantomime review in the *Nottingham and Midland Counties Daily Express* in late January 1884 reported that 'Topical allusions are worked up to date, and encores for "Oh, what a fibber that boy must be," and the "Nonsense – Fact I assure you," duet, are plentiful enough.'[2] The Nottingham reviews in particular emphasised the importance and expectation of good topical songs as well as the allusions contained in the scripts. One such song even became the subject of a brief exchange of letters in a Nottingham newspaper, when a member of the audience felt that the song's length fell short of expectation. The letter, signed 'PITTITE', complained that John Chamberlain, the performer, 'delivered two or three verses, and those only after persistent *encores*, and then concluded by singing that he did not know any more. Such remarkable brevity in a topical song is only playing the fool with an audience.' Chamberlain responded the next day, stating that the 'seven verses I sang should surely be considered enough to satisfy even so exacting a person as your correspondent'.[3]

Although these songs and duets were signalled, the content of such songs was only very occasionally printed in full in the book of words, and although the reviews sometimes gave an example of a verse or two it is often assumed that these songs were not written down or published. However, there are examples from Nottingham and Manchester of topical songs written by the pantomime authors. Naturally, they may not have been performed and would have been subject to considerable alterations during the run, but these examples offer another insight into the possibilities of pantomime referencing. The sample verses below are from a manuscript copy of the 1877 production of *Blue Beard* by Goodyer and Uthermann for the Theatre Royal, Nottingham, although it would of course have been added to during the run. It was sung by the eponymous character in Scene 7.

'When the World Turned Upside Down'

2.

We'd never have any bribery, elections would be pure,
We'd ne'er have any taxes, nor troubles to endure.
There'd ne'er be any lawyers, or bailiffs in the town
There'd be some most peculiar things when the world &c.
　　When the world &c
　　When the world &c
　　They'd whitewash the roof of the Market place
　　When the world &c

3.

The Castle would be altered in a proper sort of way
The Trent would run with new milk and honey every day
And Narrow Marsh would be the finest place in the town
And Millstone Lane a paradise when the world turned &c
　　When the world &c
　　When the world &c
　　There'd be a Clifton Statue
　　When the world &c

4.

To Sylverton's large Chapel our betting men would flock
Inside the Council Chamber they would put a new Clock
A pound of Mutton Chops would cost less than half a crown
And 'Bung' would stop the Beer tap when the world &c
    When the world &c
    When the world &c
    Then Annibal would turn Good Templar
    When the world &c

5.

About a new Stipendiary there'd ne'er be a stir
They'd make a Lord Chief Justice of Mr Petti – fer
And Goldsmith he would be a king and wear a splendid crown,
And Bentley'd be a bishop when the world turned upside down
    When the world &c
    When the world &c
    They'd finish the building of Smith's bank
    When the world &c

6.

The mayor would dance the Can-Can and Gilpin do a fling
While Billy Nicholl loudly The hundredth Psalm would sing
And Robinson would never give away five hundred pounds
And Mundella would be in the House of Lords, when &c
    When the world &c
    When the world &c
    When the world &c
    Then Trevitt would be an alderman
    When the world &c

7.

All Yeomanry reviews would take place in the rain
Saull Isaac would be member for Nottingham again,
Mark Meller's long orations would be at once put down
And Jolly Death would be Town Clerk when the world &c

When the world &c
When the world &c
David Heath would be in Parliament
When the world &c

8.

Walter Gregory in the market every Sunday night would
preach
And Thackeray would never try and make another speech
While dear old Captain White, I'll bet you fifty pound,
You'd find no change in him at all when the world &c
    When the world &c
    When the world &c
    Then Foster would take in Figaro
    When the world &c

9.

We'd ne'er have any debtors who their creditors would do
We'd ne'er have appreciative audience like you
We'd never have a singer of such wonderful renown
As I, who thank you one and all – when the world &c
    When the world &c
    When the world &c
    I'd pr'aps be able to sing you some more
    When the world &c[4]

The following year, a song whose title had been used for topical songs up and down the country, 'When Trade's So Bad', was written for Nottingham audiences. Once again surviving in manuscript form, it was written by F.R. Goodyer, although the manuscript displays evidence of two different hands for the main script as well as for this song. The song as written runs to fifteen verses and, in the original, covers a range of topics from local poverty and illness to international policy and back again to local issues of the council and marketplace preachers. The second line of each verse is the refrain of 'Can you wonder when trade's so bad':

Just now through the land this is the great cry …
And people exclaim with a groan and a sigh …
Our dear friend the butcher and also the baker,
The lawyer, the doctor, the candlestick maker,
Are grumbling, and so is the poor undertaker …
At York Street's the place where economy's killed …
They're trying their best a new workhouse to build …
It's not the poor want it, no that's all a sell,
But it's nice for the architects I've heard tell,
And a job for the lawyers and builders as well …

The weather is one perpetual shower …
And treaties are copied for Tenpence an hour …
There's lock-outs and striking in every quarter,
For the poor workhouse children it seems to be thought a
Treat – just a bun and two buckets of water …

Upon the Trent Bridge there's something has grown …
It's said they are lions all chiselled in stone …
They move us to tears much rather than smiles
To look at 'em, greatly one's temper it riles,
Than lions they're far more like cats on the tiles …

A market place nuisance there's been a long time
                              It's a wonder as trade's so bad
For not being stopped there's no reason or rhyme
                              Unless because …
In the Market on Sundays there's preaching red hot,
I'd like to dispense 'em with powder and shot,
Or bring out the fire engines – and *douse* all the lot
                              No matter if …

There's some of the Council have been to *Paree*
                              Don't you wonder when …
It wasn't the Great Exhibition to see
                              That's no wonder …

They want to inspect a far different sight
'Twas to see the French streets by electrical light,
And this at a time when money's so tight
Don't you wonder …[5]

The dialect song that Edwin Waugh was asked to write for the Second Edition of the pantomime *Puss in Boots* was, as I discussed in the main section of Chapter 3, not performed, due to its 'plaintive' nature. However, the brief notice of this matter in the *Manchester Weekly Times* included the full text of the song, whose verses included the following:

Good lorjus days, what times are these,
For clemmin' an' for cowd;
For doleful looks, an' wintry nooks,
Where folk are poor an' owd;
For hopeless care an' dark despair,
An' gloomy want o' trust;
For fireless hearths, an' cupboards bare,
An' bitter want o' crust.

   Chorus.
But, bide lads, bide,
For a happier tide;
An' keep yor hearts out o' yor shoon;
Through thick an' thin
We'n ne'er give in
There's a bit o' blue sky up aboon!

There never wur sich mournful cries
O' famine yerd afore;
John Chinaman's bin clemmed to death,
And India's suffered sore;
Yor mills may weel be stonnin' still,
Yor markets weel be slack;
For when folk's nipt for want o' meight,
They'n nought to spare for th' back.

Sich strikes, an' rows, an' breakages
There never yet wur known;
Sich frettin', an' sich chettin', an'
Sich bitter starvin' moan;
These knavish pranks i' trusted banks
Are spreadin' ruin round;
An' every hour, the tradin' ranks
Are crashin' to the ground [...]⁶

The Ben Brierley song, written for the same pantomime, was printed in a booklet accompanying the book of words, the full text of which is as follows:

I'll tell yo' in rhyme
Of a very quare time
This owd England of eaur's i'th' year seventy-eight,
For what we're o' gone through
An' what we're goin' on to,
Is enough to make ony mon strip him to fight.
We've pinin' an' clemmin',
As if ther's a famine,
When at th' same time there's plenty o' things I'th' land;
An' th' fratchin an' th' bother,
O'er this thing an' th' tother,
Is moore than onyone's patience con stond [...]

There's Gladstone and Dizzy,
At fratchin' keep busy –
It bother me which o' these two is to blame,
They're like two owd snickets,
A playin' at wickets –
One in, an' one fieldin' – that's their little game,
But I'll tell Queen Vic-tory,
If hoo cares for her glory –
An' we know of a *good* name hoo's preciously fond –
Hoo should send Ab – o'th – Yate

To be th' yead man o' th' State,
Then that would be summat one's patience could stond.[7]

Notes

1. Featured in an advertisement, *Manchester Weekly Times*, 1 January 1881, p. 1. I have only found one example of a topical song – entitled 'In 1901' – being the sole focus of an advertisement. It appeared in the *Nottingham and Midland Counties Daily Express*, 13 February 1882, p. 2, repeated in the *Nottingham Daily Express*, 14 February 1882, p. 1.

2. 'Local Amusements: Theatre Royal', *Nottingham and Midland Counties Daily Express*, 29 January 1884, p. 7.

3. *Nottingham Journal*, 12 February 1879, p. 3, and 13 February, p. 2.

4. 'When the World Turned Upside Down', reproduced courtesy of the British Library, from BL: Brit. Mus. Add. Ms. 53197R: F.R. Goodyer and Hain Uthermann, *Blue Beard* (1877), Scene 7, pp. 46–7. The identifiable references include the following: In verse 3: Nottingham Castle was in the process of being reopened as an art gallery; the Trent was the main river supplying Nottingham and there was an ongoing problem regarding sanitation and pollution of the river; Narrow Marsh and Millstone Lane were two of the poorest slum areas in the town; the statue of Sir Robert Clifton had been commissioned but not yet created – the money for it had been raised by 1879 (source for the Clifton reference: R. Iliffe and W. Baguley, *Victorian Nottingham: A Story in Pictures*, xi, p. 11, citing the *Jackdaw*, 16 May 1879). In verse 4: Sylverton [*sic*] was a Baptist preacher; the Council Chamber Clock, according to other pantomime references at this period, rarely worked correctly. In verse 5: Smith's Bank was in the Market Place in central Nottingham. In verse 6: Billy Nicholl was a converted gambler who preached in the town; John Robinson was a local businessman and philanthropist who provided an annual dinner for the poor; Mundella was an MP, the principal protagonist behind moves for industrial arbitration and the 1880 Education Act; Trevitt was a local lace manufacturer and had been a councillor (source for Trevitt reference: Iliffe and Baguley, xi, p. 10, citing a comment in the *Jackdaw* for 16 May 1879). In verse 7: Jolly Death was a private investigator of 4, Brighton Street, Peas Hill, Nottingham (from placard dated 1879, illustrated in Iliffe and Baguley, xi, p. 35). In verse 8: Captain White of the local volunteers, the Robin Hood Rifles.

5. BL: Brit. Mus. Add. Ms. 53212R: F.R. Goodyer and Hain Uthermann, *Babes in the Wood* (1878), Scene 4, pp. 27–31. Song reproduced by permission of the British Library.

6. 'Song for the Times', supplement to the *Manchester Weekly Times*, 25 January 1879, p. 27. 'Lorjus' = Lord Jesus; 'clemmin' = starving; 'cowd' = cold; 'shoon' = shoes; 'aboon' = above; 'stonnin' = standing.

7. Brierley Song, from the 1878 pantomime *Puss in Boots*. 'Eaurs' = ours; 'fratchin' = arguing; 'snickets' = squabbling children, usually girls.

4

The politics of the pantomime

By the late 1850s, pantomimes encompassed both visual and verbal referencing that reflected local, current and ongoing concerns, as well as specific celebrations of regional culture and civic achievement. In so doing, theatre managers responded to the traditions of the genre whilst also creating productions that had a particular significance for local audiences. The promotion of 'our' theatre, so necessary in the competition for status and spectacular success, was thereby given additional relevance in the expression of local concerns, which aimed to create a sense of ownership – of the theatre and the performance – for those audiences. In raising issues, theatre managers, writers and performers naturally commented on representative groups and figures in the local community, the day to day politics of municipal activity and the party politics of government. This chapter then explores the political aspect of regional pantomime, the engagement with local allegiances and the responses from local audiences and the official and informal censors of pantomime.

Visual political references and caricature

The death of Grimaldi and the perceived decline of the harlequinade after the repeal of the Licensing Act in 1843 did not immediately reduce this portion of the pantomime to what critics have supposed was an inert repetition of staid visual jokes. On the contrary, as I outlined in Chapter 1, the harlequinade remained important into the 1860s, and continued to feature pertinent visual satires that drew various reactions from the local population. In the Manchester Queen's Theatre pantomime of 1859, one of the harlequinade scenes concerned a recent corruption scandal at the Wakefield and Gloucester elections. It formed the first of five scenes, drew on an event that had disgraced men from both political parties and, according to one reviewer, 'for its political significancy' was 'probably the best scene of the five'.[1] Visual references and satire were not confined to the harlequinade. In the opening, images, caricatures and symbolic motifs were regularly integrated into scenes. The Nottingham pantomime of *Cinderella* (1882) featured a 'panorama of celebrities', the wide range of national and local figures included Gladstone, the Prince of Wales, Henry Irving, Sir James Oldknow (the Mayor of Nottingham) and Mr Tarbottom, the Borough Surveyor. It was not well received, however, not because of what and who it represented, but because 'the artist has not been happy in his elaboration of it'.[2] The panorama had simply illustrated the well-known figures with no evident accompanying comments or inferences. More pointed and successful references could be made through caricature; the masks referred to in Chapter 1 were not only worn by supernumeraries to represent demons, comic cooks and sailors, but they could also be worn to lampoon leading figures and politicians. In 1872, the Manchester Theatre Royal production of *Bluff King Hal* included a 'procession of illustrious characters', including Gladstone, 'the Emperor of Germany, Bismark, Gambetta, Thiers, MacMahon, Sir Garnet Wolseley, the King of Ashantee, John Bright and other Ministers, Mr. Disraeli, and the inevitable "Claimant"'. 'These gentlemen,' the *Manchester Guardian* reported, 'have the disproportioned heads of modern caricature.'[3]

John Russell Stephens states that there were 'strict rules' issued by the Lord Chamberlain's office 'outlawing the portrayal of notable personalities'.[4] The official cautions that could be sent to theatres were concerned to prohibit any aspect of the satirical representation of individuals. For example, a warning sent to the Alexandra Theatre, Liverpool in 1876 insisted that the manager 'Omit generally, names of living persons, or personal allusions. The representations of living persons whether by mask or make up is not permissible on the stage.'[5] However, such warnings appear to have had little impact on pantomimes. The transpontine Surrey Theatre pantomimes of 1867 and 1868 included caricature references to Disraeli and Gladstone and, as late as 1893, the *Birmingham Daily Post* included a reprinted article from the London *Standard*, which detailed the main expenditure for managers in pantomime. 'The Cost of Pantomime' detailed scenery and costumes including political masks, such as a 'Gladstone' or a 'Bismark', which cost about two to three pounds apiece.[6]

The fact that these masks were being actively promoted indicates that their use in performance was widespread, although presumably beyond the West End theatres which were under the immediate licensing jurisdiction of the Lord Chamberlain, both in relation to the plays staged there as well as the licensing of the theatre building. Certainly there is no evidence that the official warnings regarding visual caricature were heeded at provincial theatres. A 'behind the scenes' article in the *Birmingham Daily Mail* even described the process of making such masks, promoting their appearance in the 1873 pantomime of *Beauty and the Beast*: 'Out of a box come some capital masks of the immortal countenances of Messrs. Disraeli, Lowe and Gladstone and on a modelling board lies the pale clay face of a local dignitary.'[7] In performance, the opening scene of the pantomime introduced

> The Mayor of Birmingham, the Prime Minister, the Right Hon. Robert Lowe, the Right Hon. John Bright, and Mr. Disraeli.... The representation of Mr. Chamberlain, Mr. Gladstone, and Mr. Bright were not so good as might have been the case, but Mr. Lowe and Mr. Disraeli were capitally caricatured.[8]

The Theatre Royal management at Birmingham therefore not only ignored official guidelines regarding make-up and caricature of leading politicians but added to the fun in 1873 by including a dance banned by the Lord Chamberlain: 'After various comments … they join in the "Conspirators' Chorus," from "La Fille de Mdme Angot," finishing with a can-can in the most ludicrous style.'[9] Similarly, in previewing the 1877 Theatre Royal pantomime, the *Birmingham Daily Mail* was able to report that in the opening scene, 'Monsieur Lesseps, the Foreign Secretary, and the Prime Minister further enliven the proceedings with a grotesque dance and breakdown.'[10] The feature was reviewed with relish in the *Birmingham Daily Post*, which highlighted the fact that, once again, the 'political caricatures' took part in a can-can.[11] At the Prince's Theatre, Manchester the concept of a 'political ballet' with characters made up as 'prominent statesmen' was still proving popular in 1889.[12] And in Nottingham a similar 'political *pas de quatre*' took place in the 1890 pantomime *Puss in Boots* at the Theatre Royal. According to the *Nottingham Daily Guardian*, the dance was 'of a most diverting character':

Four of the male members of the company 'made up' to resemble eminent statesmen, but wearing abbreviated skirts as affected by ladies of the *corps de ballet*, burlesque … the well-known Gaiety dance which became so universally popular last pantomime season. The new *pas* was twice re-demanded last night and evidently suited the taste of the house.[13]

As a result of the 1843 Act, all theatres were required to submit new or adapted scripts (including any details of stage 'business') for inspection and licensing. Evidence from the Lord Chamberlain's Day Books shows that several of the pantomime texts submitted by the Manchester, Birmingham and Nottingham theatre managements were indeed licensed with a 'General caution against offensive "gag" & caricatures of living persons'.[14] The Birmingham pantomime of 1877 was one of those that had been cautioned and yet, as evinced in the review, the warning went unheeded. The conflicting evidence of the official memoranda and the inclusion of masks in local pantomimes has been partly resolved by John Russell Stephens, who has highlighted a more moderate and variable tone in the application of censorship to caricature in the period. Despite the written warnings, the Examiner of Plays, Edward Piggott (in office between 1874 and 1895), 'believed that many prominent individuals actually revelled in the thought of stage caricature, and, if there were no direct political intent, [he] was usually prepared to let the matter pass'.[15]

Proving direct political intent must surely have been a difficult issue. In the Prince's Theatre pantomime of 1873, a vegetable garden provided an unusual opportunity for political images: 'in the myriad carrot and turnip beds, one may trace comic suggestions of the faces and favourite attitudes of men familiar in public life'.[16] These suggestions were indeed simply caricature and were unaccompanied by any written verbal references (although of course actors may have introduced 'gag' when occasion arose). Newspaper reviews, as in this instance, occasionally offer additional glimpses of the performance and *mise-en-scène* that are not evident in the manuscripts or books of words. Another example can be found in relation to the Comedy Theatre pantomime of 1885, the text of which included relatively mild political allusions, engaging with both of the main political parties. However, the visual motifs, which are unspecified in the book of words, were rather more specific. The reviewer of the *Manchester Weekly Times* commented that

> It was certainly bold to give the huge features of the nefarious giant the semblance of Mr. Chamberlain, but even there some compensation was had in the scene where the giant looked down from aloft upon the apprentice boy Juggins – for the nonce putting on the appearance of Lord Randolph Churchill – and asked him, 'What's your Indian policy?'[17]

A more problematic visual representation occurred in 1883, in a pantomime at the Grand Circus in Peter Street, Manchester. Legally, music halls and circuses were not permitted to perform full, spoken pantomimes as the genre was classed along with the legitimate drama, to be performed only at licensed theatres. This particular production adhered to the legal restrictions on their use of the spoken word, and the juvenile performers enacted the story of *Cinderella* in dance and mime, but in the ball scene the guests, attired in 'masks and fancy costumes', included members of the English and European royal families, Gladstone, Bright, Disraeli and Lord Wolseley. As represented by children, with no accompanying words, these were harmless and presented figures from both of the main political parties, but the masked characters also included Mr Bradlaugh, the MP for Northampton. Bradlaugh was the subject of political scandal as he had refused to take the oath of allegiance on taking his seat in Parliament. Although no spoken references were made in the pantomime, he was still represented 'as a sort of pariah at a Royal ball, and his company will have nothing to do with him. Capt. Gossett and his assistants are called in, and after a stirring fight Mr. Bradlaugh is ejected from the ballroom.'[18] I mention this pantomime, not to divert the argument into the circus ring and away from the legitimate theatre, but to point up the fact that – as the Georgian harlequinades demonstrated so astutely – political representations, even when performed by children, will still carry a certain weight of interpretation. The Lord Chamberlain's perception of caricature was therefore somewhat naïve. Similarly, whilst the caricatures in some of the pantomimes may not have made overt political comments, the 'appearance' of such luminaries as Disraeli and Gladstone dancing the can-can in the Birmingham production was hardly a flattering salutation to their work. Furthermore, the inclusion of caricature was not necessarily mentioned in the submitted texts. The warning sent to the Theatre Royal at Birmingham in 1874 would have responded to character names in the book of words, which actually detailed 'Lesseps', 'Lord D–y' and 'Earl B–d'.[19] As mentioned above, the use of personal names on stage was not permitted and the thinly veiled 'Lord Derby' and 'Earl Beaconsfield', here, would have done little to persuade the Examiner of Plays that the full names and caricatures were not going to be given in performance. Therefore, although warnings could be sent and leniency could be practiced, there was little that could be done if caricatures were not brought to the attention of the Examiner of Plays. Stephens acknowledges that even though the authorities were perfectly aware of the actual and potential referencing in pantomime, the productions 'proved very difficult to control by means of pre-production censorship, since [they] relied on being up-to-date'.[20]

Additional potential for satire must also have existed in the fact that pantomime stories regularly included fictional royalty and their court officials, which allowed for interpretations not evident in the submitted text. The frequent inclusion of a 'Lord Chamberlain', for example, cannot have been completely innocent, especially when given appellations such as 'Lord Fussy Bussel'.[21] In the 1893 version of *Babes in the Wood* at the Theatre Royal, Manchester, the character of the 'Lord Chamberlain' entered and introduced the 'Baron' dressed as Henry Irving, thus providing a double opportunity for illicit caricature.[22] As all theatres had to submit their plays and revised editions for licensing, for the reading of which the Lord Chamberlain charged a fee, the following exchange also has satirical potential. It occurred in the 1890 pantomime *Puss in Boots* by T.F. Doyle (performed at the Nottingham Theatre Royal), and took place between the Princess's suitors and the Lord Chamberlain.

Sir P. You look very overworked, old man.
Cham. Well, this isn't a very easy life.
Sir D. No.
Cham. No, you see there's such difficulty in collecting the fees.[23]

The school examination scene in pantomimes became a popular site for verbal referencing, with the rapid question and answer exchanges reflecting local issues and political opinions. In reviews of the 1885 pantomime at the Theatre Royal, Birmingham, the schoolroom exchanges were overshadowed for some critics by the *mise-en-scène*. The *Gazette* promoted it as 'an elaborately set scene of a Board School, copied from one of the buildings erected by the Birmingham School Board'.[24] In turn, the reviewer of the *Birmingham Daily Mail* previewed the same scene as being 'one of the great hits of the pantomime':

> It is a realistic representation of the interior of a Board school, the graduated rows of desks, the wainscotted walls, and all the mural accessories being represented sometimes with fidelity, and in some cases utilised for comic effect. England and Scotland are painted so as to look like Mr. Gladstone in a Scotch cap.[25]

A later review in the *Birmingham Daily Gazette* added that 'Lord Randolph Churchill and Mr. Joseph Chamberlain also figure in an exaggerated form.'[26] Whilst the reports permit glimpses of a lost production, the political bias of the two newspapers is also evident. The sole caricature of Liberal leader Gladstone was noted in the Liberal *Mail* and, given the newspaper's support of Chamberlain's brand of Radical Liberalism, it is no surprise that it was Gladstone who was perceived as suitable for 'comic effect'. The Conservative *Gazette*, on the other hand, was quick to point out the additional pictures of Chamberlain and the troublesome Churchill whose personal politics ranged across the floor of the house.

Satire and the spoken word

The visual caricatures occurred of course alongside spoken references, also subject to the Examiner of Plays' inspection. Stephens, in his discussion of nineteenth-century censorship, notes that in textual references,

> The list of personalities whose names were proscribed on the stage is extensive. It ranges down from the Queen and the royal family to members of the government, foreign sovereigns and dignitaries, contemporary theatrical personalities, indeed, to anyone whose name

was a topic of public interest. All references to Queen Victoria were ruthlessly excised even if they were complimentary. So, too, with members of the Cabinet.[27]

It may be thought that if visual references escaped the Examiner, the text would not. However, there was considerable variation in the regularity with which pantomime scripts were submitted. For example, according to the Day Books, there is no record of submissions from the Nottingham Theatre Royal managers for the whole period 1866–74, 1876 or 1890; from the Comedy Theatre in Manchester in the 1890s; from the Birmingham Theatre Royal for 1866, 1868–73, 1886 or 1888; or from the Birmingham Prince of Wales Theatre for its pantomimes of 1887 and 1888. Stephens highlights the fact that manuscripts are missing from the Lord Chamberlain's collection, and may have been loaned out from his office to theatres for copying.[28] Furthermore, some scripts may have been lost, due either to the original storage methods at St James's Palace or, later, to twentieth-century reorganisation. Importantly, though, recent research suggests that sometimes provincial theatres simply did not submit scripts to the Lord Chamberlain's office, but instead loaned out their librettos directly to other provincial theatres charging them a fee for re-use.[29] If that was the case, then not only was the Examiner becoming less rigorous in applying censorship to visual representations, but provincial theatre managements were quite clearly withholding pantomime scripts from examination, as well as ignoring official warnings. For example, in response to the text of the 1877 pantomime *The Forty Thieves*, submitted by Mercer Simpson from the Theatre Royal, Birmingham, the Examiner of Plays had issued a caution against caricature. This warning, as I earlier illustrated, was ignored and the politicians' song and dance was a celebrated feature of the production. The manager had also been instructed to 'omit sc. 1 from "Enter Alde Lesseps" (stage direction) to (Prime Min) "She will have her way"'.[30] However, this speech regarding Lesseps and foreign policy survived in the book of words and featured in performance despite the official sanctions. The *Birmingham Daily Mail* reported that in the first scene, 'Monsieur Lesseps, Lord Derby and the Earl of Beaconsfield appear … and indulge in a little bantering chaff.'[31] Yet again, official censorship had failed to curtail the pantomime.

Veiled references to local councillors and politicians may not have been picked up on by the Examiner of Plays or, again, were simply not included in the submitted text, but they occurred regularly in many of the provincial pantomimes. At the Nottingham Theatre Royal in the 1870s and early 1880s, F.R. Goodyer's style of pantomime satire was insightful, as seen in the education references discussed above, but also widely regarded as inoffensive where political or local figures were concerned. As a well-known local businessman he no doubt did not wish to offend others in the town. However, George Dance, also a local man, writing for the same theatre in the late 1880s, appears to have been less concerned about potential offence, attacking a range of local figures with far broader satirical brushstrokes than those used by Goodyer. Dance's career as an author quickly moved beyond Nottingham; unlike Goodyer his pantomime scripts were not the work of a local businessman, but that of the professional author, for whom local sensitivities were not necessarily of import. According to his biographer W. Macqueen-Pope, Dance 'had an unutterable contempt for all officials of every kind … He warred with bank managers, town and county councils, and all those dressed in a little brief authority'.[32] The 1887 Nottingham version of *Babes in the Wood* by Dance exists in three editions: the copy submitted to the Lord Chamberlain's office, and two differing books of words, presumably produced for the first night and again later in the run. In Scene 4, a conversation about cookery turned to more political ingredients (Jelley was the name of a local councillor):

Tab.   Can you turn an oxtail into jelly, eh?
Friar.   Of course I can, I do it every day.
Tab.   But can you turn a Jelley, my young man,
     Into a Sheriff! At Nottingham they can.

This portion of dialogue is in all three editions of the book of words, and was not commented on by the Examiner of Plays. The third version (which was not submitted) continued the conversation:

Friar.   How was it done? It seems quite strange to me;
     To such knowledge I'd like the *golden* key.

Tab.　　Here's the receipt (*reads*). First a punch-bowl take
　　　Drop in the Sheriff you're about to make;
　　　A *liberal* dash of wine's a great expedient,
　　　And *butter* is a *radical* ingredient.
　　　You give the thing a *yellow* tinge, of course,
　　　And flavour it with Aldermanic sauce.
Friar.　　But is it palatable?
Tab.　　　　　　　　Well, a-hem! –
　　　They'll swallow *anything* in Nottingham![33]

Audiences: avoiding offence

One of the warnings that could be sent to managers by the Lord Chamberlain recognised the multiple viewpoints of the audiences. Managers could be 'recommended to omit in representation any personalities or other topical allusions, which may be calculated to give offence to any portion of a mixed audience, and thereby to provoke ill feeling and disorder'.[34] It was generally recognised that party political comments could be problematic during or just before the year of a general election: the Manchester Comedy Theatre pantomime of 1885, for example, included projected lantern illustrations of politicians, which showed men from both main parties and were greeted by 'uproarious cheering and counter-cheering'.[35] Political allusions in the same production pertaining to the recent general election were also included and referenced both main parties; the *Manchester Weekly Times* observed that the comments 'were for the most part, colourless, or if the favour seemed in one line to go to one party, in the next line it went to the other, and so no one could feel aggrieved'.[36] Concerns about political allusions at other times also featured in newspaper articles throughout the period, and the need to balance a taste for satire with a desire not to offend party feelings amongst audience members was occasionally urged in the press. Although a balanced presentation of political views was by no means at the core of all pantomime scripts, certain theatre managements and writers did adopt this approach. The Manchester Theatre Royal pantomime of 1861 began with a traditional dark scene in which, according to the *Manchester Weekly Times*, two adversaries enter: 'and then step forth "Pot" and "Kettle," their old feud still to settle; "Pot" with his Conservative views blackguarding "Kettle" for his progressive instincts, and the latter returning his remarks with an equal amount of Kettledom phraseology'.[37] In a review of the Queen's Theatre pantomime of 1877, the *Manchester Guardian* noted the array of local referencing in the pantomime and commented that the 'judicious impartiality of the authors … who satirise all alike, is greatly to be commended' although the reviewer slyly emphasised the Liberal support in the theatre: 'it is refreshing to find that the sympathies of the audience at the people's theatre in Bridge Street are for the most part on the right side in all these questions'.[38] In 1884, the Queen's Theatre was praised for the political comments being provided by a '"cross-bench" mind'.[39] And similarly, the *Era* review of *Sinbad* at the Theatre Royal, Sheffield in the same year, noted that the author, Fred Locke,

> Has been admirably backed up by some local genius, who has managed to sport at every Sheffield folly that has flown during the last twelve months with shafts of ridicule tempered by good nature and a commendable leaning towards both sides of politics.[40]

What some of these reviews highlight – whatever the politics of the newspaper may try to infer – is the fact that cross-party references would still attract simultaneous yet differing responses. The aforementioned parade of national and international politicians and dignitaries that took place during *Bluff King Hal* at the Manchester Theatre Royal in 1872 did not pass in front of a passive audience. The *Manchester Guardian* reported how the 'appearance of these characters has caused an extraordinary commotion among the audiences during the past week, and the theatre has at times seemed rather a political arena than a place of amusement'.[41] The *Guardian* comments infer a range of responses not simply within a single performance but across the week. The procession included a range of political colours, and whilst perhaps intending to provide a fair (if not officially condoned) representation of notable figures, the inclusion effectively encouraged active responses and engagement by the audiences. The reviewer's comments do not infer that riotous responses were made but that the theatre represented an 'arena', a forum in which all political views were represented. The audience willingly engaged in the occasion with, no doubt, the usual cheers, counter-cheers and hisses and no complaints were made. The fact that the procession was kept in the production for over a week (and presumably for much of the run) demonstrates that the manager was not persuaded to withdraw the item.

The 'gag'

References in pantomime could be initially orchestrated by the writer in the text, or by the producer in rehearsals, but keeping the pantomime references up to date during the run, in topical songs and interpolated 'gag', tended to be the preserve of the performers. At a performance of the pantomime at the Manchester Theatre Royal in 1874, one performer misjudged his elaboration of a joke in the topical song and created controversy when he offended the religious sensitivities of certain members of the audience.

> It is stated that a stormy scene occurred in the Theatre Royal, Manchester, on Saturday evening, on the production of the Christmas Pantomime of 'Red Riding Hood.' Mr. Aynsley Cook, who was playing the part of the Wolf, introduced a topical song, of which the refrain was ''Tis a fraud,' a reference to Moody and Sankey, the American Evangelists. This local hit was not approved by a section of the audience, who hissed the singer, while others applauded with equal eagerness. Mr. Cook accepted the challenge, and in the lulls of the hissing shouted defiantly the names of Moody and Sankey alternately. This added fuel to the storm, and he sang the stanza a second time very loudly. He was apparently about to do so a third time, but the other actors left him unsupported, and he retired from the stage.[42]

The pantomime was unlicensed and there is no extant book of words, so it is unclear whether the song was written by the author or the performer, but by taking matters into his own hands and repeating what was clearly offensive to parts of the audience, Cook was displaying an example of what the Lord Chamberlain sought to avoid. The chorus certainly achieved – as with many political comments – the usual combination of responses, but in attempting to conduct the audience in those responses Cook crossed the permissible boundary of active participation. The other performers evidently realised this and distanced themselves from his actions.

There were also occasions of potential misinterpretation. At the Plymouth theatre in 1868, the local newspapers charted a lively response to the antics of Clown in the Theatre Royal pantomime *Little Red Riding Hood*. As David Mayer has detailed, the anarchic Clown had always railed against authority, particularly figures such as the night watchman (and later the policeman), and a comedy military drill sequence was invariably included in one of the harlequinade scenes. In the second scene of the Plymouth version, the Clown parodied some of the drills of the Royal Marines stationed at the port. The Colonel Commandant took extreme offence at the allusions and banned all officers from attending the pantomime, sending a patrol to form a cordon around the theatre. The *Western Morning News* found the incident both amusing and puzzling as no direct comment or insult had been made against individuals, merely aspects of the drill. The affair seems to have died away quite quickly after assertions were made by the theatre manager that no offence had been intended, and the Colonel had cancelled the banning order on his men by early January. However, the scene did not draw complaints from the immediate audience, which included men from the Royal Marines, and the local paper was mystified as to how the Colonel could read a personal insult into a slapstick routine (detailed in the review of the first-night performance). The one person who had been offended had not attended the performance, and therefore in including the scene the actor playing Clown, and the theatre management, had apparently judged their audiences correctly.[43]

In 1867, the writers and performers of the pantomime *Gulliver's Travels* at the Manchester Theatre Royal could not ignore the crucial electoral Reform Act of that year. The pantomime was based on the version by H.J. Byron; the theatre manager Thomas Chambers, who had written and adapted all of the pantomimes for his theatre in the 1860s, revised Byron's work but does not appear to have submitted his own version for licensing. Certain of the political references in the book of words represented Gulliver as supportive of the Conservative party, then in power. For example, when he meets the Emperor of Lilliput, he relates the latter's diminutive size to his politics: 'A minister of state – not very big, / Less of the Tory statesman than the *wig*.'[44] Later in the story, when Gulliver is confronted by the Brobdingnagians, he states:

Formidable, not forbidding! I feel bolder –
I've little dread of this compound householder.
Now for the lodger franchise, though adverse on
Enfranchising what J. S. Mill terms 'person' …[45]

In drawing up the electoral Reform Bill, the Conservative Prime Minister Benjamin Disraeli had been persuaded by radical elements of the Liberal party to include compound householders and lodgers as new electors. In fact many of the elements of the Bill were introduced by Liberal rather than Conservative members of parliament; Disraeli, although recognising the need for reform, had initially been less enthusiastic about extending the vote to working men ('Enfranchising what J. S. Mill terms "person"'). The pantomime references therefore display a subtle understanding of the intricacies of the politics behind the Bill. In his adventures, Gulliver's assumed Conservative sentiments are highlighted in the way he asserts himself over the 'wig' or Whig/Liberal Lilliputian, and in his fearlessness when in the face of larger opposition (such as Disraeli faced in Parliament in preparing the Reform Bill). However, in performance Mr Righton, who was playing the title character, decided to add his own political commentary in one scene. In a fishing scene,

a shark is hooked, which bites off the head of one of the sailors, and in his stomach is found a curious collection, including a copy of the Reform Bill, which prompts Gulliver to say, 'If he can swallow that he can swallow anything.' This joke is not in Mr. H. J. Byron's libretto, and we believe Mr. Righton deserves all the credit of it.[46]

It is unclear whether the intentional placing of the property 'Reform Bill' had prompted the actor's response, or whether Mr Righton had conceived the whole idea. The Conservative *Manchester Courier* merely commented that Righton had made 'a pardonable piece of "gag"', suggesting an excusable mistake but, according to the *Guardian*, the verbal and visual joke was notable in a text that was singularly devoid of humour.[47] Approval from the Liberal *Guardian* suggests that the placing of the Bill inside the shark was not a comment against the extended franchise, but – particularly accompanied by Righton's speech – was a comment on the fact that Disraeli had claimed the reform success for his own party despite the fact that the majority of the amendments and improvements to it had been introduced by Liberal politicians. The reviewer did not deny that Gulliver may have represented Conservative principles, but read irony into the performance. Alternatively, of course, Righton may have misunderstood a requirement for political consistency in the portrayal of Gulliver and made the comment as a pro-Liberal one, directly criticising Disraeli.[48] The review in the *Manchester Weekly Times* also repeated the shark joke, but it did not attribute the delivered lines to any one actor. The speech evidently took place, but as neither of the Liberal newspapers repeated any of Gulliver's other political comments, there remains the suggestion of a bias towards the Conservative party in this script.

The press and pantomime satire

In much the same way that reviewers both delighted in describing the pantomime spectacle and yet expressed relief when a theatre resumed its programme of serious drama, the press had a curious attitude to pantomime satire. Although local reviews and previews delighted in quoting large excerpts of satirical speeches and could complain if insufficient references were made or indeed if references were omitted altogether, debates were conducted in local and national newspapers as to the propriety of satirising noted figures and party policies. In general, editorials and letters to papers such as the *Era*, the *Pall Mall Gazette* and the *Illustrated London News* scorned the Examiner of Plays' attempts to censor pantomimes, but there were times when reviewers disapproved of comments in the annual productions. As mentioned above, press disapproval of pantomime satire tended to occur more regularly in years when a general election was about to take place, but concern was also raised at other times regarding international affairs. The *Birmingham Daily Mail* in 1876 contained an article entitled 'Politics in Pantomime'. In this piece, the writer marked the limits of suitable satire in the Christmas productions:

> Sometimes a sop is thrown to the thinking portion of the audience, in the shape of what is called in playbills 'a topical allusion'; but even this is introduced, generally, without much wit and in an arrangement of verse whose rhyme and metre are secondary in importance to the joke itself.

Of late years this feature of pantomimes has been developed rather freely, and the stage has become, in a fashion, the censor of what takes place in the outside world. We find no fault with this. The managers of theatres are generally shrewd enough to see where they can get a laugh from their audience by allusion to some local blunder or national folly … but when questions of national policy are introduced at a critical moment, and party passions are inflamed by one-sided appeals, the stage travels beyond its functions and requires the application of a wholesome check.

The author cited references that were being made in pantomimes (not just in Birmingham) to the contemporaneous conflict between Russia and Turkey and the possibility of British armed involvement. He criticised those pantomime managers who encouraged patriotic appeals for war, citing the horrors of the Crimean War as a check to such expressions. However, he also referred to the representation of political figures and partisan comments:

We never sympathised with the ridiculous sensitiveness of the late Government in forbidding the caricatures of Messrs. GLADSTONE, LOWE, and AYRTON in *The Happy Land*. The stage may legitimately ridicule unpopular acts and, within well-defined bounds, unpopular public men. The less there is of this, perhaps, where party feeling is involved, the better. The theatre, after all, is not a place of political instruction.… An occasional joke in reference to passing political events may be pardoned; but we strongly deprecate the introduction of partisan appeals at times of grave crisis …[49]

The article focused on the dangers of encouraging emotional reactions to references to Russia or Turkey, and the potential for 'provok[ing] a disturbing element of mingled applause and hisses'. Whilst the mixed audience responses to political representations were perceived as lively but harmless, the engagement of audiences in comments concerning potential war was seen as dangerous. However, the appeal against stirring up a patriotic enthusiasm for conflict in the Eastern Question was ignored by pantomime writers and in 1877, despite his approval of the local referencing at the Queen's Theatre, the *Manchester Guardian* reviewer found cause to criticise the references – at the Queen's and at the Theatre Royal – to the Eastern Question. The reviewer disliked the appeal to 'cheap applause' and argued that in this 'our amusements ought at least to be neutral'.[50]

The public as censor

Despite the existence of official censorship and debates in the press, political and satirical referencing in provincial pantomimes continued apace. Indeed, the leniency of the Examiner of Plays had perhaps turned to weariness towards the end of the century. At the hearing of the 1892 Select Committee on Theatres and Places of Entertainment, Edward Piggott related his decreasing concern with pantomime censorship. With particular reference to topical allusions he stated: 'To tell you the truth, I never interfere with them now in pantomimes. That was in former years. It was done on account of certain disloyal allusions. It was done, and there was an end to it, and the thing has never been done again.'[51] Stephens has argued that, by the end of the century, the censors were more concerned with controversial plays in the West End than the pantomime, although they were still aware of the licence that could be taken in the performances. Insofar as the censorship of pantomimes was addressed at the 1892 Committee hearing, William Archer, who was called as a witness, regarded a shift of emphasis from official watchfulness to that of the general public to be more reliable; in other words, relying on the audience for moral control of the pantomime. According to Archer, audiences were 'the only really effective censor, because the only censor who is always on the spot, and always hears and sees the intentions of the actor and the author'.[52] In theory this idea seemed practicable. The licensing of provincial theatre buildings was outside the Lord Chamberlain's jurisdiction, but if a complaint was made to him about a performance, he could issue a formal warning to the theatre manager. Amongst the Lord Chamberlain's correspondence with provincial managers, however, there is no evidence of complaints being made by members of the public about political references in the pantomimes at the Birmingham, Manchester or Nottingham theatres.

Whilst members of the public may not have deemed it worthwhile complaining to the Lord Chamberlain, their opinions could be voiced through letters to the local newspapers. The Manchester and Birmingham newspapers did carry occasional letters regarding the decorum of dancers' dresses and the perceived ill effects of the 'immoral' music hall songs, but complaints against political references in specific productions were only very occasionally made. A series of letters to the *Manchester Guardian* in early 1881 charted a lively debate over the impromptu inclusion of caricature 'gag' in the pantomime of *Blue Beard* at the Theatre Royal, but in general little comment was registered by members of the public. In Nottingham, only two pantomimes – those of 1865 and 1868 – were criticised for their political references. In the 1868 pantomime *Babes in the Wood*, the author included a lengthy reference to the 'late election' of 1867 and the successful candidate, Sir Robert Clifton.

> WEL. Oh yes; Sir Robert Clifton's safely seated!
> QUEEN. So old a general couldn't be defeated.
>   If the esteem he's held in don't secure him,
>   His lovely aide de camp must still ensure him.
> BUSY B. Pray who is that?
> QUEEN. The question makes me frown;
>   Go ask the good folk living in the town
>   Who 'twas with winning smile, their homesteads visited,
>   And gained their votes almost before solicited:
>   And if consent some few still had a doubt of it;
>   Ask who's bright eyes, completely 'witched them out of it!
>   From whom, life's way, the poor oft get a lift on;
>   You'll get but one reply – 'Twas Lady Clifton![53]

Sir Robert Clifton was a well-known and popular local figure but one whose involvement in local politics attracted a certain amount of notoriety. In the mid-nineteenth century Nottingham politics had been dominated by the Whig party, whose candidate for the 1861 election was the Tory, Lord Lincoln.[54] Clifton, a man known to be in favour of moderate reform, stood in opposition as an independent Tory candidate, supported by a Chartist-Liberal faction, and won the election. Then in 1865, a group of radical Whig-Liberals broke away from the Whig caucus and formed an independent party with Clifton as their candidate, along with Samuel

Morley a prominent local hosiery manufacturer and orthodox Liberal. Both men were successful but the election as a whole was corrupt and 'both candidates were unseated after bribery was proved'.[55] Two years later, Clifton stated publicly that he would not stand at the 1868 election, but entered at the eleventh hour. His political partner was Col. Charles Wright, who was known to refer to Clifton as his 'General' (thus linking directly to the pantomime speech). On the day of the election, voting went against Clifton but, according to accusatory letters in the *Nottingham and Midland Counties Daily Express*, free beer had been supplied in the town centre by him to influence voters' decisions. Further letters made additional allegations of complicity between Seely (the Whig candidate) and Clifton.

The *Express*, a Liberal paper, condemned the pantomime speech in its first review of the production on 28 December. On the following day a letter was printed in the same paper from the pantomime author W.J. Thompson who claimed a misrepresentation had taken place:

> The policy of introducing political allusions in public entertainments is justly questioned, and in the speeches complained of I have studiously avoided doing so. But taking advantage of the license of pantomime, I have merely endeavored [sic] to pay a *personal compliment*.[56]

The exchange of letters in the *Express* continued throughout the first week of the run between the author and his anonymous critics. One, signing himself 'ARISTIDES', remarked that he had been 'Very glad … to hear the nauseous toadyism about Clifton unmistakeably hissed when I was present [at the pantomime]'.[57] Importantly, the complaints were only from one part of the audience and from the one Liberal paper. The same paper had complained about similarly supportive sentiments for Clifton in the 1865 pantomime, but on that occasion had acknowledged that both cheers and hisses had been heard in the audience. The 1868 speech was specifically reprinted in the newspaper because the audience was being noisy, although the type of noise was not explained; was it therefore the noise of complaint or approval?[58] Eventually the matter was settled by a letter from the theatre lessees, Mrs J.F. and Miss K. Saville, stating that in their 'desire … to please *all* and *offend none*' the lines had been removed from the production.[59]

The incident raises an interesting issue regarding pantomime references. In terms of political allegiances, the 1865 and 1868 pantomimes expressed specific support for Clifton, an independent Tory MP who opposed the powerful Whig caucus in the town. The management decision to support the aristocratic Clifton may have related to the legacy of theatrical patronage in the provincial town, but after 1868 and for the next sixteen years, political references in the Nottingham pantomimes maintained a cross-party and subdued level of satire. The author for much of this period was F.R. Goodyer, a writer of whom it was said 'There is more of good nature than of bitterness in all he says, and in no instance has he allowed his playful muse to carry him beyond the limits of good taste'.[60] His engagement and subtle approach to local politics evidenced a specific managerial decision and, indeed, the relatively small catchment area of local audiences may have precluded overt and potentially alienating political statements. However, by the 1880s Nottingham was witnessing municipal growth as well as the local effect of the 1884 electoral reform act. The appointment of George Dance as the pantomime author may well have been in response to growing demands for

External view of the Theatre Royal, Nottingham, with statue of Samuel Morley, *c*.1895.

municipal and political accountability from audiences more willing to see and hear local leaders lampooned.

As in Birmingham (discussed below), Liberalism dominated Manchester politics from the 1840s, but whilst Radical Liberalism was the driving force in the first decade of Victoria's reign, after the 1840s Manchester Liberals were, according to the historian Alan Kidd, 'inherently conservative'.[61] Indeed, local Radical MPs were voted out of office in 1857 when Liberal foreign policy was seen as too aggressive, and from this date there was a noticeable shift to the right, with the first Conservative MP voted into office in 1868.[62] Kidd notes that many in the Manchester business and middle classes were drawn to Disraeli's Conservative party after the Liberal divides over Irish Unionism in the 1880s, and after the electoral reform of 1884 many new working-class voters were also attracted to the Tory party.[63] The diverse political allegiances in Manchester created a range of attitudes in the principal theatres. For example, the extant scripts and books of words exhibit praise and scorn for Liberalism in its various forms. The opening dark scene of the Manchester Theatre Royal production of *Sinbad the Sailor* in 1894 attacked Lord Rosebery, the then Liberal Prime Minister who, despite his inherited title, was keen to abolish the House of Lords.[64]

> *Davy.*   The House of Lords at last has got to go;
>   At least Lord Roseberry has threatened so.
>   But that's a sop to Cerberus, my hearty,
>   By Cerberus I mean the Irish party.
>   The Liberals will quickly turn their coats.
> *Oceanus*   Whene'er they see *that* 'cry' has cost them votes …[65]

Conservative politicians and policies were similarly decried when opportunity offered and, towards the end of the century, the emerging Socialist and Labour movements occasionally featured in pantomime. Whilst the long-established Tory and Liberal parties with their familiar leaders and political ideologies allowed for a variety of comments and representation in pantomime, the new – and for some – unfamiliar politics of socialism were addressed with little serious support. At the Theatre

Royal, Manchester, the ruffians Jeremiah Jenkins and William Williams in the 1893 production of *Babes in the Wood* considered a political career:

> [*Williams*]   I wouldn't be a Hem P, Lardy dardy,
>   But one o' them labour blokes like Queer Hardy.
> *Jenkins*   'E doesn't labour, mate
> *Williams*   Which right you are.
>   Strikes and spouting pay him better far.[66]

The number of theatres in Manchester enabled a range of perspectives, but the frequent changes of management at each theatre also affected the style of referencing in the pantomimes. The personal politics of managers and lessees naturally influenced the party political tone of satire, and therefore sustained political allegiances across the whole period from 1860 to 1900 are difficult to ascertain. At the Theatre Royal, for example, there are occasional years or short periods when a single party allegiance is evident in the scripts, such as the pro-Tory comments in 1867 and 1881 (*Little Bo Peep*). The Second Edition of the latter, written under Captain Bainbridge's management, was criticised by the *Manchester Weekly Times*: 'the allusions in verse, and many of the jokes and gags, are controversial in the sense of being all on one side, and they have the natural and no doubt desired result of exciting loud demonstrations of conflicting opinion'.[67] However, under the management of Thomas Ramsey at the end of the century, pro-Liberal comments were made in the productions of 1892, 1893 and 1896. The 1893 pantomime in particular is interesting in terms of the nuances of inter-party divisions then occurring in Liberal politics, between Gladstone's old school of Liberalism and the ideas of new, young politicians such as Lord Rosebery.

At the Queen's Theatre, where regional identity played such an important role in the pantomimes, the productions of the mid-1860s appeared to support Liberal politics. In *Kafoozalum; or, the Beau, the Beauty, and the Babah* of 1866, the good fairy announced – to the approval of the *Manchester Guardian* – that:

> Mine is a Liberal government – don't fear;
> We admit no Conservative members here.

A reform bill we mean to pass this session
In spite of all the Tory opposition.[68]

In the 1870s, political references continued to centre on the Liberal party, in particular the problems its leaders faced regarding Irish nationalism. Pantomimes featured references to Obstructionists (in the 1877 and 1879 productions), Home Rule campaigners (mentioned in every pantomime), and Republications (cooked by the Giant in the 1880 version of *Jack the Giant Killer*).[69] However, in the mid-1880s pantomime references at this theatre became distinctly pro-Tory. The lessee and manager of the theatre in the early 1880s were Joseph Salter and James Curtis Emerson respectively, and whilst their own politics would normally have dictated the tone of pantomime referencing, it is possible that the potentially largely working-class audience at the Queen's, together with the significant shift in working-class political support in Manchester after the 1884 election, may on these occasions have influenced the managerial decision. The author of the 1883 and 1884 pantomimes was J. Wilton-Jones, whose distinctly pro-Tory scripts also featured at the Leeds Grand Theatre in 1885. In a review of the latter, the *Era* commented that 'Some objection being taken to the Conservative tendencies of the dialogue an impartial sprinkling of political skits is now introduced at the expense of both the great political parties.'[70]

Opened in 1886, the new Comedy Theatre pantomimes initially sustained a pro-Tory party allegiance, and indeed, such a move may have been easier to establish for the management of a new theatre. The first pantomime, produced under the management of John Heslop and written by Wilton-Jones, featured a politically-minded 'Dame':

DAME. (*with dignity*) I'd have you know, sir, I'm a Primrose Dame
   I've joined the League, so mind you keep your station.
   This humble roof's my 'Local Habitation.'
BARON. The League?
DAME. Just so. The Tories are in power
   United by a simple little flower.
   When Gladstone tries the Tories' game to 'blew,'
   The little yellow primrose pulls 'em through.[71]

Similarly, the hero 'Dick Whittington' in the 1887 pantomime (also by Wilton-Jones) hailed from Manchester and promoted the Conservative policy of Fair Trade, whereas the wicked 'Vizier' in R. Newman's script for *Aladdin* (1888) was one of the (Liberal) opposition. By 1890 the theatre had a new manager, Pitt Hardacre, whose chosen pantomime author for the remainder of the century was the local journalist William Wade. With the exception of pro-Conservative sentiments in the 1891 production, his pantomime scripts moved away from party political commentaries to focus on local civic references and city issues. Hardacre had obviously decided that a more general tone suited his theatre audiences, and preferred his pantomimes to appeal to local families, a policy underlined by his choice of advertisements for the pantomime books of words. In each of the extant books there is a full page advertisement for the *Manchester City News*. This paper was recognised locally as being non-political. Its prospectus claimed 'that it was a "family paper," and "will altogether avoid the introduction of party politics."'[72]

There is evidence also that, as at many theatres in the late nineteenth century, political references, especially in the topical song, were becoming the province of the comedians. The decline in written partisan references cannot be solely attributed to the period post-1890, however. There are scripts for the Manchester theatres prior to this date which either exhibit little in the way of political referencing or contain criticisms that are applicable across the political spectrum. For example, Edwin Waugh's 1866 pantomime of *Robin Hood* included a speech calling for the enfranchisement of the working class by the 'Friar' (a dialect character), but also a wide-ranging attack on the political factions in parliament. In Scene 8, the character of the 'King' complained:

Oh, what a job to guide this groaning nation,
Between first this, then that, administration!
Apostate Radicals, and timid Whigs;
And Tory-Liberals, with their slipp'ry rigs;
Dull dwellers in Adullums's wretched cave –
Who, round a diff'rent – leader – sneaking rave;
And one lot and another. Oh the pain!
When will my country cut the *juggler* vein.[73]

Management policy and audience collusion

In Chapter 3 I discussed the engagement of particular authors by theatre managers, and suggested that the choice was made not as an arbitrary selection of cheap local 'hacks' but rather in relation to their authors' local knowledge and standing. In addition to a knowledgeable portrayal of relevant local issues such as education and poverty, their engagement could also relate to the political affiliations of the theatre, not simply by writing suitable scripts in accordance with managerial demands, but in terms of a shared political belief. Whilst political expression at the Manchester theatres could be affected by changes in management, and at the Theatre Royal, Nottingham by the need to be circumspect in the face of a limited catchment area of potential audiences, the longevity of managements at the Theatre Royal and at the Prince of Wales Theatre in Birmingham enabled significant and sustained political affiliations that were shared by their authors.

Birmingham held a unique place in the political life of nineteenth-century Britain: its Liberal politicians and civic leaders shaped the town and played a prominent part on the national political stage. The managers of the two theatres each adhered to different factions of Liberalism, the distinctive note of each dictating the political references in their pantomimes. This sustained allegiance was supported personally and professionally by two of the authors engaged by the Theatre Royal management, who between them wrote pantomimes for a period of over twenty years: Charles Millward and James J. Blood. The case studies below address the style and content of their pantomime references but also highlight the crucial issue of audience responses. Whilst newspapers reviewed these pantomimes according to their own partisan allegiances and audiences naturally included people with all shades of political interests, the combined and sustained expressions of managers and authors at each theatre drew little comment from members of the public who appear to have accepted and even colluded in the political stance of the annual productions.

Political case studies

The Theatre Royal, Birmingham

From the early 1870s the focus of political comments at the Birmingham Theatre Royal pantomimes lay in the civic and political status of the town that was brought about by the work and influence of Joseph Chamberlain. Chamberlain was not a local man, but after settling in Birmingham in the 1850s he had established himself as a successful businessman who was also interested in social reform. In 1869 he co-founded the National Education League, the moving force behind the Education Act of 1870 which transformed the provision of primary education, and in 1873 he was elected Mayor of Birmingham, a post he retained for three successive years.[74] As Mayor he instigated and oversaw major improvements and redevelopment in the town and his stance as a Radical Liberal symbolised the political developments that were to dominate Birmingham for the remainder of the nineteenth century. In 1876 he was elected MP for Birmingham, and although he now moved on the national political stage, he retained close links with Birmingham.[75] This allegiance was reciprocated by the town: Chamberlain's status and that of the town were closely linked and his progress was charted with unfailing interest by the principal theatre, the Theatre Royal.

On gaining the civic seat in 1873, his achievement and establishment in the town were celebrated in the book of words for that year's pantomime, *Beauty and the Beast*. A fictional cast list was headed by 'A Chamberlain of great renown' to be played by 'Mr. MAYOR'. The blurred boundary between the world of pantomime and the reality of nineteenth-century civic politics was a recurring feature of the productions at the theatre, notably in versions of *Dick Whittington* (which are discussed below). However, the pantomimes also contained direct political allusion and comment. The 1873 production did not simply celebrate Chamberlain's new mayoral role; in the opening dark scene, an exchange between the Spirit of Discord and the Sphynx extended the theme:

DIS.   A *mayor's* nest you've disturbed, but to our gain
He has too long in Council *Chamber lain,*
A nobler destiny awaits him. He
May be the Sheffield blade's keen edged M.P.
He's full of work, and will some day be –
SPHYNX.   Hold!
That future may be guessed at, but not *told*.[76]

In this pantomime even the antagonistic characters expressed support for Chamberlain. This speech not only celebrated his immediate success but referred to the fact that he was due to stand for the Sheffield parliamentary seat in the forthcoming 1874 general election. The lines further engaged the audience in thought-provoking word-play. The phrase 'He / May be' asserted their role as electorate: Chamberlain's future would indeed be up to them, but the next line, 'will some day be –', was suggestively completed in performance by visual representations of Chamberlain together with leading figures from the current Liberal government and Cabinet, including John Bright, the long-serving Birmingham MP, Prime Minister Gladstone and Lowe, the Chancellor of the Exchequer. Disraeli, the leader of the Conservative opposition, also made an appearance, but the visual emphasis was on Liberal party power. Therefore, the combination of political characters and the open-ended speech directed the audience to consider Chamberlain's longer term and 'nobler destiny'. The scene clearly indicated that Chamberlain *would* take his place in the political pantheon in the future, even if the specifics could only be 'guessed at, but not *told*'. The verbal and visual references raised no complaints and the only voice of dissent was that of the Conservative *Gazette* which, in its review of the opening-night performance, took the opportunity to

> enter our protest against the political element in pantomimes … let us have our annual treat with our little ones without being called upon to applaud a bid for any political party. Here we have Bright eulogised – Chamberlain idolised and Dizzy told he is a humbug. Speaking not as a Conservative, but as a pantomime-goer, we protest against it. Heaven knows we have enough of politics in most matters.[77]

It is unlikely that this particular reviewer was speaking purely as a pantomime-goer, but other members of the audience seemed undisturbed by the references and the correspondence columns of both the Conservative and the Liberal papers remained empty of accusations or counter-accusations regarding the pantomimes throughout the period. Chamberlain was in fact defeated at the 1874 election but idolising him was, it seems, *de rigueur* at the Theatre Royal. Birmingham was, historically, a Liberal town, and the theatre reflected that political stance. Indeed, references in the pantomimes did not flinch from following Chamberlain's adherence to Radical Liberalism.

At a formal dinner in October 1874, Chamberlain as Mayor had addressed members of the Birmingham Town Council. The Mayor and Council were only too aware of a forthcoming visit to the town by the Prince and Princess of Wales and Chamberlain followed established protocol at the dinner by proposing a toast to 'The Queen and Royal Family'. He then delivered a speech in which he declared himself loyal to the Royal Family and unwavering in his support of the proposed visit: 'a man might be a gentleman as well as a Republican; and even an advanced Liberal might not be unmindful of the duties of hospitality and the courtesy which every one owed to a guest'. He continued by defining his view of republicanism as that which was based on the 'unswerving faith in the value of representative institutions', decrying what was sometimes inferred to be republicanism's 'uproot[ing]' of 'existing orders'. However, his speech went on to denounce what he described as 'exaggerated loyalty' by those who 'enshrined … royal personages in … a stifling atmosphere of fulsome adulation', and who 'grew hysterical at public banquets on the occasion of the usual loyal toasts'. He also stressed his belief in meritocracy, and his speech appealed for public praise to be directed to the royal family 'for what they saw in them worthy of honest admiration' rather than 'attributing to them immaculate perfection and superhuman virtues'.[78] Chamberlain's reputation and radical ideas concerned his critics prior to the visit and it was with noticeable relief that *The Times* was able to report on the 'heartiness and loyalty' with which the royal party was greeted when it visited Birmingham on 3 November.[79]

The royal visit and Chamberlain's republicanism were made the focus of an entire scene in the pantomime of that year, *Ride a Cock Horse to Banbury Cross*. In reality, the Prince and Princess of Wales had been met at the Birmingham borough boundary by the Mayor and Mayoress, together with a full reception committee and two troops of the 12th Lancers, prior to a procession through the town. In the pantomime, the retinue of the fictional Earl of Warwick was greeted by the character of the 'Mayor', who was unmistakeably costumed to represent Chamberlain. In Chapter 3 I referred to Simon Gunn's discussion of the culture of civic parades in provincial cities and the way in which such occasions expressed the political power and hierarchies of the civic authorities. The procession in the 1874 pantomime was an unusual example of a pantomime paralleling such an event and was made uniquely possible by the overt political allegiance of the theatre to Chamberlain. During the pantomime meeting between the Earl and the Mayor, the former asked:

And now – the question – I must plainly ask –
Is yours a pleasant duty or a task?
'Tis said that you and others of your town
Would stamp out monarchy, and put kings down.
If that be true our visit might perplex you.[80]

The scene here echoed both the contemporaneous occasion and contextual views of the local and national press and yet the pantomime script went further. The Mayor's response to this question – much like Chamberlain's initial speech to the Town Council – was not limited to a simple declaration of loyalty:

We hope you will not let such rumours vex you.
The sweets of office, and a Prince's smile
Have made us very loyal – for a while.
And now I say, though some around may frown,
I hope we always may possess a *crown!*[81]

Whilst the exchange was distanced by its setting within the nursery tale and historical location of medieval Warwickshire, the references were unmistakable. By including this scene in the pantomime the theatre management had forced Chamberlain's views to the fore, refusing to modify his radical version of Liberalism either to assuage concern or in the name of amusement. The daring temporariness in the phrase 'for a while' accentuated Chamberlain's comments regarding the 'duties of hospitality', and the final line – 'I hope we always may possess a *crown!*' – concisely reiterated the closing remarks of his speech to the council in November, in which he had supported the idea of monarchy but concurrently inferred that individual monarchs should prove themselves worthy of their status.

This affirmation of Chamberlain's political views failed to raise any eyebrows in the press reviews, merely amusing the critics of all three of the main Birmingham newspapers. The lack of comment acknowledged the perceptive nature of the reference, but also signified an awareness of the theatre's political allegiance.

This allegiance to Chamberlain's Radical Liberalism recurred in pantomimes throughout the period. For example, in the 1881 pantomime *Beauty and the Beast*, a pasteboard model of a 'huge lion' interrupted the proceedings of one scene. This moment is not evident in the script but was described in reviews: one character fought and killed the 'lion', and after being successfully destroyed and cut in half, 'the severed portions then turn[ed] round to the audience and display[ed] – one a portrait of Bright and the other one of Chamberlain'.[82] The representation of a lion connoted the heraldry of England and, in showing pictures of John Bright and Chamberlain inside the destroyed lion, this image offered a layered interpretation. At one level it foregrounded the two Liberal MPs as political representatives of Birmingham, a town in the centre of England and at the centre of national industrial production, but it could also be read as a purely political image, of Liberalism as the core of English politics. The Liberal party had been returned to power in the general election of 1880 and that year had seen Chamberlain enter the Cabinet – the centre of British government – for the first time. A third reading of the image might also have suggested that the destruction of the lion symbolised the defeat of the Conservative party, historically recognised as the representative party of the English establishment.

Such was the fervour of support for Chamberlain by the management at the Theatre Royal that even errors of judgment were ignored. In the 1879 pantomime *The Fair One with the Golden Locks*, a whole scene was dedicated to the industrial success of the town and the social improvements instigated by Chamberlain. His financial skill was praised by the character Brum, who stated, 'Thanks to our *Chamberlain's* financial skill / We have just now an overflowing till.'[83] Despite the practical achievements of the town improvements, including the redevelopment of slum areas, the expenditure had in fact straitened the municipal finances, a point of interpretation not missed by the *Gazette*, whose reviewer read 'pointed sarcasm' into the speech.[84] The praise for Chamberlain in the pantomime was understandably underscored by the Liberal papers, which acted to reinforce Chamberlain's achievements rather than focus on the financial difficulties, which were in effect denied in the pantomime.

The town improvements in Birmingham had earlier been addressed in the pantomime of 1875, in a production that provided early indications that the theatre was transforming Chamberlain's career into a local legend. In the opening scene of *Puss in Boots*, a lengthy speech outlined the work done in the town, concluding that 'For this advancement, thank brave Chamberlain / The local Whittington – three times Mayor – / Good luck to him. May he be long "all there".'[85] Chamberlain's three terms as Mayor of Birmingham were seized on by the theatre management as the rationale to stage regular productions of *Dick Whittington and His Cat*, the legend of the lad who travelled to London to seek his fortune and became Mayor of London three times. Through specific references the productions celebrated the very real achievements of Chamberlain, but by drawing attention to the Birmingham Civic Chair they also managed to assert the provincial town over London. Although in the staged pantomime stories Dick Whittington indeed became Mayor of London, the emphasis remained on the Birmingham mayoral office. In the 1884 production, that focus was emphasised by Whittington's arrival as Mayor of London being accompanied by the spectacular procession of Birmingham and Midlands trades discussed in Chapter 3.

It was upon Chamberlain's entering the Cabinet as President of the Board of Trade in 1880 that the pantomime *Dick Whittington* was performed for the first of three runs in the 1880s, all making a very specific connection between the hero of the legend and the hero of Birmingham:

Lord Mayor *three* times! And may it be my fate,
To be an M. P. and Minister of State!
The thought of that makes me so gay and *bright*
I might have in a *chamber lain* all night![86]

The theatre management engaged the successful music-hall star Vesta Tilley to play Dick in both the 1884 and 1888 versions of this pantomime. In so doing, her repeated appearance in the role established a sense of continuity and a reiteration of sentiments that underscored Chamberlain's own successive achievements and local popularity. In the 1888 version of *Dick*

Whittington, the character of Dick in the final triumphant scene appeared on a real white horse, the civic hero defeating wrong and surviving slander and assault in the world of the pantomime at a time in the late 1880s when Chamberlain, Birmingham's own civic legend, was fighting political battles in Westminster; in 1886 he had left the Liberal party over the issue of Irish Home Rule (promoted by the Liberal leader, Gladstone), and aligned himself with rebel Conservatives to form the Liberal Unionist party.

Chamberlain's dominance of civic matters in Birmingham engendered a powerful sense of allegiance in the town that was eagerly reflected in productions at its oldest established theatre. Such an affiliation may have been due to personality as well as the practical effects of his social reform, but the admiration of Chamberlain in the pantomimes was not simply the effect of a single personality. After 1886, his alliance with Conservative MPs did not affect the regard in which he was held in Birmingham, but neither did it alter the political stance of the Theatre Royal pantomimes. Liberal political support ran deep in Birmingham, and although the Chamberlain years of the 1870s had a ready-made hero for their pantomimes, the theatre continued to express political support for the party throughout the 1880s, which can be evidenced in periods of Conservative as well as Liberal government. Indeed, the Theatre Royal pantomimes frequently contained negative comments about local and national Conservative figures that were not always confined to humorous or harmless jokes. For example, in the aforementioned 1874 pantomime *Ride a Cock Horse to Banbury Cross*, the character 'Guy, Earl of Warwick' delivered a long speech in Scene 7, in which he promoted political hypocrisy:

> To 'pubs' make promises; abstainers laud;
> The church uphold, and then Dissent applaud....
> Go in for working men; for masters stick up,
> And o'er every grievance make a 'kick up' …

The speech could have passed as a general and satirical commentary on election promises, but it was concluded by the Mayor – already established as representing Chamberlain – stating of Sir Guy, 'From those strong sentiments, thus indicated, / It strikes me, you are growing *Dizzy – pated!*'[87] The implication of the speech was therefore instantly shifted from one of general cynicism to a specific attack on the policies of 'Dizzy' (Disraeli), the then Conservative Prime Minister. The following year, after the lengthy speech praising Chamberlain's town improvements, characters concluded that 'Our Tory rulers have not brightly shone.'[88] And the 1876 pantomime *Sinbad the Sailor*, with its Eastern setting, provided ample opportunity to criticise Disraeli for his foreign policy in the Balkans. A more local example could be found in the Conservative alderman and former Mayor, Henry Hawkes, who was an active opponent of Chamberlain. Hawkes was treated with disdain in the local Liberal press and became a regular target in the Theatre Royal pantomimes. For example, in the 1882 pantomime *Sinbad the Sailor*, the demon character of the Old Man of the Sea cursed the Liberal caucus (the ruling civic body of the local Liberal party that had been established by Chamberlain): 'But I will kill it, since my plans it baulks, / And leave its *Car-cus* to be pecked by *Hawkes*.'[89]

Whilst responses to the pantomime references by local reviewers were naturally aligned to the political stance of their newspapers, complaints by those reviewers about comments and images in the pantomimes were on the whole limited. It might be assumed that regular attacks on the Conservative party leaders and policies and local civic dignitaries would have resulted in more regular responses from the *Gazette*, but in general the paper refrained from engaging with what may have been judged adverse comments. Such an attitude – as I have already suggested – implies that the newspapers were perfectly aware of the theatre's stance on political issues. It was well known, for example, that two of the principal writers of the Birmingham pantomimes in this period, Charles Millward and James J. Blood, were themselves Liberal supporters. Millward aligned himself with Radical Liberalism and although he was not a local man, his political leanings suited those of the theatre management. Blood, who was local, was also a member of the Liberal Arts Club in Birmingham, of which Chamberlain was for a time chairman. The Arts Club had been 'initiated under the auspices of Mr. Mercer Simpson', the Manager of the Theatre Royal, and its members made use of rooms on the theatre premises.[90] Blood even introduced membership of the Arts Club as an aspiration for one of his characters in *The Forty Thieves*:

ABDUL. What are you doing here?
CASSIM. Oh! – don't *you* know;
    I want to join the Arts Club.[91]

An acceptance of the political preferences in pantomime references at the Theatre Royal may therefore explain the relatively subdued response from the Conservative *Gazette*. The local Liberal papers were naturally in accord with the sentiments expressed in the annual pantomimes, in particular the *Birmingham Daily Post*, whose owner J.T. Bunce was a noted local supporter of Chamberlain. However, an addition to the pantomime of 1887 prompted an unusually negative response in the *Post*. That response further highlights both the expectation of political affiliation and the manner in which the pantomimes staged that affiliation.

In December 1887 the theatre management staged the pantomime *Little Goody Two Shoes*, starring Miss Jenny Hill, the 'Vital Spark' of the music halls. In the newspaper reviews of the opening-night performance, Hill's patriotic song 'The Old Flag' was applauded by all the Birmingham papers, but her topical song 'England for the English' was less well received by both the principal Liberal papers. The *Birmingham Daily Mail* thought it contained 'bunkum words and tawdry sentiments', thankfully glossed over by Hill's performance of 'dash and spirit', but the *Birmingham Daily Post* was incensed:

> [as] for a song in praise of the many virtues of Fair Trade – well, we suppose that it is hopeless to expect that music-hall performers will ever understand how ridiculous is the figure which they cut in their attempt to pose as the political instructors of their audience. However, we have no doubt that Miss Hill knows as much of political economy as the majority of the Fair Trade party.[92]

The *Birmingham Daily Gazette*, however, applauded the 'patriotic song, in which Free Trade, "all one-sided though," comes in for a very drastic denunciation'.[93] The reason Miss Hill's song divided the critics depended on the subtle difference between the words 'Free' and 'Fair' Trade. Free Trade was a policy that had been adopted by both political parties in the course of the nineteenth century, but by the mid-1880s there was a more defined division between the Liberal adherence to Free Trade, and the protectionist measures – or Fair Trade – which were championed by members of the Conservative party. During the national depression of the 1880s, the varied trades and industries in Birmingham were not universally affected, and whilst Free Trade did encourage foreign competition, Liberal opposers of Fair Trade were more concerned about the rising prices of necessities, especially food, which might have occurred if protectionist trade tariffs were introduced. There had been considerable debate in Birmingham in 1887 regarding the two policies, the Free Trade argument being led, with letters in the press, by the longstanding Liberal MP John Bright. The divided reception of the pantomime song by the reviewers was therefore naturally aligned to the political stance of their newspapers, but the extended attack in the *Post* was also a complaint against Conservative principles being introduced in relation to heroic sentiments.

The Theatre Royal pantomimes contained a variety of political references, from overt caricature to subtle asides, but a singular trend in this period was to align party politics with character types. In other words, the heroes supported Liberal policies and politicians whilst the human villains and supernatural demons claimed Conservative principles. This dichotomy was illustrated in the 1887 pantomime in which the villain was named King Counterfeit, a Conservative who, when defeated in battle at the end of the story, remained adamant that he '*Stuck to my colours, and so dyed true blue*'.[94] He and his cohorts attacked Liberal policies and at one point he disguised himself as a pedlar, selling items representing the Liberal party, such as 'Gladstone axes' and Chamberlain monocles, a reductive symbolism which suggested that Liberalism comprised only token power and political representation. Conversely the Principal Boy, 'Sterling', represented the plucky and hardworking Liberal Birmingham working man. The heroic Liberal character type had been effectively represented by Vesta Tilley in the 1879 pantomime *The Fair One with the Golden Locks* and again in the two productions of *Dick Whittington* in 1884 and 1888. Therefore, although an anti-Free Trade song could have been sung in the 1887 production, it should not have been sung by the hero. The song, copyrighted to Hopwood and Crew of London, was not written by the author of the pantomime James J. Blood, and was an uneasy addition that clearly failed to take account of the complexity of the trade issues that had been debated in Birmingham during the preceding months. The complaint voiced in the *Post* review did not criticise the theatre management or the author, but steadfastly focused on the political illiteracy of the 'music-hall performer'. In particular the reviewer attacked Hill for what he perceived as her 'attempt to pose as the political instructo[r]' of the audience, a statement that raises an important issue regarding the reception of political references by audiences at the Theatre Royal.

In terms of audience reaction, different responses were occasionally noted by critics. For example, in the 1868 pantomime of *Ali Baba and the Forty Thieves*, an illustration of 'leading personages', including Disraeli, Gladstone and Bright, elicited both 'cheers and counter-cheers' from the audience.[95] As a major theatre in a large town, attracting audiences from a wide topography across town, suburbs and county as well as further afield, the Theatre Royal management could not dictate the political nature of its audiences, and naturally a range of political understanding would be part of a large audience's cultural experience. However, even if individual members of the audience held varying political ideas, the sustained political emphasis of the Birmingham pantomimes would have become part of the range of expectations experienced by many of the theatre-goers visiting the pantomime. A large section of the regular theatre-goers at the Theatre Royal would have begun, over time, to expect a Liberal emphasis in the political referencing of the pantomimes. The correspondence columns of the local newspapers charted lively debates among a range of readers, from politicians to urban working men and farmers, but references in the local pantomime prompted no written responses. Despite the fact that topical speeches were reprinted in previews and reviews to alert readers to political referencing and to provide suitable interpretations, potential and actual audience members remained apparently unperturbed by the attitudes expressed in the Christmas production. As I indicated earlier, no local complaints were made to the Lord Chamberlain's office about any of the Theatre Royal pantomimes in this period, which suggests a level of complacency by Birmingham audiences. Both David Mayer and, more recently, Millie Taylor have noted how pantomime has always 'poked fun at authority figures'[96] but the references at Birmingham could range from quite serious accusations to simple caricature. If these references had engaged in simply 'pok[ing] fun' at all political parties and politicians, the occasional more pointed attack might have caused comment from members of the audience, but the sustained tone combined with the lack of complaint suggests strongly that, even allowing for a range of political allegiances amongst the audiences, there existed an established knowledge by many that this theatre management supported the Liberal party. Such knowledge made the audiences not complacent, but complicit. Within that context of expectation and complicity, the accusation made in the *Birmingham Daily Post* that Jenny Hill's anti-Free Trade song was an attempt to educate the audience takes on a different tone. If many in the audiences at the Theatre Royal were aware of the political motivations behind the pantomime referencing, the fear expressed by the *Post* was, perhaps, that Hill was trying to *re*-educate them, against the established principles which governed the remainder of the production.

As mentioned in this case study, the assertion of Radical Liberalism in the Theatre Royal pantomimes was reflected in the allocation of political creeds to character types. However, amongst the Liberal/Conservative representations there was another layer of political referencing, which related to the Liberal Prime Minister, W.E. Gladstone. Chamberlain's radicalism distanced him from the party leader, increasingly so over the issue of Irish Home Rule. Therefore, although Gladstone was the leader of the Liberal party, the local allegiance to Chamberlain took precedence in references to the Liberal party in the Theatre Royal pantomimes. In *The Queen of Hearts* (1883), Gladstone was caricatured as 'Farmer Radish'. Neither the script nor the reviews give an indication that this character had any lines – let alone political statements – but 'Farmer Radish', a minor character, was 'made up to represent the "Grand Old Man," so familiar in modern politics … wearing the cartooned collar, which amusingly increases in size as the pantomime goes on'.[97]

The Prince of Wales Theatre and Liberal politics

In contrast to the 1883 caricature at the Birmingham Theatre Royal, the 1884 pantomime at the nearby Prince of Wales Theatre presented a different version of Gladstone. In *The Forty Thieves*, the leading character Ali Baba introduced himself, and was referred to throughout, as a 'Grand Old Man' (the popular nickname for Gladstone). Ali Baba was not represented as a silent joke as at the Theatre Royal but as the central character, and whilst he was a comic creation, he was an affectionate portrayal, not a fool. His passion for lengthy speeches provided a running joke but, whilst he expressed concern about parliamentary bills, the income tax, redistribution and parliamentary divisions, he remained the hero of the pantomime. As opposed to the Ali Baba figure at the Prince of Wales Theatre, therefore, the creation of Farmer Radish at the Theatre Royal as not only a minor, but apparently a silent character, was pointed. Birmingham was a Liberal town but the types of Liberalism supported locally – and reflected in the pantomimes – differed. At the Theatre Royal the working partnerships of the manager Mercer Simpson with the writers Charles Millward and James J. Blood advocated Chamberlain's Radical Liberalism. Conversely, at the Prince of Wales Theatre a very different Liberal allegiance was expressed in the annual productions. At that theatre, Chamberlain's radicalism was opposed, and authors such as the local man T. Edgar Pemberton, who wrote the 1884 version of *The Forty Thieves*, instead advocated the more traditional Liberal politics of Gladstone: the elder statesman was here applauded not lampooned.

The allegiance of the Prince of Wales Theatre pantomimes to Gladstonian Liberalism predated James Rogers's management of the theatre. The first manager, Mr Swanborough, engaged the author Martin Duttnall to write all but one of his Christmas productions. Whilst reviews highlighted Swanborough's efforts to stage a suitably spectacular pantomime, they also noted his inferred political allegiance to the Liberal party. In Duttnall's 1865 text, the fairy queen proclaimed that

> full soon
> The air will be o'erladen with *per*fume.
> Let it be so, and may each odour rare
> So *per*meate our city's murky air,
> That Pestilence, in Cattle, Bird, or Man,
> May ne'er be found in dear old Birmingham;
> And may its social atmosphere be quite
> As clear as its political – and Bright ...[98]

The somewhat tenuous path to the concluding couplet nonetheless highlights the necessity of including – at whatever literary cost – relevant political allusions. Later in the same scene, a reference was made to the late Prime Minister, Viscount Palmerston:

Enter a PALMER.

Palmer. Daughter, the nation claims ye for its own!

Queen.   His accents sound like to a *name well known*

     And loved in England; 'tis a *Palmers-tone!*

Iron K[ing] The jaunty trusty brave old English lion,

     For whose successor we indeed may sigh on ...[99]

The *Birmingham Daily Post* applauded the 'well-written lines' honouring the popular Prime Minister who had led two Liberal governments, from 1855–8 and from 1859 until his death in 1865.

In 1866, James Rogers took over the lesseeship of the theatre, to be succeeded by his son, Captain Rogers, in the mid-1880s. During that time the Rogers family committed their pantomimes to the Liberal cause, as had Swanborough. As Simpson at the Theatre Royal hosted the Arts Club, so both James and Captain Rogers entertained local political and civic dignitaries in the 'smoke-room' of the Prince of Wales Theatre. E. Lawrence Levy, in his book *Birmingham Theatrical Reminiscences*, went so far as to suggest that at the regular meetings of local Liberal figures 'many a municipal and other policy was initiated'.[100] The pantomimes at the Prince of Wales Theatre sustained the pattern of political referencing in favour of the more mainstream Liberal party; scripts either ignored or downplayed Chamberlain's local achievements and were opposed to the control exerted by the Radical Liberal caucus in the town. For example, Chamberlain's achievement regarding the enactment of the Artisan Housing Bill in Birmingham was applauded in that year's pantomime ('all honour due') but the comment was not extended. In the 1883 book of words for *Cinderella*, approval for Chamberlain's patent laws ('By those the worker who *invents* is able / To reap the profit – not the rich man's table') was mixed with two attacks on his Bankrupt's Bill, and the word 'Radical' was considered an insult by one of Cinderella's sisters.[101] The pantomime story of *Dick Whittington* at the Prince of Wales also lacked the local emphasis and political inferences of productions at the Theatre Royal. In the 1891 Prince of Wales version, the concluding Lord Mayor's Procession was visibly rooted in London, featuring a procession of nations, a band dressed as Grenadier Guards accompanying Britannia, and girls dressed as the Horse Guards.

Whilst the London patent theatres did attempt to avoid censorship regulations (for example, with the references to Chancellor Lowe, mentioned in the article), the threat of fines and potential theatre closure made these theatre managers cautious. The *Hornet* article noted a few subtle 'bits of quiet satire' in the Drury Lane production of that year and 'no Politics' at all in that at Covent Garden. Indeed an overview of reviews in *The Times* and the *Era* between 1865 and 1878 (the period in which the Lord Chamberlain attempted tighter censorship controls) offers little evidence that the patent theatres were breaking any rules. The *Times* review of the Covent Garden pantomime of 1873 also found that it was 'rather sparing of allusions' and of Drury Lane in 1876 that 'the dialogue' was 'singularly free from those allusions to passing events which elsewhere are awaited with so much eagerness'.[105] Political allusions at Covent Garden that year appear to have been contained within a topical song, which the reviewer notes was not in the book of words and would have evaded censorship more easily.[106] By contrast, the provincial pantomime writers and performers continued to include 'bold speeches'. Perhaps not always lengthy speeches but – especially at the Birmingham theatres – sustained and thematic political agendas, outspoken references, and allegations against named individuals, which occurred with a regularity that would have been hard to control. The *Hornet* claim is perhaps exaggerated, but the sustained tone and thematic references woven into dialogue together with the pantomime subject matter and visual references (evident for the historiographer only in newspaper reviews) created not only the boldness of provincial pantomime, but also a significant part of its regional identity.

Notes

1. 'The Christmas Pantomime at the Queen's Theatre', *Manchester Weekly Times*, 24 December 1859, p. 5.
2. '*Cinderella* at the Theatre Royal', *Nottingham Daily Guardian*, 27 December 1882, p. 8.
3. 'Queen's Theatre', 26 December 1872, p. 8, and 'The Pantomimes: Theatre Royal', 26 December 1873, p. 8, both in *Manchester Guardian*.
4. J.R. Stephens, *The Censorship of English Drama 1824–1901* (Cambridge, 1980), pp. 10, 116.
5. The warning was sent to the theatre on 30 November 1876 (*Register of Lord Chamberlain's Plays*, vol. iv, 1873–76, p. 111).
6. 'The Cost of Pantomime', *Birmingham Daily Post*, 27 December 1893, p. 2.
7. 'Behind the Scenes at Pantomime Time. By "the Odd Man Out"', *Birmingham Daily Mail*, 20 December 1873, p. 4.
8. 'The Theatre Royal', *Birmingham Daily Post*, 27 December 1873, p. 5.
9. *Ibid.*
10. 'The Pantomimes', *Birmingham Daily Mail*, 21 December 1877, p. 3.
11. 'Theatre Royal', *Birmingham Daily Post*, 27 December 1877, p. 5.
12. 'Prince's Theatre', *Manchester Guardian*, 23 December 1889, p. 8.
13. 'Theatre Royal', *Nottingham Daily Guardian*, 3 February 1891, p. 7.
14. BL: Brit. Mus. Add. Ms. 53706: The Lord Chamberlain's Day Books, v, p. 13. See also Stephens for a selection of the Lord Chamberlain's cautionary memorandums, in Appendix C of *Censorship*, p. 160, and p. 183, n. 12. The term 'gag' was usually applied to impromptu or unscripted comic business on stage.
15. Stephens, *Censorship*, p. 117.
16. 'Prince's Theatre – "Cinderella"', *Manchester Weekly Times*, 3 January 1874, p. 4.
17. '"Jack and the Beanstalk" at the Comedy', *Manchester Weekly Times*, 26 December 1885, p. 6.
18. 'Pantomime at the Grand Circus', *Manchester Weekly Times*, 29 December 1883, p. 7.
19. Charles Millward, *The Forty Thieves* (1877), Brit. Mus. Add. Ms. 53319/P, p. 1.
20. Stephens, *Censorship*, p. 117.
21. 'The Pantomimes: "Sleeping Beauty"', *Manchester Guardian*, 26 December 1863, p. 5.
22. MA: Th792.094273 Ma86: Theatre Royal, Manchester, *Pantomime Books*, vol. ii, Fred Locke, *Babes in the Wood* (1893), book of words, Scene 10, p. 62.
23. NLSL: L79.8: T.F. Doyle, *Puss in Boots* (1890), book of words, Scene 3, p. 16.
24. 'The Birmingham Pantomimes: *Robinson Crusoe* at the Theatre Royal', *Birmingham Daily Gazette*, 23 December 1885, p. 5.
25. 'The Christmas Pantomimes: *Robinson Crusoe* at the Theatre Royal', *Birmingham Daily Mail*, 26 December 1885, p. 3.
26. 'Theatre Royal', *Birmingham Daily Gazette*, 28 December 1885, p. 4.
27. Stephens, *Censorship*, p. 116.
28. *Ibid.*, p. 2.
29. I am indebted to Mrs Kathryn Johnson, curator of the Lord Chamberlain's Plays collection at the British Library, for sharing this aspect of her research with me in conversation (March 2002). An example of provincial theatres loaning scripts can be found in the financial records of the Theatre Royal, Nottingham. In 1866, the manager of the Manchester Theatre Royal, Thomas Chambers, loaned a copy of his pantomime *Aladdin* (script plus music) to the Nottingham theatre

proprietors. The script was then re-worked slightly for Nottingham audiences, but the revised edition was not submitted to the Lord Chamberlain for licensing. The Nottingham management paid Chambers directly for both documents, although the music had only been on loan. See above, Chapter 2, endnote 84 for details of the payment.

30. BL: Brit. Mus. Add. Ms. 53706: The Lord Chamberlain's Day Books, v, p. 64.

31. 'The Pantomimes', *Birmingham Daily Mail*, 21 December 1877, p. 3.

32. W. Macqueen-Pope, *Shirtfronts and Sables: A Story of the Days When Money Could be Spent*, (London, 1953), pp. 86–7. The career of Dance (later Sir George Dance) has been well recorded, in particular by W. Macqueen-Pope, who was Dance's private secretary in London between 1908 and 1914. J. Davis and V. Emeljanow's '"Wistful Remembrancer": The Historiographical Problem of Macqueen-Popery', *New Theatre Quarterly*, 17 (2001), p. 302 first drew my attention to Macqueen-Pope's *Shirtfronts and Sables*.

33. NLSL: L79.8: George Dance, *Babes in the Wood* (1887), book of words, Scene 6, p. 33.

34. Signed by E.F.S. Piggott, the memorandum is taken from BL: Brit. Mus. Add. Ms. 53,706: Lord Chamberlain's Day Books, v, p. 1.

35. '"Jack and the Beanstalk" at the Comedy', *Manchester Weekly Times*, 26 December 1885, p. 6.

36. *Ibid.*

37. 'The Christmas Pantomimes: The Royal: "Beauty and the Beast"', *Manchester Weekly Times*, 28 December 1861, p. 3.

38. 'Queen's Theatre', *Manchester Guardian*, 27 December 1877, p. 5.

39. 'The Christmas Pantomimes: The "Queen of Hearts" at the Queen's Theatre', *Manchester Guardian*, 18 December 1884, p. 5.

40. 'Provincial Theatricals: Sheffield', *Era*, 3 January 1885, p. 17.

41. 'The Pantomimes', *Manchester Guardian*, 9 February 1874, p. 7.

42. 'Scene at the Manchester Theatre', *Bristol Mercury*, 26 December 1874, p. 3.

43. 'Plymouth under Martial Law: Extraordinary Proceedings', *Western Morning News*, 30 December 1868, p. 2, 'The Marines and the Pantomime', *Western Morning News*, 31 December 1868, p. 3, and 'Correspondence', p. 4.

44. William Brough, *The Wonderful Travels of Gulliver* (1867), book of words, [no scene], p. 9.

45. *Ibid.*, p. 14. A 'compound householder' was one whose rates were included in his rent.

46. 'The Christmas Pantomimes', *Manchester Guardian*, 21 December 1867, p. 5.

47. 'The Pantomimes', *Manchester Courier*, 21 December 1867, p. 5.

48. Generally speaking, pantomimes tended to either attack all political parties equally, with no single character taking a party line, or they could present specific party allegiances defined by certain characters. Where the latter occurred, characters maintained their allocated loyalties (see the issue of the Jenny Hill song in Birmingham later in this chapter). The problem I suggest in relation to Righton is that he may have momentarily forgotten that Gulliver was supposed to be Conservative.

49. 'Politics in Pantomime', *Birmingham Daily Mail*, 22 December 1876, p. 2. *The Happy Land* was written by W.S. Gilbert and the issues surrounding his incorporation of political satire are discussed by John Russell Stephens in *The Censorship of the British Drama*, pp. 119–24.

50. 'The Christmas Pantomimes', *Manchester Guardian*, 17 January 1878, p. 6.

51. *Report from the Select Committee* (1892), p. 333, in answer to question 5211.

52. *Ibid.*, p. 237, in answer to question 3946.

53. W.J. Thompson, *Babes in the Wood* (1868), book of words, Scene 2, p. 11.

54. The details of Nottingham politics are taken from Church, *Economic and Social Change*, pp. 218–21.
55. *Ibid*., p. 219.
56. *Nottingham and Midland Counties Daily Express*, 29 December 1868, p. 4.
57. *Ibid*., 31 December 1868, p. 4.
58. For an illuminating discussion of theatre noise, see Reid, 'Popular Theatre', pp. 74–7.
59. *Nottingham and Midland Counties Daily Express*, 1 January 1869, p. 4.
60. 'The "King of the Peacocks"', *Nottingham Daily Guardian*, 4 January 1873, p. 3.
61. Kidd, *Manchester*, p. 72.
62. *Ibid*., pp. 68, 72.
63. *Ibid*., pp. 158, 171.
64. *Oxford Dictionary of National Biography*, vol. xlv, pp. 370–83.
65. MA: Th792.094273 Ma86: Theatre Royal, Manchester, *Pantomime Books*, vol. ii, Fred Locke, *Sinbad the Sailor* (1894), book of words, Scene 1, p. 9.
66. MA: Th792.094273 Ma86: Theatre Royal, Manchester, *Pantomime Books*, vol. ii, Fred Locke, *Babes in the Wood* (1893), book of words, Scene 2, pp. 22–3.
67. 'Theatre Royal. "Second Edition" of *Bo Peep*', *Manchester Weekly Times*, 4 March 1882, p. 6.
68. 'Queen's Theatre', *Manchester Weekly Times*, 22 December 1866, p. 5.
69. Obstructionists were Irish nationalist politicians who opposed Gladstone.
70. 'Provincial Theatricals: Leeds', *Era*, 16 January 1886, p. 15.
71. *Little Red Riding Hood* (1886), book of words, Scene 2, pp. 17 and 18.
72. A.J. Lee, 'The Management of a Victorian Local Newspaper: the *Manchester City News*, 1864–1900', *Business History* 14/2 (1973), pp. 131–48 (p. 132).
73. MA: Th792.094273 Ma83 and Ma83/A: Prince's Theatre, Manchester, *Pantomime Books*, vol. i, Edwin Waugh, *Robin Hood and Ye Merrie Men of Sherwood* (1866), book of words, Scene 8, p. 31.
74. *Oxford Dictionary of National Biography*, vol. x, pp. 924–5.
75. *Ibid*., p. 926.
76. BCL: L28.1.64589: Charles Millward, *Beauty and the Beast* (1873), book of words, Scene 1, p. 3.
77. 'Theatre Royal', *Birmingham Daily Gazette*, 27 December 1873, p. 5.
78. 'Dinner to the Birmingham Town Council', *Birmingham Daily Post*, 7 October 1874, p. 5.
79. Quoted in 'The London Press on the Royal Visit', *Birmingham Daily Post*, 5 November 1874, p. 6.
80. BCL: L28.1.314833: Charles Millward, *Ride a Cock Horse to Banbury Cross* (1874), book of words, Scene 3, p. 9.
81. *Ibid*.
82. 'The Theatre Royal Pantomime', *Birmingham Daily Post*, 27 December 1881, p. 5.
83. BCL: L28.1.64592: Charles Millward, *The Fair One With the Golden Locks* (1879), book of words, Scene 1, p. 5.
84. 'The Theatre Royal Pantomime', *Birmingham Daily Gazette*, 24 December 1879, p. 5.
85. BCL: L28.1.64591: Charles Millward, *Puss in Boots* (1875), book of words, Scene 1, p. 3.
86. BCL: L28.1.64593: Charles Millward, *Dick Whittington* (1880), book of words, Scene 4, p. 12. The '*bright*' in line 3 alludes to John Bright, who was a Liberal MP for Birmingham from 1857 until his death in 1890. He was often linked with Chamberlain in pantomime references.

87. BCL: L28.1.314833: Charles Millward, *Ride a Cock Horse to Banbury Cross* (1874), book of words, Scene 7, p. 16.

88. BCL: L28.1.64591: Charles Millward, *Puss in Boots* (1875), book of words, Scene 1, p. 4.

89. BCL: L28.1.69240: F.W. Green, *Sinbad the Sailor* (1882), book of words, Scene 1, p. 2.

90. E.L. Levy, *Birmingham Theatrical Reminiscences: Jubilee Recollections (1870–1920)* (Birmingham, [1920]), pp. 29, 89.

91. BCL: L28.1.112840: J.J. Blood, *The Forty Thieves* (1890), book of words, Scene 7, p. 21.

92. 'The Pantomimes: *Goody Two Shoes* at the Theatre Royal', *Birmingham Daily Mail*, 27 December 1887, p. 4; and 'Theatre Royal – *Goody Two Shoes*', *Birmingham Daily Post*, 27 December 1887, p. 5.

93. 'Theatre Royal. *Goody Two Shoes*', *Birmingham Daily Gazette*, 27 December 1887, p. 5.

94. BCL: L28.1.125961: J.J. Blood, *Little Goody Two Shoes* (1887), book of words, Scene 7, p. 27.

95. 'Christmas Amusements: Theatre Royal, *Ali Baba and the Forty Thieves*', *Birmingham Journal*, 2 January 1869, p. 5.

96. M. Taylor, *British Pantomime Production*, p. 142.

97. 'Boxing-Day Amusements: Theatre Royal', *Birmingham Daily Gazette*, 27 December 1883, p. 5.

98. BL: Brit. Mus. Add. Ms. 53047: Martin Duttnall, *Little Bo Peep* (1865), book of words, Scene 2, p. 5.

99. *Ibid.*

100. Levy, *Birmingham Theatrical Reminiscences*, p. 32.

101. BL: Brit. Mus. Add. Ms. 263: T.F. Doyle, *Cinderella* (1883), book of words, Scene 5, p. 13, Scene 4, p. 7, Scene 5, p. 13, Scene 7, p. 17.

102. Davis and Emeljanow, *Reflecting the Audience*, p. 80.

103. BCL: LF28.60828: 'Newspaper Cuttings: Birmingham Drama', ii, 1866–1876: clipping entitled 'Politics of the Pantomime', *Hornet*, 24 January 1874.

104. *Ibid.*

105. 'Covent Garden', *The Times*, 27 December 1873, p. 5, and 'Drury Lane', *The Times*, 27 December 1876, p. 5.

106. 'Covent Garden', and 'Drury Lane', *The Times*, 27 December 1876, p. 5.

Conclusion

> Though in London spectacle goes a long way towards making a pantomime a success, in the provinces something more is required by audiences.[1]

In the light of contemporaneous and cited claims regarding the financial importance of the annual pantomime, the purpose of this book has been to examine how theatre managers in the provinces tried to ensure the necessary house receipts; in other words, how they attracted audiences to their local theatres. It is clear that pantomime was not always financially successful. In a small town that was undergoing poor trade and social hardship, as well as for a second or third theatre trying to compete for audiences in a larger city, a lack of income at the doors and box office could severely affect the preparations for the pantomime as well as the door sales of the actual production. Therefore, theatre managers had to adapt their resources and productions to meet the times and the competition as well as responding to local expectations. In providing the necessary elements of the genre and conforming to the cultural expectations of spectacle, the resourceful manager could create new traditions: the use of large crowds of supernumeraries to compensate for a lack of beautiful scenery, for example, or equally large groups of children, dancing in picturesque costumes. Those managers who had the means to ensure regular scenic spectacle could afford for the press reviewer to visit backstage, to promote the quantity of labour, fabulous sets and inventive mechanical effects. At each end of the spectrum, managers drew on promotional materials to reinvent the pantomime according to their financial ability; the adjusted style of productions became local traditions, specific to each theatre, which were recognised and advocated in the local press.

Whilst the local identity of pantomime in part rested on these stylistic differences brought about through the necessity of competition and financial survival, local and regional identity – achieved through the expression of a range of relevant issues and concerns, and aspects of the regional cultural inheritance – was also a crucial element of the script, aspects of the *mise-en-scène* and performance. Such inclusions did not present a homogeneous interpretation of local features; evidence in the books of words and reviews shows that at Manchester, for example, not all characters in the various productions spoke with a regional accent, and other styles of dance were performed as well as the clog. Instead productions created local identity through the referencing of a variety of interest groups in the local and regional communities. These references sought to engage with and comment on important and not so important events and personages that had amused or incensed local feeling. Very occasionally solutions or actions were suggested, but these were more generally deflected into comic business or a change of subject. Speeches rarely if ever sought to intervene or propose serious social solutions. In this example from the Theatre Royal, Manchester, the speech is concluded by the entrance of a symbolic figure and the local problem is shifted to the national issue of free trade:

> A miner's not content with what he earns
> *Put down* the agitator, that's the plan,
> Then workmen will be happier to a man.
> Then you will see a revolution made;
> A good one too, and here he is   [fig. of GOOD TRADE]
> *King M*. If I can help it that you'll never see,
> All your good trade's gone out to Germanee.[2]

The political referencing of provincial pantomime, as demonstrated in Chapter 4, varied from theatre to theatre. The range of 'bold speeches', and visual satires on national and civic politicians, occurred in all pantomimes. The unique political status and recent radical history of Birmingham were complemented by longevity of managements and the regular engagement of specific pantomime authors at the two main theatres, which created a very particular political identity for the pantomimes. Over time audiences (and press) became accustomed to the slant of expressions at each theatre, and political reputation formed part of the pantomime-going experience; indeed, the acceptance of this situation highlights a collusive relationship between audiences and management. At the Theatre Royal in Nottingham, the large number of pantomime references in the period adopted a cross-party approach to political references; with a relatively small audience topography, managers could not afford to offend their clients, as the example from the mid-1860s illustrated. At Manchester, the range of references utilised at each theatre effectively reflected the range of political ideas in the urban 'metropolis', but the frequent changes of management at each of the main theatres often precluded the development of allegiances witnessed at Birmingham.

The long-term engagement of authors and the patterns of manager/ author collaborations clearly point to a defined commercial strategy. Authors such as Goodyer, Anderton, Dance, Millward and Blood were men whose work, be it business, professional authorship or journalism, could be promoted in alignment with the status of the theatre. Men who were known for their writing and for their local or political affiliations presented scripts that were knowledgeable about and in tune with local affairs, be they the role of local politicians on the national stage, the activities of the School Board or the inefficiencies of the municipal authorities. The preference of managers for particular writers appears to have been a nationwide pattern. In R.J. Broadbent's *Annals of the Liverpool Stage*, he refers to a Mr H.B. Nelson, the 'sole proprietor and manager' of the Prince of Wales Theatre in Liverpool from 1896 to 1900. According to Broadbent, all of Nelson's pantomimes were written by one author, J. James Hewson.[3]

Most of the pantomimes at the Comedy Theatre in Manchester were written by William Wade for the manager Pitt Hardacre. Wade was acting editor and dramatic critic for the *Umpire* for twenty years as well as Assistant Editor for the *Manchester Examiner* in the 1890s, and he wrote twenty-two pantomimes for theatres in the city, chiefly the Comedy.[4] Despite his work at the *Examiner* (a paper somewhat to the left of the *Guardian*), Wade's scripts – owing to the dictates of Hardacre – lacked political commentary, and the texts instead contained more subtle references to the civic issues of Manchester. He took his role as pantomime author lightly, and some of his books of words are interspersed with self-referential comments. In the book for *Goody Two Shoes* in 1892, he submitted an apology:

In the first place, the book is far too long. Happily one half of it will neither be spoken nor acted. The plot is complicated, and will be wholly lost among the oddities of the comedians; the jokes are far away above the Shakespearean student's appreciation, and altogether there is too much value for the money. I may add in conclusion, in response to many touching appeals, that I regret it is now too late to withdraw the production, as I have already been paid for it.

And on a later page:

[NOTE. – Should the audience demand it, the management desire to say that an effigy of the author, richly stuffed with chestnuts, will be suspended from the flies at the end of each performance, in order that those caring to do so may mark their appreciation of his efforts with brick bouquets. Please see that the tributes do not mark the orchestra.][5]

In one respect, Wade's observations were accurate; pantomime scripts did get altered and cut during the run. Sometimes this was done in collaboration with the author (evidenced by the occasional existence of different versions of books of words) and sometimes not, such as when making practical excisions in the performance for new acts, or when – as Wade notes – the comedians chose to add in their own material. Reviews of Wade's pantomimes at the Comedy Theatre often remarked on how much of his script remained after several weeks, his lines being generally respected by the performers. Wade, in entering into the spirit of pantomime humour, specifically allowed room in his scripts – as Anderton did for his pantomimes in Birmingham – for the increasing amount of comic business (and variety acts) that he knew would be added in by performers in the emerging style of pantomimes of the 1890s. The recognition of this by Anderton and Wade once again demonstrates that the provincial pantomime author, in addition to providing a script with appropriate references and jokes for a particular theatre, was acutely aware of the changing commercial necessities of productions, a fact sometimes ignored by critics of the pantomime author's role.

Wade's appreciation of the nature of pantomime performance in 1892 foreshadowed further changes to the provincial pantomime at the end of the nineteenth century. The status of some of the theatres was evidently still of import: in 1907 the Theatre Royal, Manchester was still being described in advertisements as the 'Home of Pantomime', and in 1918 (at which point the theatre was the only one in Manchester regularly staging pantomime) *Cinderella* was advertised as 'John Hart's Annual "Royal" Production'.[6] Further, the taste for spectacle continued but the lengthy ballets and processions declined and the abilities of the music-hall comedians and 'rollicking fun' became a more prominent feature of promotional materials, including reviews. By the late 1890s and with the increase in touring productions being hosted at many theatres, plus the emphasis on stars and comedians adding their own material, the quantity of social references in the books of words became noticeably reduced. The newspaper reviews also became briefer; a different style of reporting merely summarised the comic value of the main performers, and the lengthy columns of descriptions of the scenery and excerpts of topical speeches were no longer a feature of the regional pantomime review. This is not to say that social referencing and, by implication, the reflection of a local identity was excluded, but historiographically, it is more difficult to locate. If the local social referencing and political emphasis of pantomimes did decline after 1900 it may have been due to one of several possible factors: firstly, the increasing control of referencing, in songs and 'business', by the visiting stars who would not have had the detailed local knowledge of earlier writers. Secondly, as the country moved into a state of war in 1914, although theatre managements were encouraged to keep their venues open to boost morale, and indeed pantomimes were produced at regional theatres throughout the First World War, political speeches and attacks on the government may have been deemed inappropriate. But I would propose a third possibility. Simon Gunn, in his discussion of the civic metropolises of the nineteenth century, notes the decline of middle-class bourgeois culture after 1900. Whilst I do not regard this as directly related to the decline of pantomime satire, there are elements of his concluding remarks that are pertinent. He notes the decline in civic ceremonies and processions and the simultaneous 'gradual disappearance of the regular, detailed reporting of promenades, "street types" and fashionable events' (the last linking directly to my own observations on the reduced pantomime reviews); and municipal growth and the building of the civic centres was complete by the late nineteenth century.[7] The second half of the nineteenth century had witnessed the emergence and growth of the civic city, rapid change in the local environment and the developing political involvement, at local and national level, of an expanding electorate. It was a period that required comment and reflection in the pantomimes, by managers and writers who understood their audiences. It is possible that after 1900 the accurate reflection of local issues was no longer needed, mirroring somewhat the decline in the regional satirical journals that had been published in the last quarter of the nineteenth century. The 'Politics of the Pantomime' had declined because – as with those journals – they were no longer an intrinsic part of the provincial expression of urban culture.

Notes

1. 'Pantomime Songs', *Nottingham Daily Express*, 23 December 1887, p. 6.
2. BL: Brit. Mus. Add. Ms. 325: Harry F. McClelland, *Jack and the Beanstalk* (1895), Scene 1, p. 1.
3. R.J. Broadbent, *Annals of the Liverpool Stage, from the Earliest Period to the Present Time* (Liverpool, 1908), p. 292.
4. Manchester Local Studies Library: 'Newspaper Cuttings. Vic-Walker': Untitled newspaper cutting [handwritten date of 1909] regarding William Wade.
5. *Goody Two Shoes* (1892), book of words, pp. 5, 11.
6. Advertisement, *Manchester Guardian*, 28 December 1907, p. 1 and 27 December 1918, p. 1.
7. Gunn, *Public Culture*, pp. 190, 192–3.

Bibliography

Primary sources

Newspapers
Aris's Birmingham Gazette
Birmingham Daily Gazette
Birmingham Daily Mail
Birmingham Daily Post
Birmingham Journal
Bristol Mercury
Era
Manchester Courier
Manchester Guardian
Manchester Times
Manchester Weekly Times
Nottingham and Midland Counties Daily Express
Nottingham Daily Guardian
Nottingham Evening Post
Nottingham Journal
Nottingham Review
Nottingham Weekly Guardian
Western Morning News
The Times
Tomahawk

Manuscripts and unpublished items
Birmingham Central Library (Local Studies Library):
57566: 'Bound collection of playbills for the Theatre Royal, Birmingham', 7 vols (1865–1896).
F/1 243679: 'Birmingham Miscellaneous': Blood, J.J., *Robinson Crusoe* (1885)

L28.1 4401948C: *Birmingham Theatre Royal Pantomimes 1856–1892* (bound collection):

> Millward, Charles, *Sinbad the Sailor or, the Red Dwarfs, the Terrible Ogre, and the Old Man of the Sea* (1865), L28.1.64583
>
> —— *Aladdin and the Wonderful Lamp* (1866), L28.1.64584
>
> —— *Robinson Crusoe* (1867), L28.1.243337
>
> —— *Blue Beard* (1869), L28.1.64585
>
> —— *Dick Whittington* (1870), L28.1.64586
>
> —— *The Fair One with the Golden Locks* (1871), L28.1.64587
>
> —— *The Fairy Fawn* (1872), L28.1.64588
>
> —— *Beauty and the Beast* (1873), L28.1.64589
>
> —— *Ride a Cock Horse to Banbury Cross* (1874) [3 variants], L28.1.314833
>
> —— *Puss in Boots* (1875), L28.1.64591
>
> —— *Sinbad the Sailor* (1876), L28.1.67562
>
> —— *The Forty Thieves* (1877), L28.1.202317
>
> —— *Robinson Crusoe* (1878), L28.1.98582
>
> —— *The Fair One with the Golden Locks* (1879), L28.1.64592
>
> —— *Dick Whittington and His Cat* (1880), L28.1.64593
>
> Millward, Charles and Clay T.C., *Beauty and the Beast* (1881), L28.1.64594
>
> Green, F.W., *Sinbad the Sailor* (1882), L28.1.69240
>
> Hall, Frank and Blood, J.J., *Queen of Hearts* (1883), L28.1.64595
>
> Blood, J.J., *Dick Whittington and His Cat* (1884), L28.1.92007
>
> —— *Cinderella* (1886), L28.1.92008
>
> —— *Little Goody Two Shoes* (1887), L28.1.125961
>
> —— *Whittington and His Cat* (1888), L28.1.243338
>
> —— *Aladdin* (1889), L28.1.243339
>
> —— *The Forty Thieves* (1890), L28.1.112840
>
> Thorn, Geoffrey, *Sinbad the Sailor* (1891), L28.1.243340
>
> Locke, Fred, *Cinderella* (1892), L28.1.125962

LF28.1 57541: Theatre Royal, Birmingham. Play Bills Etc. (1853–1878)

LF28.60828: 'Newspaper Cuttings: Birmingham Drama', ii, 1866–1876: Clipping entitled 'Politics of the Pantomime', *Hornet*, 24 January 1874.

London: British Library: Lord Chamberlain's Plays:

Anderton, John, *Cinderella* (1889), Brit. Mus. Add. Ms. 53443E

—— *The Babes in the Wood* (1890), Brit. Mus. Add. Ms. 53465D

—— *Dick Whittington* (1891), Brit. Mus. Add. Ms. 53489N

—— *Little Goody Two Shoes* (1895), Brit. Mus. Add. Ms. 53587

—— *Puss in Boots* (1898), Brit. Mus. Add. Ms. 53674O

—— *Sinbad the Sailor* (1899), Brit. Mus. Add. Ms. 53699G

Blood, J.J., *Robinson Crusoe* (1885), Brit. Mus. Add. Ms. 53349D

Dallas, J.J., *Jack and Jill* (1883), Brit. Mus. Add. Ms. 256

Davis, Alfred, *Harlequin Graceful and the Fair One with the Golden Locks, or the Dame who Lived in a Shoe, and the Little Old Man in the Moon.* Brit. Mus. Add. Ms. 531806B

Doyle, T.F., *Cinderella* (1883), Brit. Mus. Add. Ms. 263

—— *Aladdin* (1884), Brit. Mus. Add. Ms. 53329B

Duttnall, Martin, *Little Bo Peep; or, Queen Butterfly's Ball and King Grasshopper's Feast in Birmingham in the Olden Time* (1865), Brit. Mus. Add. Ms. 53047

Goodyer, F.R and Uthermann, Hain, *Blue Beard* (1877), Brit. Mus. Add. Ms. 53197R

Goodyer, F.R and Uthermann, Hain, *Babes in the Wood* (1878), Brit. Mus. Add. Ms. 53212R

Goodyer, F.R and Uthermann, Hain, *Jack and the Beanstalk* (1879), Brit. Mus. Add. Ms. 53229D

Green, F.W., *Aladdin* (1879), Brit. Mus. Add. Ms. 53226L

Horsman, C., *Whittington and His Cat* (1865), Brit. Mus. Add. Ms. [1865]

Locke, Fred, *Cinderella* (Birmingham submission), Brit. Mus. Add. Ms. 53516C

Locke, Fred, *Sinbad the Sailor* (1894), Brit. Mus. Add. Ms. 53564G

McClelland, Harry F., *Jack and the Beanstalk* (1895), Brit. Mus. Add. Ms. 325

Millward, Charles, *The Forty Thieves* (1877), Brit. Mus. Add. Ms. 53197P

Paulton, Harry, *Gulliver's Travels* (1885), Brit. Mus. Add. Ms. 53350M

Pemberton, T. Edgar, *The Forty Thieves* (1884), Brit. Mus. Add. Ms. 53329D

Reece, Robert, *The Yellow Dwarf* (1878), Brit. Mus. Add. Ms. 53210A

Wade, William, *Beauty and the Beast* (1887), Brit. Mus. Add. Ms. 239

Wilton-Jones, J., *Little Red Riding Hood* (1883), Brit. Mus. Add. Ms. 264

Wilton-Jones, J., *The Queen of Hearts* (1884), Brit. Mus. Add. Ms. [1884]

Lord Chamberlain's Day Books, ii, Brit. Mus. Add. Ms. 53703

Lord Chamberlain's Day Books, iii, Brit. Mus. Add. Ms. 53704

Lord Chamberlain's Day Books, iv, Brit. Mus. Add. Ms. 53705

Lord Chamberlain's Day Books, v, Brit. Mus. Add. Ms. 53706

Lord Chamberlain's Day Books, vi, Brit. Mus. Add. Ms. 53707

Manchester Archives and Local Studies Library:

'Newspaper Cuttings: Vic-Walker': [anonymous] Untitled newspaper cutting [handwritten date of 1909] regarding William Wade

BR F052 M13A, 1878–9 Vol 2.47 MF 81920: [anonymous] 'Our Album: Alfred Thompson, Esq', *Momus* (Manchester, 1878–9), p. 2.

Manchester Archives: Theatre Collection:

Th792.094273 Ma 1: Comedy [Gaiety] Theatre, Manchester, *Pantomime Books*:

> J. Wilton-Jones, *Little Red Riding Hood* (1886); J. Wilton-Jones, *Dick Whittington* (1887); R. Newman, *Aladdin, or, the Tramp of a Scamp for a Lamp* (1888); W. Wade, *Cinderella* (1889); W. Wade, *Fair One with the Golden Locks, Or, the Hazard of a Dye* (1891); W. Wade, *Goody Two Shoes* (1892); W. Wade, *Cinderella* (1895); W. Wade, *Whittington and his Cat* (1897); W. Wade, *Little Bo Peep* (1899); W. Wade, *Robinson Crusoe* (1900);

Th792.094273 Ma77: Palace Theatre, Manchester, *Pantomime Books*:

> J.J. Dallas, *Jack and Jill* (Manchester, 1897)

Th792.094273 Ma80: Queen's Theatre, Spring Gardens, *Pantomime Books*:

> J.H. Doyne, *Aladdin* (1860); J.H. Doyne, *Valentine and Orson* (1861); Frank Maitland, *The Invisible Prince* (1862); Charles Horsman, *Sinbad the Sailor* (1863); William Seaman, *Harlequin King Humpty Dumpty* (1864); *Whittington and His Cat* (1865); J.H. Doyne, *Harlequin and Kafoozalum* (1866); *Harlequin Guy Fawkes* (1867); James Shepley, *A Apple Pie and Little Boy Blue; or, Harlequin Jack-in-the-Box and the World of Toys* (1868)

Th792.094273 Ma 82: Queen's Theatre, Bridge Street, *Pantomime Books*:
James Shepley, *Ali Baba and the Forty Thieves* (1870); Alfred Maltby, *Robinson Crusoe* (1874); J.J.B. Forsyth, *Jack and the Beanstalk* (1877); J.J.B. Forsyth, *Old Mother Goose* (1879); J.T. Denny, *Aladdin* (1881); John F. McArdle, *Beauty and the Beast* (1882); J. Wilton-Jones, *Little Red Riding Hood* (1883); J.P. Taylor, *Blue Beard* (1888); T.F. Doyle, *Robinson Crusoe* (1889); T.F. Doyle, *Sinbad the Sailor* (1893); Eric J. Buxton, *Red Riding Hood* (1896)

Th792.094273 Ma83: Prince's Theatre, Manchester, *Prince's Annual Season 1876–77: Illustrated Account of the Pantomime 'Sinbad or, Harlequin Old Man of the Sea and the Diamond Fay of the Enchanted Valley of the Roc'*

Th792.094273 Ma83 and Ma83/A: Prince's Theatre, Manchester, *Pantomime Books*, 3 vols:
vol. i: Pyngle Lane, *Mother Goose* (1864); Edward Robertson Ward, *Little Bo Peep* (1865); Edwin Waugh, *Robin Hood* (1866); William Brough, *Gulliver's Travels* (1867); William Brough, *Frogee Would a-Wooing Go* (1869); [Alfred Thompson], *Harlequin Blackbird* (1870)

vol. ii: *Forty Thieves* (1878); *Puss in Boots* (1884), *Ali Baba and the Forty Other Thieves* (1884); William Wade, *Robinson Crusoe* (1886); William Wade, *Beauty and the Beast* (1887); George Dance, *Sinbad the Sailor* (1888); George Dance, *Little Bo Peep* (1890) [2 versions]; J. Wilton-Jones and Thos. W. Charles, *Little Red Riding Hood* (1894)

vol. iii: J. Wilton-Jones and Thos. W. Charles, *Robinson Crusoe* (1895); John J. Wood, *Puss in Boots* (1897); J. Hickory Wood and A.M. Thompson, *Sinbad the Sailor* (1898); A.M. Thompson and Robert Courtneidge, *Robinson Crusoe* (1902); J. Hickory Wood, *The Forty Thieves* (1903)

Th792.094273 Ma86: Theatre Royal, Manchester, *Pantomime Books*, 2 vols:
vol. i: Thos. Chambers, *Cinderella* (1860); Thos. Chambers, *Beauty and the Beast* (1861); Thos. Chambers, *The House That Jack Built* (1862); T. Chambers and W.S. Hyde, *Sleeping Beauty* (1863);

Thos. Chambers and W.S. Hyde, *Puss in Boots* (1864); *Valentine and Orson* (1868); John Strachan, *Sinbad the Sailor* (1869)

vol. ii: T.F. Doyle, *Blue Beard* (1886); T.F. Doyle, *Old Mother Goose and the Sleeping Beauty* (1887); T.F. Doyle, *The Forty Thieves* (1888); George Dance, *Dick Whittington* (1889); Horace Lennard, *Aladdin* (1890); Fred Locke, *Little Red Riding Hood and Bonnie Boy Blue* (1892); Fred Locke, *Babes in the Wood* (1893); Fred Locke, *Sinbad the Sailor* (1894); *Aladdin* (1897); Arthur Sturgess and Arthur Collins, *Babes in the Wood* (1898); A.H. Smith, *Jack and the Beanstalk* (1901); J. Hickory Wood and William Wade, *Mother Goose* (1904)

Th792.0942733 L522/9: Duffy, H.A., *Manchester Pantomimes Annual: Containing Stories by all the leading artistes at the Royal, Prince's and Queen's Theatres* (Manchester, 1892)

Th.792.4273 H4: [various] *Hardacre's Annual, Christmas 1892* (Manchester, 1892, published on behalf of J. Pitt Hardacre, lessee of the Comedy Theatre)

Nottingham Local Studies Library:

L79.8: Loose collection of books of words (Theatre Royal, Nottingham):

Anonymous, *The House That Jack Built* (1865)

Anonymous, *Aladdin; or, Harlequin and the Geni of the Wonderful Lamp* (1866)

Thompson, W.J., *Babes in the Wood; or, Harlequin Cock Robin, Prince Charley and His Pretty Bluebell* (1868)

[Strachan, John], *Little Goody Two Shoes! and Her Queen Anne's Farthing; or, Harlequin Old King Counterfeit and the World of Coins* (1869)

Strachan, John, *Harlequin Robinson Crusoe or, Man Friday, Jack Frost and the King of the Carribee Islands* (1870)

Hughes, F., *The Forty Thieves or, Harlequin Open Sesame and the Enchanted Home of the Arabian Nights* (1871)

Goodyer, F.R., *Little Red Riding Hood; Or, Harlequin Neptune, the Wehr Wolf, Old Dog Tray, the Fairy Golden Gossamer, and the Wonderful Head* (1873)

—— *Little Bo Peep and Boy Blue; Or, Harlequin Jack in the Box,*

Tom Thumb, and the Norfolk Giant (1874)

—— *Dick Whittington and His Cat* (1880)

—— *Robinson Crusoe and His Man Friday* (1881)

—— *Cinderella* (1882)

—— *Little Bo Peep* (1883)

—— *The Forty Thieves* (1884)

—— *Little Red Riding Hood* (1885)

Dance, George, *Aladdin, or the Wonderful Lamp* (1886)

—— *Babes in the Wood* (1887)

—— *Sinbad the Sailor* (1889)

Doyle, T.F., *Puss in Boots; Or, the Marquis! The Miller! And the Mouse!* (1890)

Maddock, Arthur L., *Robinson Crusoe; Or, the Good Friday Who Came on Thursday Half-Holiday* (1891)

Locke, Fred and Jay-Penne, A., *Cinderella* (1892)

L80.2 GOOD1: Goodyer, F.R., *Odds and Ends*

RL79.8: Loose Collection of playbills (Theatre Royal, Nottingham) 1860–1900

RQL 79.8: Theatre Scrapbook 1865–1943

Nottinghamshire Archives:

M8806: Receipted Bills, Mounted (September to December 1865)

M8807: Receipted Bills, Mounted (December 1865 to August 1866)

M8808: Receipted Bills, Mounted (September 1866 to April 1867)

M8809: Day Book of Accounts for Administration of Nottingham Theatre Royal, 1866–7

M8812: Ledger of Accounts for Administration of Nottingham Theatre Royal, Sept to Dec 1865

M8814: Salary Book No. 2 (1866–1867)

M8817: Stage Door Book, 1865–1867

M8822: Collection of Loose Bills from 1865

Public Records Office:

LC 3/89–109: Lord Chamberlain's Registers of Letters

LC1/327, LC1/341–343, LC1/418, LC1/435, LC1/453, LC1/508: Lord Chamberlain's Letters Received

Secondary sources

Allen, G.C., *The Industrial Development of Birmingham and the Black Country 1860–1927* (London, 1929)

Allen, R.G., 'Topical Scenes for Pantomime', *Educational Theatre Journal*, 17 (1965), pp. 289–300

Altick, R.D., 'Past and Present: Topicality and Technique', in J. Clubbe (ed.), *Carlyle and His Contemporaries: Essays in Honour of Charles Richard Sanders* (Durham, 1976), pp. 112–28

Anonymous, 'My Pantomime', *All the Year Round*, 10/14 (1863), pp. 272–6

Armstrong, I., *Victorian Glassworlds: Glass Culture and the Imagination 1830–1880* (Oxford, 2008)

Ashton, G., 'The First Two Hundred Years', in Benyon (ed.), *The Theatre Royal Nottingham*, pp. 3–14

Auslander, P., *Liveness: Performance in a Mediatized Culture* (Oxford and New York, 2008)

Bailey, P., *Popular Culture and Performance in the Victorian City* (Cambridge, 1998)

—— 'Theatres of Entertainment/Spaces of Modernity: Rethinking the British Popular Stage 1890–1914', *Nineteenth Century Theatre*, 26/1 (1998), pp. 5–24

Bakhtin, M., *Rabelais and His World*, trans. H. Iswolsky (Cambridge, MA, 1968)

Balme, C.B., *The Cambridge Introduction to Theatre Studies* (Cambridge, 2008)

Barker, K., 'The Performing Arts in Five Provincial Towns 1840–1870', unpublished PhD thesis (University of Leicester, 1982)

—— 'Bristol at Play 1801–1853: A Typical Picture of the English Provinces?', in Mayer and Richards (eds), *Western Popular Theatre*, pp. 91–103

—— *The Theatre Royal, Bristol, 1766–1966: Two Centuries of Stage History* (London, 1974)

Barrett, D., 'The Dramatic Authors' Society (1833–1883) and the Payment of English Dramatists', *Essays in Theatre*, 7/1 (1988), pp. 19–33

Baudrillard, J., *The Consumer Society: Myths and Structures* (London, 1998)

Beckett, J., *The Book of Nottingham* (Buckingham, 1990)

—— *The East Midlands from AD 1000* (London, 1988)

Bennett, S., *Theatre Audiences: A Theory of Production and Reception*, 2nd edn (London, 1994)

Benyon, R. (ed.), *The Theatre Royal Nottingham 1865–1978: A Theatrical and Architectural History* (Nottingham, n.d.)

Blank, B., 'My Pantomime', 'The Era Almanack for 1878', in bound volume *The Era Almanack 1874–1879* (no publication details), pp. 33–7

Booth, M.R., 'Studies in Nineteenth Century British Theatre 1980–1989', *Nineteenth Century Theatre*, 20/1 (1992), pp. 46–57

—— *Theatre in the Victorian Age* (Cambridge, 1991)

—— *Victorian Spectacular Theatre 1850–1910* (London, 1981)

—— (ed.), *English Plays of the Nineteenth Century*, vol. v: *Pantomimes, Extravaganzas and Burlesques* (Oxford, 1976)

Bowlby, R., *Just Looking: Consumer Desire in Dreiser, Gissing and Zola* (New York, 1985)

Brace, C., 'Finding England Everywhere: Regional Identity and the Construction of National Identity, 1890–1940', *Cultural Geographies*, 6/1 (1999), 90–109

Bradby, D., James, L. and Sharratt, B. (eds), *Performance and Politics in Popular Drama: Aspects of Popular Entertainment in Theatre, Film and Television 1800–1976: Papers Given at a Conference at the University of Kent at Canterbury, September 1977* (Cambridge, 1980)

Bratton, Jacky, *New Readings in Theatre History* (Cambridge, 2003)

Briggs, A., *History of Birmingham*, 2 vols (London, 1952), vol. ii: *Borough and City 1865–1938*

Broadbent, R.J., *Annals of the Liverpool Stage, from the Earliest Period to the Present Time* (Liverpool, 1908)

—— *A History of Pantomime* (London, 1901)

Brunton, J., 'A Dance to the Music of Time', *Bygones: Nottingham Evening Post Special Publication*, 17 (1998), pp. 20–1

Calvert, Mrs C., *Sixty Eight Years on the Stage* (London, 1911)

Carlson, M., *Theories of the Theatre: A Historical and Critical Survey from the Greeks to the Present*, expanded edn (Ithaca, NY, 1994)

Cavanagh, J., *British Theatre: A Bibliography 1901–1985* (Romsey, 1989)

Chambers, J.D., *The Workshop of the World: British Economic History 1820–1880*, 2nd edn (Oxford, 1974)

Cheesmond, Robert, 'Oh No It Isn't: A Functionalistic Re-definition of Pantomime', in R. Merkin (ed.), *Popular Theatres? Papers from the Popular Theatre Conference* (Liverpool, 1996), pp. 220–39

Church, R.A., *Economic and Social Change in a Midland Town: Victorian Nottingham 1815–1900* (London, 1966)

Clinton-Baddeley, V.C., *Some Pantomime Pedigrees* (London, 1963)

Cohen, T., 'High and Low Art, and High and Low Audiences', *Journal of Aesthetics and Art Criticism*, 57 (1999), pp. 137–43

Connolly, L.W., 'The Censor and Early Nineteenth-Century English Pantomime', *Notes and Queries*, 22 (1975), pp. 394–6

Cowan, A. and Steward, J. (eds), *The City and the Senses: Urban Culture Since 1500* (Aldershot, 2007)

Cowgill, R. and Holman, P., *Music in the British Provinces 1690–1914* (Aldershot and Burlington, VT, 2007)

Crompton-Rhodes, R., *The Theatre Royal, Birmingham 1774–1924: A Short History* (Birmingham, 1924)

Crump, J., 'Provincial Music Hall: Promoters and Public in Leicester, 1863–1929', in P. Bailey (ed.), *Music Hall: The Business of Pleasure* (Milton Keynes, 1986), pp. 53–72

—— 'Patronage, Pleasure and Profit: A Study of the Theatre Royal, Leicester 1847–1900', *Theatre Notebook*, 38 (1984), pp. 77–88

Cunningham, J.E., *Theatre Royal: A History of the Theatre Royal, Birmingham* (Oxford, 1950)

Davenport Adams, W.A., *A Dictionary of the Drama: A Guide to the Plays, Playwrights, Players and Playhouses of the United Kingdom and America, from the Earliest Times to the Present*, vol. i, A–G (London, 1904)

—— *A Book of Burlesque: Sketches of the English Stage Travestie and Parody* (London, 1891)

Davis, J. (ed.), *Victorian Pantomime: A Collection of Critical Essays* (Basingstoke, 2010)

—— 'Boxing Day', in Davis and Holland (eds), *The Performing Century*, pp. 13–31

—— 'Imperial Transgressions: The Ideology of Drury Lane Pantomime in the Late Nineteenth Century', *New Theatre Quarterly*, 12 (1996), pp. 147–55

—— (ed.), *Plays by H.J. Byron* (Cambridge, 1984)

Davis, J. and Emeljanow, V., *Reflecting the Audience: London Theatregoing 1840–1880* (Hatfield, 2001)

—— '"Wistful Remembrancer": The Historiographical Problem of Macqueen-Popery', *New Theatre Quarterly*, 17 (2001), pp. 299–309

—— 'New Views of Cheap Theatres: Reconstructing the Nineteenth Century Theatre Audience', *Theatre Survey: The Journal of the American Society for Theatre Research*, 39 (1998), pp. 53–72

Davis, T.C., *The Economics of the British Stage 1800–1914* (Cambridge, 2000)

—— 'Editorial', *Nineteenth Century Theatre*, 24/1 (1996), pp. 36–41

—— 'Reading for Economic History', *Theatre Journal*, 45 (1993), pp. 487–503

—— 'The Theatrical Employees of Victorian Britain: Demography of an Industry', *Nineteenth Century Theatre*, 18/1 and 2 (1990), pp. 5–34

Davis, T.C. and Holland, P. (eds), *The Performing Century: Nineteenth Century Theatre's History* (Basingstoke and New York, 2007)

Davis, T.C. and McConachie, B., 'Introduction', *Theatre Survey*, 39 (November 1998), pp. 1–5

Davis, T.C., and Postlewait, T. (eds), *Theatricality* (Cambridge, 2003)

Davison, P., Meyersohn, R. and Shils, E. (eds), *Literary Taste, Culture and Mass Communication*, 14 vols (Cambridge, 1978–80), vol. viii: *Theatre and Song* (1978)

Debord, G., *Society of the Spectacle*, trans. D. Nicholson-Smith (New York, 1998)

De Bres, K. and Davis, J., 'Celebrating Group and Place Identity: A Case Study of a New Regional Festival', *Tourism Geographies*, 3/3 (2001), pp. 326–37

Dickenson, S.-J., 'Oh Yes It Is! A Practical Exploration of the Validity of the Role of Pantomime', in R. Merkin (ed.), *Popular Theatres? Papers from the Popular Theatre Conference* (Liverpool, 1996), pp. 240–51

Dodd, A.H., 'History in Pantomime', *History*, 12 (1927–8), pp. 215–26

Egerton Leigh, Lieut. Col., *A Glossary of Words Used in the Dialect of Cheshire* (originally published 1877; Wakefield, 1973)

Edwards, J.R., *British History 1815–1939* (London, 1977)

Eigner, E.M., *The Dickens Pantomime* (Berkeley, CA, 1989)

—— 'Imps, Dames and Principal Boys: Gender Confusion in the Nineteenth-Century Pantomime', *Browning Institute Studies*, 17 (1989), pp. 65–75

Feather, J., *Publishing, Piracy and Politics: An Historical Study of Copyright in Britain* (London, 1994)

Featherstone, A., '"Crowded Nightly": Popular Entertainment Outside London during the Nineteenth and Early Twentieth Centuries', unpublished PhD thesis (Royal Holloway, University of London, 2000)

Featherstone, S., ''E Dunno Where 'E Are: Coster Comedy and the Politics of Music Hall', *Nineteenth Century Theatre*, 24/1 (1996), pp. 7–33

Fitzgerald, P., *The World Behind the Scenes* (London, 1881)

Fitzsimmons, L., 'The Theatre Royal, York in the 1840s', *Nineteenth Century Theatre and Film*, 31/1 (2004), pp. 18–25

Foulkes, R., *The Calverts: Actors of Some Importance* (London, 1992)

Fowles, J., *Advertising and Popular Culture* (Thousand Oaks, CA, 1996)

Freshwater, H., *Theatre & Audiences* (Basingstoke, 2009)

Frow, G., *'Oh Yes, It Is!': A History of Pantomime* (London, 1985)

Galbraith, G.R., *Reading Lives: Reconstructing Childhood, Books, and Schools in Britain, 1870–1920* (New York, 1997)

Gallagher, C. and Greenblatt, S., *Practicing New Historicism* (Chicago and London, 2000)

Gans, H.J., *Popular Culture and High Culture: An Analysis and Evaluation of Taste*, rev. edn (New York, 1999)

Garner, Jr, S.B., *The Absent Voice: Narrative Comprehension in the Theater* (Urbana, 1989)

Gaull, M., 'Pantomime as Satire: Mocking a Broken Charm', in S.E. Jones (ed.), *The Satiric Eye: Forms of Satire in the Romantic Period* (New York, 2003), pp. 207–24

Geertz, C., *The Interpretation of Cultures: Selected Essays* (London, 1993)

Golby, J.M. and Purdue, A.W., *The Civilisation of the Crowd: Popular Culture 1750–1900*, 2nd edn (Stroud, 1999)

—— *The Making of the Modern Christmas* (London, 1986)

Graham, J., *An Old Stock-Actor's Memories* (London, 1930)

Gray, D., *Nottingham: Settlement to City*, 2nd edn (East Ardsley, 1969)

Greenblatt, S., 'Resonance and Wonder', in P. Collier and H. Geyer-Ryan (eds), *Literary Theory Today* (Ithaca, NY, 1990), pp. 74–90

Guilford, E.L. (ed.), *Memorials of Old Nottinghamshire* (London, 1912)

Gunn, S., *The Public Culture of the Victorian Middle Class: Ritual and Authority and the English Industrial City* (Manchester, 2000)

Halliday, A. (ed.), *Comical Fellows; or, the History and Mystery of the Pantomime: With Some Curiosities and Droll Anecdotes Concerning Clown and Pantaloon, Harlequin and Columbine* (London, 1863)

Hammond, P., 'Cultural Identity and Ideology', http://myweb.lsbu.ac.uk/philip-hammond/1999b.html, pp. 1–14

Handbook of Birmingham. Prepared for the Members of the British Association, 1886 (Birmingham, 1886)

Heinrich, A., *Entertainment, Propaganda, Education: Regional Theatre in Germany and Britain between 1918 and 1945* (London, 2007)

Heinrich, A., Newey, K. and Richards, J. (eds), *Ruskin, the Theatre and Victorian Visual Culture* (Basingstoke and New York, 2009)

Hochberg, S., 'Mrs Sparsit's Coriolanian Eyebrows and Dickensian Approach to Topicality', *Dickensian*, 87 (1991), pp. 32–6

Holland, P., 'The Play of Eros: Paradoxes of Gender in English Pantomime', *New Theatre Quarterly*, 13 (1997), pp. 195–204

Hopkins, E., *Childhood Transformed: Working-Class Children in Nineteenth-Century England* (Manchester, 1994)

Hudson, J., *Wakes Week: Memories of Mill Town Holidays* (Stroud, 1992)

Hughes, A., 'The Lyceum Staff: A Victorian Theatrical Organization', *Theatre Notebook*, 28 (1974), pp. 11–17

Hurt, J.S., *Elementary Schooling and the Working Classes 1860–1918* (London, Toronto and Buffalo, 1979)

Iliffe, R. and Baguley, W., *Victorian Nottingham: A Story in Pictures*, 20 vols (Nottingham, 1970–83)

Jackson, R., *Victorian Theatre* (London, 1989)

Joyce, P., *Visions of the People: Industrial England and the Question of Class 1848–1914* (Cambridge, 1991)

Kaplan, C., 'The Only Native British Art Form', *Antioch Review*, 42 (1984), pp. 266–76

Kaplan, J., 'A Puppet's Power: George Alexander, Clement Scott, and the Replotting of *Lady Windermere's Fan*', *Theatre Notebook*, 46 (1992), pp. 59–73

Kennedy, D., *The Spectator and the Spectacle: Audiences in Modernity and Postmodernity* (Cambridge, 2009)

Kershaw, B., 'Oh for Unruly Audiences! Or, Patterns of Participation in Twentieth-Century Theatre', *Modern Drama*, 42 (2001), pp. 133–54

Kershaw, C., 'Dan Leno: New Evidence on Early Influences and Style', *Nineteenth Century Theatre*, 22/1 (1994), pp. 30–55

Kidd, A., *Manchester* (Keele, 1993)

Kift, D., *The Victorian Music Hall: Culture, Class and Conflict*, trans. R. Kift (Cambridge, 1996)

Langford, J.A., *Birmingham: A Handbook for Residents and Visitors* (Birmingham, [1879])

Lascelles and Hagar's Commercial Directory of the Town and County of the Town of Nottingham (Nottingham, 1848)

Law, M.J., 'Aspects of Theatre in Liverpool, 1850–1900', Abstract, 16 December 2000, http://www.thesis.com/idx/036/it036006918.htm

Lee, A.J., 'The Management of a Victorian Local Newspaper: the *Manchester City News*, 1864–1900', *Business History*, 14/2 (1973), pp. 131–48

Lennox, Lord W.P., *Plays, Players and Playhouses at Home and Abroad with Anecdotes of the Drama and the Stage*, 2 vols (London, 1881)

Levy, E.L., *Birmingham Theatrical Reminiscences: Jubilee Recollections (1870–1920)* (Birmingham, [1920])

Macqueen-Pope, W., *Shirtfronts and Sables: A Story of the Days When Money Could be Spent* (London, 1953)

Manchester Faces and Places: An Illustrated Record of the Social, Political and Commercial Life of the Cotton Metropolis and Its Environs (1890–1906) [periodical]

Manchester Press Club, The, *Fifty Years of Us: A Jubilee Retrospect of Men and Newspapers* (Manchester, 1922)

Mander, R. and Mitchenson, J., *Pantomime: A Story in Pictures* (London, 1973)

Matthews, B., *A Book about the Theater* (New York, 1916)

Mayer, D., 'Supernumeraries: Decorating the Late-Victorian Stage with Lots (& Lots & Lots) of Live Bodies', in Heinrich, Newey and Richards (eds), *Ruskin, the Theatre and Victorian Visual Culture*, pp. 154–68

—— 'Some Recent Writings on Victorian Theatre', *Victorian Studies*, 20 (1977), pp. 311–17

—— *Annotated Bibliography of Pantomime and Guide to Study Sources* (London, 1975)

—— 'The Sexuality of English Pantomime', *Theatre Quarterly*, 4 (1974), pp. 55–64

—— *Harlequin in His Element: The English Pantomime 1806–1836* (Cambridge, MA, 1969)

—— 'The Pantomime Olio and Other Pantomime Variants', *Theatre Notebook*, 19 (1964), pp. 22–8

Mayer, D. and Richards, K. (eds), *Western Popular Theatre: The Proceedings of a Symposium Sponsored by the Manchester University Department of Drama* (London, 1977)

McCord, Norman, *British History 1815–1906* (Oxford, 1991)

McGrath, John, *A Good Night Out: Popular Theatre, Audience, Class and Form*, 2nd edn (London, 1996)

Meisel, M., *Realizations: Narrative, Pictorial and Theatrical Arts of Nineteenth-Century England* (Princeton, NJ, 1983)

Meller, H. (ed.), *Nottingham in the Eighteen Eighties* (Nottingham, 1971)

Messinger, G.S., *Manchester in the Victorian Age: The Half-known City* (Manchester, 1985)

Millward, J. in collaboration with Booth, J.B., *Myself and Others* (London, 1923)

Mitchell, B.R. with the collaboration of Deane, P., *Abstract of British Historical Statistics* (Cambridge, 1962)

Moody, J., *Illegitimate Theatre in London 1770–1840* (Cambridge, 2000)

—— 'The State of the Abyss: Nineteenth Century Performance and Theatre Historiography in 1999', *Journal of Victorian Culture*, 5 (2000), pp. 112–28

Morley, J., 'The Struggle for National Education', *The Fortnightly Review*, New Series 14, (July–December 1873), pp. 143–62, 303–25, 411–33

Morris & Co's Commercial Directory and Gazetteer of Nottingham and District (Nottingham, 1877)

Morris & Co's Commercial Directory and Gazetteer of Nottinghamshire with Grantham, Chesterfield, and Gainsborough (Nottingham, 1869)

Morrow, J.C., 'The Staging of Pantomime at Sadler's Wells 1828–1860', unpublished PhD thesis (Ohio State University, 1963)

Morson, G.S. and Emerson, C., *Bakhtin: Creation of a Prosaics* (Stanford, CA, 1990)

Moynet, M.J., *French Theatrical Production in the Nineteenth Century* (1873), trans. and augmented A.S. Jackson with M.G. Wilson, ed. M.A. Carlson (New York, 1976)

Nadal-Klein, J., 'Reweaving the Fringe: Localism, Tradition, and Representation in British Ethnography', *American Ethnologist*, 18/3 (1991), 'Representations of Europe: Transforming State, Society and Identity', pp. 500–17 (accessed 17 June 2008)

Newey, K., 'Early Nineteenth-Century Theatre in Manchester', *Manchester Region History Review*, 17/2 (2006), pp. 1–19

Nicoll, A., *A History of English Drama 1660–1900*, 6 vols, 2nd edn (Cambridge, 1952–9), vol. v: *Late Nineteenth-Century Drama 1850–1900* (1959)

Norwood, J., 'The Britannia Theatre: Visual Culture and the Repertoire of a Popular Theatre', in Heinrich, Newey and Richards (eds), *Ruskin, the Theatre and Victorian Visual Culture*, pp. 135–53

O'Brien, J., *Harlequin Britain: Pantomime and Entertainment, 1690–1760* (Baltimore, 2004)

—— 'Harlequin Britain: Eighteenth-Century Pantomime and the Cultural Location of Entertainment(s)', *Theatre Journal*, 50 (1998), pp. 489–510

Oxford Dictionary of National Biography, ed. H.C.G. Matthews and B. Harrison, 60 vols (Oxford, 2004)

Paasi, A., 'Region and Place: Regional Identity in Question', *Progress in Human Geography*, 27/4 (2003), pp. 475–85

Parker, J. (ed.), *Who's Who in the Theatre: A Bibliographical Record of the Contemporary Stage* (London, 1912)

Pemberton, T.E., *The Theatre Royal Birmingham, 1774–1901: A Record and Some Recollections* (Birmingham, 1901)

Pickering, D., *Encyclopedia of Pantomime* (Andover, 1993)

Planché, J.R., *The Recollections and Reflections of J.R. Planché: A Professional Autobiography*, 2 vols (London, 1872)

Postlewait, T., *The Cambridge Introduction to Theatre Historiography* (Cambridge, 2009)

Postlewait, T. and McConachie, B.A. (eds), *Interpreting the Theatrical Past: Essays in the Historiography of Performance* (Iowa City, 1989)

Purkiss, D., *Troublesome Things: A History of Fairies and Fairy Stories* (London, 2000)

Reid, D.A., 'Popular Theatre in Victorian Birmingham', in Bradby, James and Sharratt (eds), *Performance and Politics in Popular Drama*, pp. 65–89

Report from the Select Committee on Theatrical Licenses and Regulations; Together with the Proceedings of the Committee, Minutes of Evidence, and Appendix (Shannon, 1970; 1st edn 1866)

Report from the Select Committee on Theatres and Places of Entertainment; Together with the Proceedings of the Committee, Minutes of Evidence, Appendix, and Index (Shannon, 1970; 1st edn 1892)

'The Report of the Royal Commission on Copyright' (1875), in *The Royal Commissions and the Report of the Commissioners* (London, 1878)

Richards, T., *The Commodity Culture of Victorian England: Advertising and Spectacle 1851–1914* (Stanford, CA, 1990)

Robbins, N., *Slapstick and Sausages: The Evolution of the British Pantomime* (Tiverton, 2002)

Robinson, J., 'Becoming More Provincial? The Global and the Local in Theatre History', *New Theatre Quarterly*, 23/3 (2007), pp. 229–40

Rodway, P.P. and Slingsby, L.R., *Philip Rodway and a Tale of Two Theatres. By His Daughters* (Birmingham, 1934)

Root, Jr, R.L., *The Rhetorics of Popular Culture: Advertising, Advocacy, and Entertainment* (New York, 1987)

Rowell, G., *The Victorian Theatre: A Survey* (Oxford, 1967)

Ruston, A., 'Richard Nelson Lee and Nelson Lee Junior, Authors of Victorian Pantomime: A Bibliographical Checklist', *Nineteenth Century Theatre*, 18/1 and 2 (1990), pp. 75–85

—— 'Richard Nelson Lee and the Victorian Pantomime in Great Britain', *Nineteenth Century Theatre Research*, 11/2 (1983), pp. 105–17

Ryan, K. (ed.), *New Historicism and Cultural Materialism: A Reader* (London, 1996)

Saintsbury, G., *Manchester* (London, 1887)

Salberg, D., *Once Upon a Pantomime* (Luton, 1981)

Sayers, R.S., *A History of Economic Change in England 1880–1939*, repr. edn (Oxford, 1973)

Scott, C., *The Drama of Yesterday and Today*, 2 vols (London, 1899)

Scott, C. and Howard, C., *The Life and Reminiscences of E.L. Blanchard, with Notes from the Diary of Wm. Blanchard*, 2 vols (London, 1891)

Seebohm, F., 'National Compulsory Education', *Fortnightly Review*, New Series 8 (1 July – 1 December 1870), pp. 103–13

Senelick, L., 'Politics as Entertainment: Victorian Music-Hall Songs', *Victorian Studies: A Journal of the Humanities, Arts and Sciences*, 19 (1975), pp. 149–80

Seville, C., *Literary Copyright Reform in Early Victorian England: The Framing of the 1842 Copyright Act* (Cambridge, 1999)

Shepherd, S. and Womack, P., *English Drama: A Cultural History* (Oxford, 1996)

Showell's Dictionary of Birmingham (Birmingham, 1885)

Soundscape Productions for BBC Radio 4, 'Oh No It's Not!' (5-part series transmitted 23 December 2003 – 2 January 2004)

Speaight, G., 'New Light on "Mother Goose"', *Theatre Notebook*, 52 (1998), pp. 18–23

—— 'Harlequinade Turn-ups', *Theatre Notebook*, 45 (1991), pp. 70–84

Stephens, J.R., *The Profession of the Playwright: British Theatre 1800–1900* (Cambridge, 1992)

—— *The Censorship of English Drama 1824–1901* (Cambridge, 1980)

Sullivan, J.A., 'Local and Political Hits: Allusion and Collusion in the Victorian Pantomime', in J. Davis (ed.), *Victorian Pantomime: A Collection of Critical Essays* (Basingstoke, 2010)

—— 'Pantomime Libretti and the Victorian Reading Audience', in G. Allen *et al.* (eds), *Making an Audience: Reading Textual Materiality* (forthcoming, 2011)

—— 'Managing the Pantomime: Productions at the Theatre Royal Nottingham in the 1860s', *Theatre Notebook*, 60/2 (2006), pp. 98–116

—— 'The Business of Pantomime: Regional Productions 1865–1892', unpublished PhD thesis (University of Nottingham, 2005)

Summerfield, P., 'Patriotism and Empire: Music-hall Entertainment, 1870–1914', in J.M. Mackenzie (ed.), *Imperialism and Popular Culture* (Manchester, 1986)

Sutherland, G., *Elementary Education in the Nineteenth Century* (London, 1971)

Talbot, P.A., 'The Macclesfield Theatre Company and Nineteenth-Century Silk Manufacturers', *Theatre Notebook*, 54 (2000), pp. 24–42

Taylor, M., *British Pantomime Production* (Bristol and Chicago, 2007)

Thompson, D., *England in the Nineteenth Century*, 14th edn (Harmondsworth, 1970)

Townsend, A.R. and Taylor, C.C. 'Regional Culture and Identity in Industrialised Societies: the Case of North-East England, *Regional Studies*, 9/4 (1975), pp. 379–93

Troubridge, St V., *The Benefit System in the British Theatre* (London, 1967)

Upton, C., *A History of Birmingham* (Chichester, 1993)

Vicinus, M., *The Industrial Muse: A Study of Nineteenth Century British Working-Class Literature* (London, 1974)

Wade, W., 'The Story of My Life and How I Fell into Writing Pantomimes', *Hardacre's Christmas Annual* [1892]

Wagner, L., *The Pantomimes and All About Them: Their Origin, History, Preparation and Exponents* (London, 1881)

Walton, J.K. and Poole, R., 'The Lancashire Wakes in the Nineteenth Century', in R.D. Storch (ed.), *Popular Culture and Custom in Nineteenth-Century England* (London and New York, 1982), pp. 100–24

Ward and Lock's Illustrated Guide to, and Popular History of Birmingham and Its Vicinity: Its Institutes, Manufactures, and Chief Public Buildings (London and New York, [1892])

Wardle, D., *Education and Society in Nineteenth-Century Nottingham* (London, 1971)

Wearing, J.P., *American and British Theatrical Biography: A Directory* (Metuchen, NJ, 1979)

Weltman, S.A., 'Pantomime Truth and Gender Performance: John Ruskin on Theatre', in D. Birch and F. O'Gorman (eds), *Ruskin and Gender* (Basingstoke, 2002), pp. 159–76

White, F. and White, J., *History, Directory and Gazetteer of the County and of the Town and County of the Town of Nottingham* (Sheffield, 1844)

White, W., *History, Gazetteer and Directory of Nottinghamshire*, 2nd edn (London, 1885–6)

Williams, G.J., 'The Arch Street Theatre and Charles Sprague: The "Gentleman of this City" Who Was Not', paper given at the American Society for Theatre Research Annual Conference, Durham, NC, 23 November 2003

Willson-Disher, M., *Clowns and Pantomimes* (London, 1925)

Wilson, A.E., *Pantomime Pageant: A Procession of Harlequins, Clowns, Comedians, Principal Boys, Pantomime-Writers, Producers and Playgoers* (London, 1946)

—— *Christmas Pantomime* (London, 1934)

Wilson, M.S., 'Columbine's Picturesque Passage: The Demise of Dramatic Action in the Evolution of Sublime Spectacle on the London Stage', *The Eighteenth Century: Theory and Interpretation*, 31 (1990), pp. 191–210

Wyke, T. and Rudyard, N., *Manchester Theatres* (Manchester, 1994)

Index